SNAKES IN SUITS

Also by Robert D. Hare, Ph.D.

*Without Conscience: The Disturbing World
of the Psychopaths Among Us*

SNAKES IN SUITS

When Psychopaths Go to Work

Paul Babiak, Ph.D., and Robert D. Hare, Ph.D.

ReganBooks
An Imprint of HarperCollins *Publishers*

HarperCollins books may be purchased for educational, business, or sales promotional use. For information please write: Special Markets Department, HarperCollins Publishers Inc., 10 East 53rd Street, New York, NY 10022.

FIRST EDITION

Designed by Sarah Gubkin

Printed on acid-free paper

Library of Congress Cataloging-in-Publication Data has been applied for.

ISBN 10 0-06-083772-1
ISBN 13 978-0-06-083772-3

06 07 08 09 10 / 10 9 8 7 6 5 4 3 2 1

In memory of Cheryl, and Paul

CONTENTS

Contents

PREFACE

Most workers are honest, loyal, law-abiding citizens, concerned with making a living, contributing to society, and raising a family in a fair and just world. Others, though, are more selfish, concerned only about themselves with little regard for fairness and equity. Unfortunately, there are some individuals in the business world who allow the responsibilities of leadership and the perks of power to override their moral sense. A rise in the number of reports of abuse in major corporations should not be a surprise, given the increased access to unrestricted power, resources of startling proportions, and the erosion of ethical standards and values.

Some who have faltered may have experienced a weakened moral sense of "right" in the face of excessive temptation and easy access to power. Others may feel justified in reaping the rewards in proportion to the size of the organization they lead, arguing that their extravagances seem excessive only to those who have little hope of being so rewarded. Still others have embraced the self-serving mantras that "greed is good" and that success at any cost to others is justifiable and even desirable. But another group exists, one whose behaviors and attitudes are potentially much more destructive to the organization and its employees than those noted above who are motivated by greed or big egos. This group, the subject of this book, displays a personality disorder rooted in lying, manipulation, deceit, egocentricity, callousness, and other potentially destructive traits. This personality disorder, one of the first to be described in the psychiatric literature, is psychopathy.

A dozen or so personality disorders have found their way into the psychiatric nomenclature. What makes psychopathy unique is that its defining characteristics and traits often lead to behaviors that conflict with the generally accepted norms and laws of society. Some people with psychopathic personalities are in prison because of their crimes against people and property. Others are in prison for committing economic or white-collar crimes, such as fraud, embezzlement, or stock manipulation. These are crimes against businesses and institutions, as well as the employees who work in them.

In addition to the problems their abusive behaviors cause to spouses, friends, and family members, individuals with a heavy dose of psychopathic traits are potentially harmful to professional relationships. For example, their grandiosity, sense of entitlement, and lack of personal insight lead to conflict and rivalry with bosses and coworkers, and their impulsivity and "live in the moment" philosophy lead them to keep repeating these and other dysfunctional, antisocial behaviors, despite performance appraisals and training programs. Many experts believed that these traits alone make it difficult for psychopaths to have successful long-term careers in industry. At least that was the conventional wisdom until we did our research.

One might think that conning or bullying traits in a job applicant would be so obvious to employers that such candidates would not be hired for important jobs, especially those where the ability to get along with others is critical. One might also think that abusive, deceitful behavior toward coworkers would eventually lead to disciplinary action and termination. But, based on the cases we have re-viewed, this often is not the case.

There are four possible reasons for this. First, some core psycho-pathic personality traits—we might call them talents—may seem attractive in job applicants, and contribute to their success at being hired. For example, psychopaths can be very charming, able to talk their way past even the most seasoned interviewers. When it is to their advantage, they can display a charisma that can disarm and be-guile even the most wary individuals. Just as those who have unwit-tingly married a psychopath find themselves trapped in a web of deceit, abuse, and pain, so too can a company make a faulty hiring decision and find itself with a serious problem on its hands down the road. Psychopaths are skilled at social manipulation, and the job in-terview is a perfect place to apply their talents.

Second, some companies quite innocently recruit individuals with psychopathic tendencies because some hiring managers may mistak-enly attribute "leadership" labels to what are, in actuality, psycho-pathic behaviors. For example, taking charge, making decisions, and getting others to do what you want are classic features of leadership and management, yet they can also be well-packaged forms of coer-cion, domination, and manipulation. Failing to look closely beneath the outer trappings of stereotypical leadership to the inner working of the personality can sometimes lead to a regrettable hiring decision.

Third, the changing nature of business itself is also a contribut-ing factor to the increase in psychopathic persons being hired. "Bu-reaucracy" as a business model evolved early in the last century to address the problems inherent in coordinating and optimizing the efforts of large numbers of people who were performing many inter-related job functions. As business competition became more sophis-ticated, these support systems became more complex, and their supporting infrastructure grew in size. As a result, bureaucracies typ-ically employed a large number of people, had multiple processes and procedures, and were expensive to run. These characteristics earned them a reputation for being almost too big to be effective.

Since then, organizational structures and processes have evolved considerably, with the most dramatic changes taking place during the early 1970s and 1980s, the beginning of what may be called "the organization wars." During this time corporate takeovers, acquisitions, mergers, and breakups led to great social and financial upheaval in the business world. The desire to create sleek, lean, efficient companies was a good one, and long overdue in many industries. Eventually, in order to survive, many companies shed their old-style, bureaucratic policies and structures for a flatter, more free-form, faster-paced organizational environment. During the 1990s, this new, "transitional" organizational style—fewer layers, simpler systems and controls, more freedom to make decisions—became the norm. In fact, *change* became a matter of business necessity and economic survival. Competing successfully now required the quick generation and movement of new information. Speed and innovation were now more important than keeping track of what was already old news.

With the need to embrace change came a switch from hiring "organization men and women" who would maintain the status quo to hiring individuals who could shake the trees, rattle cages, and get things done quickly. This hiring switch inadvertently led to the selection of some individuals with psychopathic traits and characteristics. Unfortunately, the general state of confusion that change brings to any situation can make psychopathic personality traits— the appearance of confidence, strength, and calm—often look like the answer to the organization's problems. Yet, hiring individuals with these traits seemed like the right thing to do. Egocentricity, callousness, and insensitivity suddenly became acceptable trade-offs in order to get the talents and skills needed to survive in an accelerated, dispassionate business world.

Fourth, psychopathic individuals, known for ignoring rules and regulations, coupled with a talent for conning and manipulation, found these new, more flexible organization structures *inviting*. The temptation for someone with a psychopathic personality to join a new, fast-paced, competitive, and highly effective "transitional" orga-nization, especially one with few constraints or rules, is too great, and the personal rewards too significant, to be ignored. The effect of these things is that psychopaths are more attracted to work for busi-nesses that offer fast-paced, high-risk, high-profit environments.

It is very important to understand how and why the psychopath so readily manipulates people and organizations, given the increasing financial and social risk to companies wishing to survive in a chaotic business environment filled with uncertainty, constant change, and increasing regulation. In addition to financial harm to a company and its shareholders, there are also personal dangers to coworkers. There is the risk to the careers of those subjected to the emotional or physical abuse of a psychopathic coworker. For example, senior exec-utives may find their authority and security severely compromised by the "high-potential" management candidate moving up the ranks. Covert attacks and defensive maneuvers waste valuable time and en-ergy that could otherwise be focused on creativity, productivity, and profitability. In addition, bruised leadership egos and lowered morale are much harder to measure but can lead to large declines in organi-zational performance.

Unfortunately, even an organization with sophisticated hiring and promotion practices would find it challenging to defend itself against these "corporate cons." Even loyal coworkers—firsthand wit-nesses to much of the psychopath's machinations—do not always understand what is happening. And, when some do raise the red flag, they may find that no one at the top responds to it.

This book evolved out of our growing realization that lack of specific knowledge about what constitutes psychopathic manipula-tion and deceit among businesspeople was the corporate con's key to success. The scientific literature on the behavior of criminal psy-chopaths is extensive but geared to the forensic scientist and clini-cian. We hope to close some of the gaps in the current understanding of psychopaths among the business readers by using nontechnical language and case studies. We want to provide the reader with the experience of working next to a corporate psychopath by presenting the kinds of real-life situations we've encountered in our work. Because a psychopathic coworker can harm your career in seen and unseen ways, we hope that this knowledge will prepare you to defend yourself in the future.

The premise of this book is that psychopaths do work in modern organizations; they often are successful by most standard measures of career success; and their destructive personality characteristics are invisible to most of the people with whom they interact. They are able to circumvent and sometimes hijack succession planning and performance management systems in order to give legitimacy to their behaviors. They take advantage of communication weaknesses, organizational systems and processes, interpersonal conflicts, and general stressors that plague all companies. They abuse coworkers and, by lowering morale and stirring up conflict, the company itself. Some may even steal and defraud.

This book will help you peel back the layers covering the psychopath's personality. We will approach this task in several ways, leading the reader toward an understanding of what makes psychopaths tick and what behaviors can be observed in the office that might provide clues as to their true nature. We will follow the exploits of "Dave," one of the first corporate psychopaths documented in the scientific literature, as he weaves his web of deceit. His ability to present himself as a rising star and corporate savior, all the while abusing his coworkers and eventually the company, will be made transparent. We will also explain in some detail what the current thinking is about psychopathic behavior in organizations, illustrating specific traits with examples and short case histories taken from real life. This book will introduce you to the way these "snakes in suits" manipulate others; it will help you see through their games and give you pointers on how to protect yourself, your career, and your company.

We consider it important to caution the reader that, although the topic of this book is psychopathy in the workplace, *not everyone described herein is a psychopath.* The "snakes" we describe are not based on actual persons, and any resemblance to such persons, living or dead, is purely coincidental. Rather, they are profiles of generic psychopaths based upon composites of psychopathic characteristics derived from published reports, the news media, and our own research about such personalities. While we do at times refer to actual persons, such as in the sidebars, we do so only because the person's behavior is either consistent with the concept of psychopathy or illustrates a key trait or behavior that is typical of the disorder. While these individuals may or may not be psychopaths, their reported behavior provides a useful vehicle for elaborating the various traits and behaviors that define psychopathy. *The reader should not assume that an individual is a psychopath simply because of the context in which he or she is portrayed in this book.*

ACT I, Scene I

GRAND ENTRANCE

One could imagine he was arriving at a *GQ* photo shoot, judging by his smooth, strong, and confident entrance. As interview suits went, his was the finest. His smile was broad and toothy, his shirt crisp and white, and, well, the whole package was perfection.

"Hi, I'm Dave. I'm here to see Frank," he said to the receptionist, who had already noticed him, as had the other young women who had positioned themselves unobtrusively in the lobby. "I'll ring him, sir. Please have a seat," she replied. "It's good to see you again," she smiled. And it certainly was, she thought, as she smiled to herself and glared at her competition.

"Hi, Dave, good to see you again," rang Frank's voice, beaming from across the room as he approached Dave. "How was the trip in?"

"Fine, pleasant," stated Dave as he gave a firm handshake.

"We have a couple more interviews for you today," said Frank. "Just some human resources folks, and a meeting with my boss, our vice president, and then lunch and a tour of the surrounding community."

"Great, I'm ready to get started," Dave said.

Garrideb Technologies was one of those high-tech companies, born in a garage in the Midwest, that had skyrocketed to success beyond the wildest dreams of its founders. Because of the company's incredible growth, changes to the organization were sorely needed, not the least of which was the need to hire more staff. The management team went for the best talent available to keep up with the growing demands for their products and services. Few candidates had résumés with the specialized education and experience they needed, but Dave did.

The HR interviews went better than these interviews usually go. HR types tend to probe more deeply into the motivations of people than do the department interviewers, and ask for too many details about past jobs and references, but Dave was polite. "I'll stay as long as you need me," he said, smiling, "so whatever you need, please, that's why I'm here." After they were through, the HR assistant escorted Dave to the executive wing.

"Welcome, Dave, I'm glad to finally meet you," stated John, the vice president of new products, noting the attractive tie against Dave's starched shirt. "How was your trip in?"

"Excellent," stated Dave, "this is a beautiful part of the country. I can't wait to take a better look around. Your facilities are extraordinary; I've never seen such architecture."

"Thanks," responded John. "We try to make it comfortable for our staff. Success has its rewards, and we don't skimp on creature comforts."

"I've heard a bit about your strategic plan from Frank, and I've read the company brochure, but I'd like to get the details from you, as the major strategist of the company's success. How did you do all of this?" inquired Dave. Pleased with Dave's interest in the company's future, he took some slides from a binder on his bookshelf to show Dave some graphs. John launched into his exposition on his plan. "Unbelievable! You really have done a great job orchestrating everything," exclaimed Dave.

John was pleased to interact with someone who, despite his age, understood so well the intricacies of building a business. He pushed aside the suggested interview questions HR had prepared for him and asked Dave to tell him about himself. Dave obliged eagerly by describing his work history, giving plenty of examples reflecting John's respect for hard work and diligence. The extent of Dave's experience was—at age thirty-five—impressive, documented by a résumé and a portfolio most would work a career to achieve.

The interview with John went exceptionally well. As the interview ended, Dave extended his hand, smiled, and said, looking straight into John's eyes, "Thank you so much for your time. I look forward to working closely with you; I know I can help you realize your strategic vision."

"The pleasure was mine; I hope to see you again," answered John. John's secretary escorted Dave back to the lobby to wait for Frank. *One could not ask for a better candidate,* thought John as he dialed up Frank with his approval.

Frank grabbed his jacket, but as he reached the door of his office on his way to pick up Dave for lunch, his phone rang, "I'd like us all to get together later today to discuss Dave's candidacy," said the HR director.

"Oh, Melanie, that won't be necessary. John and I just agreed to offer Dave the job; I'm going to take him to lunch and make him the offer."

"But we agreed to get all the interviewers together to discuss each candidate thoroughly; and we wanted to bring back Tom, the guy from New York, for a second look also," she reminded Frank.

"That won't be necessary; clearly, one could not ask for a better candidate than Dave," he said as he hung up. Frank was happy to have found someone with the right fit for both the job and the organization, and he didn't want this one to get away.

Over lunch, Frank made the offer to Dave. Dave pushed back at the original salary offer, which was actually high in the range, and Frank agreed to sweeten the pie with a sign-on bonus and review in six months.

Frank was very pleased when Dave accepted the enhanced offer. Seeing leadership potential in him, Frank knew that Dave's style, intelligence, and technical expertise made him an ideal management candidate in this successful, rapidly growing high-tech firm. Everyone who interviewed Dave thought he was perfect; one of the people from the lab even stated that he was "too good to be true." Dave would start working for Frank in two weeks.

This scene is growing more common as companies accelerate their hiring practices to attract, hire, and retain new, high-potential talent before their competitors do. Gone are the days of the painstaking vetting process. Competition is fierce and qualified candidates few. Business now moves swiftly, and common wisdom is that those who hesitate lose. But was Dave a good hire?

We'll follow Dave and others through this book, and explore what makes them so attractive, yet so potentially damaging to an organization. We'll describe how they get in and how they move up the organization into positions of increasing power and influence, where the damage they can do to the organization and its members can be significant. We'll then offer suggestions to employees and coworkers who might be potential targets, and to managers and executives on how to secure the organization from unscrupulous manipulation.

How would you describe Dave's personality? Would you hire Dave?

1

Nice Suit. Would a Snake Wear Such a Nice Suit?

Fred led the group to O'Hare's tavern after work that night. He started a tab and ordered a round of drinks for everyone from the company. As more people arrived, there were cheers and high-fives as coworkers rejoiced about their good fortune. Fred raised his glass in a toast. Silence spread over the group as everyone turned toward him with a raised glass: "The Pit Bull is dead. Long live the Pit Bull!" he shouted to the glee of everyone there.

"Hear, hear!" they cheered as glasses were emptied and bursts of laughter and applause overtook the room. There was not a sad person in the place that night; quite a change from most Friday nights at O'Hare's over the past two years.

Things at the company had been good up until the Pit Bull arrived. Raises were excellent, bonuses generous, working condi-

tions pleasant, and the chance to work for one of the oldest and most respected names in the business was personally rewarding to many. Nevertheless, as with all good things, there was change. The CEO, "Old Man Bailey" to his friends (and most employees were his friends), had sold his financial services company to a bigger competitor two years back. However, like so many career executives, he just could not see himself quietly fading away, but needed to keep his hands in the business, so he negotiated an interim consulting position on the board to assist with the transition.

The board welcomed his advice and felt comfortable with his occasional visits to his former company's (now a division) headquarters. Bailey wanted to keep the old values he had impressed upon his people alive in the company, and hoped that they would spread to the other parts of the bigger corporation, but this was not to be. Being part of a big corporation meant that there were now many divisions and locations, and his little piece of the corporate world, as well as his ability to influence, was lessening with each acquisition. Other divisions had their own values, service lines, and ways of doing things, and the corporate staff had their own ideas about what the overall company culture ought to be like.

Although he made a point of staying out of the day-to-day running of the business, one decision in particular that bothered Bailey was the promotional transfer of Gus, a "hotshot whiz kid" according to Bailey, into the top slot as COO of the division. Bailey saw Gus as a status-conscious suck-up who hated holding people accountable, avoided confrontation, preferred to get others to do his dirty work, and was rather susceptible to flattery and attention. Bailey thought Gus spent too much time meeting with the corporate folks and not enough time getting things done in his division.

Soon pitchers of beer and bowls of peanuts were spread out over the tables in O'Hare's back room, where the group discussed the details of the Pit Bull's termination. As staff from different departments mingled, those who had heard only some of the rumors sought out more information; others wanted confirmation of the details they had heard. It was great fun to collect different bits and pieces of the story and try to assemble a picture of what had really happened.

Six months into Gus's tenure, all hell broke loose. For the first time in its long history, Bailey's division had failed to meet its targets, so much so that the market analysts were starting to make unflattering comments, endangering the reputation of the whole corporation. Making things worse, there was also the risk of a hefty, very public, and humiliating fine for noncompliance on some government work—a fact that had not reached the newspapers yet, but was sure to make headlines if not averted quickly. Bailey felt that Gus ought to be let go, and offered to run the place until a suitable, better-qualified candidate could be found. The corporate executive committee disagreed. In an effort to help Gus and be fair to him in his new role, they decided to create a new director of operations position reporting to him.

One person who caught their attention as the perfect internal candidate for the job was Helen. Helen had joined one of the other acquisitions only a year before and rose to stardom overnight. Her performance review praised her spirit, diligence, focus, energy, and natural ability. She demonstrated her worth to her management, building a reputation for making things happen, for successful project management, and for meeting deadlines. Admittedly, some collateral damage occurred along the way, but that did not seem to concern her management team, who put her on the key management watch list. Yet, despite the glowing reviews from her management, her division was expanding its head count and underperforming, all the while requesting and receiving approval for larger budgets two years in a row. Bailey wondered how the corporate folks could

*ignore these numbers and put someone who was used to spending
money in charge of a financial problem. But then, these were no
longer his decisions to make.*

*Helen did very well in the exploratory interview with the
search committee. Her dynamic and engaging manner and her
self-proclaimed ability to fix organizational problems—which
the division certainly had—made her an obvious choice for the
spot. Outside analysts would also see the appointment of such an
assertive, vibrant, and directive person to a failing high-profile
division as a very firm commitment to meeting the government's
regulatory requirements. Her style and her manner matched
what both the corporation and analysts wanted to see. The timing, the circumstances, and her abilities seemed like a good fit.*

Lynda, from accounting, sat in the corner of the room and
sipped her beer. The raucous conversation of the colleagues who sat
with her provided a soothing backdrop for Lynda's private thoughts.
"You should be happy, Lynda," said Julie, the senior member of the
audit team. "You won, and the [expletive deleted] is gone."

Lynda took a drink and smiled shyly. Just out of school, she
never thought working for a big company would be like this. The last
few months had been very rough on her. She could handle the work,
of course, and brought some new computer assessment techniques to
the department from her schooling, but the hurt she felt just would
not go away.

"Listen, Lyn, the world is made up of all kinds of people, and
you were unlucky to get a jerk on your first job. But most folks are
nice and want to do a good job—you're one of them, and you're surrounded by friends—you did the right thing; you're our hero." A collective expression of sympathy rose from the table, and Julie put her
arm around Lynda, who smiled.

Lynda had been the unlucky target of much of the abuse in the
accounting department. Perhaps it was her naïveté, her youth, or her
propensity to be honest, but even Julie could not completely shield
her from the abuse. Julie had gone to bat for Lynda when her audit

raised serious questions about what the Pit Bull was doing, but her own strength was no match for the Pit Bull.

Helen was disappointed in the offer. She expected that Gus would be let go or moved out and she would get the top job. Her division HR VP explained to her that the director job was a high-profile development position, the key position responsible for improving the day-to-day workings of the division; all would be watching to see if she could help Gus turn it around in short order. Stellar performance in her new role would go a long way to fast and significant promotions, she was told. In addition, Gus and Helen were seen as an excellent combination for the task, and while individually quite different in approach and style, they would make a very powerful team—she could learn from his experience as much as he could learn from her.

Helen said that she would consider taking the job on the condition that she receive all the support she needed to succeed, a reasonable request by all accounts. The corporation was prepared to take whatever steps were deemed necessary, and approve whatever authority was requested, in order to fix the problem and move away from this embarrassing episode in the corporation's history. In sharp contrast to the financial controls elsewhere within the corporation, therefore, Gus and Helen could have pretty much whatever resources they requested. With these assurances, and effectively a blank check, Helen agreed to take the job.

In a little over six months, the problems that had plagued the unit seemed to disappear. The service level on the government contracts rose to 95 percent delivery performance, the errors (human, computer, and procedural) that had created the problems were found and quickly corrected, and the regulatory compliance question went away quietly. Helen was singled out for public praise for saving the division. Even Gus spoke favorably about her, especially her ethical conduct, diligence, and dedication to the job.

Fred made the rounds of the small groups that formed around the room. New toasts were made as he moved in and out. Bits and pieces of heated conversation were audible through the overall din. Rick, from the mailroom, confirmed that the state police had been at the back door to keep everyone inside: "And there were these two guys in black suits carrying out computers, files, and the contents of the shred bin," he reported. Sheila, from security, confirmed that the call had come that morning, followed by the orders to put security staff by the front door. "Yes, handcuffs," she responded to the questions from the marketing staff.

No one was surprised when Gus was moved out of his position—except, perhaps, Gus—after Helen made arguments to the executive committee members that implicated him in the original business letdown. She had clever ideas and tremendous energy, and persisted in pushing strongly for what she wanted; she constructed a plausible story line about Gus's mismanagement that solidly reinforced her business case. Helen was profoundly competitive, dramatic in her engagement with others, and just loved to take center stage and the limelight. Turning the division around gave her the platform she needed for a great career at the company. Overall, she convinced them that she possessed all the leadership traits needed to run a major business. Naturally, she was the choice to replace Gus, and was rewarded by a promotion to his position as COO.

The front door of O'Hare's opened slowly. There stood a rather large man in a long, black coat. He glanced at his wristwatch and moved toward the bar. O'Hare was at the bar that evening, and greeted the well-dressed gentleman with a nod. Taking off his black gloves, the man ordered a ginger ale in a Scotch glass with a swizzle stick. O'Hare nodded and went to make the drink.

Not everyone liked Helen, of course, and some of her staff did not trust her. She treated the junior colleagues with disdain and a measure of contempt, often deriding their abilities and competence. To those she found useful to her career, however, she was gracious, engaging, and fun. She had a talent for presenting her good side to those she felt mattered, all the while denying, discounting, discarding, and displacing anyone who did not agree with her decisions.

Helen developed a reputation for telling the corporate staff what they wanted to hear, stage-managing meetings with the executive team as if they were Hollywood productions. She insisted that her direct reports follow the agreed-upon scripts, deferring any unexpected or difficult questions to her. According to her peers, Helen was a master at impression management, and she successfully manipulated her boss, intimidated direct reports, and played up to key personalities important to her.

Picking up his drink, the man looked around the tavern. The place was quiet except for the noise from the back room. The visitor asked for another drink, putting his credit card on the bar. O'Hare poured the drink and placed it on the bar, taking the credit card to run a tab.

With the government fiasco behind her and Gus out of the way, Helen let loose some of her domineering management style. Histrionics were common during staff meetings, and participants often felt bruised, battered, and humiliated at the end of their meetings with her. She would stomp around the new office complex—which she had leased because she wanted a bigger office—without acknowledging others, barking out orders and generally intimidating, frightening, and pushing people around.

This was a total departure from the values embodied in Bailey, a man whose door was always open, and who routinely made the rounds of the staff, soliciting new ideas to improve the business. Bailey valued his people and amazed new staff with his ability to remember their spouses' names and children's sports accomplishments. Bailey was a people person who was not only extremely bright, but also knew how to make money, and he made a lot. He knew that his success—the success of the business—rested with the quality of his staff, and he shared the glory as well as the rewards with those around him.

Over the next few months, Helen hired her own group of people to replace many of her more vocal opponents on her senior staff. Relying on her own gut-feel approach to hiring talent, she would offer large sign-on bonuses to entice young, bright executives to leave their current jobs, and if she then decided—within days or weeks—that they just weren't good enough and couldn't hack it, they had to go. She fired most of the quick appointments to her management team in rapid succession as she decided they were inadequate, incompetent, or no longer needed. There was no concern about the damage she did to the careers and family lives of these people, or the legal problems she could potentially cause for the corporation.

Helen seemed able to get away with whatever she wanted, including the purchase of the latest extravagance, whether this be a computer, a new car, corporate apartment, or any other accessory that signaled the trappings of power. Helen initiated a series of expensive management conferences, held in tropical locations, with prominent keynote speakers, in which she trumpeted the division's accomplishments with her fully taking the spotlight. Her presentation of success was at odds with a continuing lack of cohesion within the division—but somehow those outside did not notice this discrepancy.

She was unwilling and perhaps unable to acknowledge that any of her decisions could have any negative consequences for the business. Questioning her behavior provoked intense reactions, as, for example, when she fired the executive coach hired by the corporation to help her smooth over her rough edges. She was never wrong but always right, being interested only in positive news. People resented the way in which she paraded about like a queen bee. She enjoyed displaying her status, power, and the ex-

ecutive privileges she enjoyed within the corporation, including the lease of a corporate jet for her travels. She had made many enemies, but many on the staff were afraid of her.

The man at the bar glanced at his wristwatch once again and looked around the room as if searching for someone. "They're in there," said O'Hare, nodding to the door to the back room. "I don't think they are expecting you, but you can go right in."

What really irked the staff was Helen's increasing absence from the office, while she had virtually lived in her office while Gus was in charge. Her second in command, Ned—a close, personal friend appointed by her to a new business development post—was often absent at the same time, provoking unkind rumors. Other, more critical rumors had him running another business on the side, in spite of the prohibitions of company policy. Ned's presence was resented, but Helen protected him and no one dared contradict or question them.

With glass in hand, the man pushed open the door to the back room slowly. No one really noticed the visitor enter, except Fred.

"Ned was found in the cafeteria getting coffee," reported Sheila. "When they put the cuffs on him, he protested, making a big scene and demanding to call his lawyer!"

"What about the Pit Bull trying to escape on the jet?" questioned Sam, who was always the last to hear the latest gossip.

Seeing who had entered the room, Fred coughed loudly in an attempt to warn the group, but few heard him. Loudly tapping his glass with his ring, he began to get the group's attention. Loud noise turned to whispers, and whispers to complete silence as more and more people took notice of the gentleman's arrival.

The fraud that had been uncovered was as clever as it was brazen. No one suspected that some of the key accounts responsible for the turnaround and growth were fictitious, and Ned and the Pit Bull were a team of fraudsters. Little did those in the office realize that some of the bigger accounts were completely phony, created by Ned to inflate the business results. No one could imagine that they had been working right next to a couple of crooks.

The gentleman searched the faces in the room and smiled at those he still recognized. Seeing Shirley at the back table, he moved toward that group. Most of the folks had already risen, but Lynda, whose back was to the door, was still deep in her thoughts. As he moved forward, the crowd parted. Standing to her side, he asked, "Are you Lynda?" Surprised out of her reverie, she turned and saw who was standing next to her.

Few companies experience the high drama that unfolded that day. Eventually, the authorities learned that Helen, using the computer access codes she had gotten from the IT server, was able to make ever so small changes to several customer accounts, gradually siphoning off assets to her offshore account. Ned, who by chance was in the office that day, had seen the state police pulling up and had had enough time to call Helen before he bolted out of his office toward the cafeteria exit and into the hands of the police. Helen was luckier. As the unmarked cars were coming down her street, she escaped out the back door of her palatial house and stole across the yard to the next street, where she always kept her second car parked and ready for just such an emergency. While the corporate jet was being watched, few imagined that she also leased a private plane at a local airstrip on the other side of town.

"Yes, sir," Lynda said, timidly.

"I wanted to thank you personally for all your help. I really do appreciate your courage and honesty."

"Mr. Bailey," said Fred, coming up behind him, "it's great to see you. Welcome to our little get-together."

"It's good to see you, too, Fred. Looks like we've run out of beer," he hinted as he took a seat next to Lynda. "The party's on me, folks," said Old Man Bailey. "Fred, could you get me another drink? O'Hare knows what I take."

2

Who *Are* These People?

Novels and movies portray psychopaths in extreme, stereotypical ways. They appear as cold-blooded serial killers, stalkers, sex offenders, con men and women, or the prototypical evil, manipulating villain, such as Dr. No or Hannibal Lecter. Reality, unfortunately, provides some support for this view, but the picture is somewhat more complex than this.

Years of research on prison populations bear out the criminality and violence implied by the term *psychopath*. We now know that both male and female psychopaths commit a greater number and variety of crimes than do other criminals. Their crimes tend to be more violent than those of other criminals, and their general behavior more controlling, aggressive, threatening, and abusive. Further, their aggression and violence tend to be predatory in nature—cold-blooded and devoid of the intense emotional upheaval that typically accompanies the violent acts of most people. This sort of aggression and violence is *instrumental*, simply a means to an end, and seldom followed by anything even approaching normal concern for the pain and suffering inflicted on others. On the other hand, much of the violence of other criminals tends to be *reactive*—a typical response to threats or situations that generate an intense emotional state. This type of violence, which includes what is often described as a crime of passion, typically is followed by feelings of remorse and guilt for the harm done to others.

Perhaps most dangerous of all from a public safety point of view, psychopathic criminals *recidivate* at a much higher rate, and do so much earlier, than do other criminals. The recidivism rate refers to the percentage of offenders that commit a new crime subsequent to release into the community. Psychopaths make up about 15 percent of the prison population. Many of the remaining 85 percent of individuals in prison might be described as sociopaths or as having antisocial personality disorder, similar, but different disorders often confused with psychopathy (see sidebar). Although the prevalence of psychopathy in the general population is relatively small—only about 1 percent—the social, economic, physical, and psychological damage done by individuals with this disorder is far out of proportion to their numbers. They are responsible for at least half of the persistent serious and violent crimes committed in North America. Yet, as we shall see, not all psychopaths turn to a life of crime, and not all criminals are psychopaths.

Psychopathy, Sociopathy, and Antisocial Personality Disorder

Many people are confused about the differences among psychopathy, sociopathy, and antisocial personality disorder. Although the terms frequently are treated as if they are interchangeable—by the general public and professionals alike—they refer to related but not identical conditions.

Psychopathy is a personality disorder described by the personality traits and behaviors that form the basis of this book. Psychopaths are without conscience and incapable of empathy, guilt, or loyalty to anyone but themselves.

Sociopathy is not a formal psychiatric condition. It refers to patterns of attitudes and behaviors that are considered antisocial and criminal by society at large, but are seen as normal or necessary by the subculture or social environment in which they developed. Sociopaths may have a well-developed conscience and a normal capacity for empathy, guilt, and loyalty, but their sense of right and wrong is based on the norms and expectations of their subculture or group. Many criminals might be described as sociopaths.

Antisocial personality disorder (APD) is a broad diagnostic category found in the American Psychiatric Association's *Diagnostic and Statistical Manual of Mental Disorders*, 4th edition (DSM-IV). Antisocial and criminal behaviors play a major role in its definition and, in this sense, APD is similar to sociopathy. Some of those with APD are psychopaths, but many are not. The difference between psychopathy and antisocial personality disorder is that the former includes personality traits such as lack of empathy, grandiosity, and shallow emotion that are not necessary for a diagnosis of APD. APD is three or four times more common than psychopathy in the general population and in prisons. The prevalence of those we would describe as sociopathic is unknown but likely is considerably higher than that of APD.

One may argue that psychopaths who live freely in society simply have not yet been caught committing a crime or engaging in socially destructive behavior. Given the psychopaths' personality features, and their inclination for breaking the rules and pushing the envelope of acceptable human behavior, there is some merit to this argument. Still, just having a psychopathic personality disorder does not make one a criminal. Some psychopaths live in society and do not technically break the law—although they may come close, with behavior that usually is very unpleasant for those around them. Some may lead seemingly normal lives, not hurting people in ways that attract attention, but causing problems nonetheless in hidden economic, psychological, and emotionally abusive ways. They do not make warm and loving parents, children, or family members. They do not make reliable friends or coworkers. Many psychopaths adopt a parasitic existence, living off the generosity or gullibility of others by taking advantage of and often abusing the trust and support of friends and family. They may move from place to place and from one source of support to another. You probably know one. You could work for, work with, or be married to someone with a psychopathic personality and not know that there is a formal psychological term for the individual who causes you so much pain and distress. He or she can be a neighbor, friend, or family member whose behavior you may find fascinating, confusing, and repelling.

So how do psychologists and psychiatrists accurately decide whether someone has a psychopathic personality? In the early days of research on psychopathy, there was no widely acceptable standard of measurement. The psychiatric criteria for use in diagnoses were vague, sometimes confusing, and could vary depending on the personal experiences of the researcher or diagnostician. This dark and murky past has cleared up considerably over the last fifty years as psychopathy has grown into one of the most researched and well-understood psychopathological variables.

A pioneer in the early years of this field was Hervey Cleckley, M.D., working as a psychiatrist in a psychiatric facility in the late 1930s. Offenders and patients were sent to psychiatric hospitals for treatment if they were believed to have some form of mental illness. Cleckley had the opportunity to study his patients carefully, and he realized that many of them did not display the usual symptoms of mental illness, but instead seemed "normal" under most conditions. He watched them charm, manipulate, and take advantage of other patients, family members, and even hospital staff. To Cleckley's trained eyes, these individuals were psychopaths.

Cleckley eventually wrote what has become a classic textbook on psychopathy, *The Mask of Sanity*. Originally published in 1941, this definitive book is now in its fifth edition (1976), and was one of the first books to present a clear picture of psychopathy. Despite having normal intelligence, Cleckley's patients often made poor life judgments and didn't learn much from their personal experiences, causing them to repeat dysfunctional or unfruitful behaviors. They lacked insight concerning themselves and the impact of their behavior on others, but this seemed not to concern them at all. They did not understand and cared little about the feelings of others, lacking both remorse and shame for the harm they did others. They were noticeably unreliable, even about important things relevant to their current situation, and seemed to have no real life goals or plans. Most obvious of all, these patients were consummate liars, being untruthful about almost everything (even inconsequential things most people wouldn't waste time and energy lying about). They were insincere, although often appearing to be very sincere to those with little experience interacting with them, particularly new staff members.

Reviews of their records showed them to be antisocial and violent for reasons that often seemed random and senseless. They could be egocentric in the extreme, and were seemingly unable to experience deep human emotions, especially love and compassion. They failed to have significant or intimate relationships. Even their sexual relations were superficial and impersonal. In fact, they seemed unable to feel intensely any of the emotions that others experience, except perhaps primitive or proto-emotions such as anger, frustration, and rage. According to Cleckley, psychopaths come across as having a superficial charm and good intelligence. Psychopaths are often entertaining and can tell creative, believable stories. They don't seem to experience delusional or irrational thinking, which often characterizes a mental disorder, and they tend not to be anxious or neurotic. On the surface, then, they appear normal, sane, and in control; in fact, many are quite likable. As Cleckley put it, "[the] psychopath presents a technical appearance of sanity, often one of high intellectual capacities, and not infrequently succeeds in business or professional activities."

The title of his book, *The Mask of Sanity*, reflected Cleckley's belief that, although psychopaths do not exhibit the obvious symptoms of mental illness, they suffer from a profound underlying disorder in which the language and emotional components of thought are not properly integrated, a condition he called *semantic aphasia*. It is tempting to try to decide if someone is a psychopath simply by watching or listening to him or her and checking off the characteristics that match Cleckley's list. Cleckley, however, never intended his list of observations to be a formal checklist for diagnosis, and had never tested his model statistically. As a clinician with many years of exposure to psychopaths, he reported those traits that seemed to him to characterize the syndrome.

Confirmation of his observations and the development of scientific methods for assessment, therefore, was left to others, one in particular being Hare, the second author of this book. He describes these efforts, outlined in his book, *Without Conscience: The Disturbing World of the Psychopaths Among Us*, as follows:

> *I worked in a maximum-security penitentiary early in my career as a psychologist in order to help finance my graduate school education. While there, I took an interest in the behavior of psychopaths, whom I occasionally met as part of my work. My initial interest was in finding out if there were any physiological differences between psychopathic and nonpsychopathic offenders. Cleckley had noted that psychopaths used language somewhat differently from most other people; their sentence structure, choice of words and tempo (or beat) were different. Others and I also had noted that psychopaths have difficulty understanding the emotional content of words that add color and interest to communication. They would often describe their most atrocious crimes with dispassion and disinterest, showing no emotion at all. Just hearing these matter-of-fact descriptions sent chills*

down the spines of many criminal investigators, even though they typically were hardened by years of work with criminals. Could there be something different going on in the psychopath's brain that might explain these differences?

I wanted to look deeper into the brain for some answers. In these early experiments, I would present psychopathic and nonpsychopathic offenders with words differing in emotional content and measured their physiological responses. High emotional content words might include "rape," "blood," or "knife," while low emotional content words might include "tree," "house," and "rock." Trained as an experimental psychologist, I knew that high-emotion words trigger physiological responses in subjects that could be measured using sensitive laboratory equipment; would the same be true of psychopaths?

The first obstacle was defining psychopathy. There was no standard and reliable assessment instrument available to researchers to measure the disorder. The diagnostic skills of the investigator, on which accuracy relied, could not be assured. Some researchers might use Cleckley's definition, others the American Psychiatric Association's Diagnostic and Statistical Manual *(DSM), then a newly published guidebook for psychiatrists, and still others might rely on their own clinical impressions. Without a consensus, how could a researcher in Canada be sure that a researcher somewhere else in the world could reproduce his research results? What if they didn't agree on which subjects were really psychopaths, and which subjects were not?*

I needed to create a research-worthy measure of psychopathy, and this new instrument had to be valid, reliable, and psychologically sound. Cleckley's list of behavioral descriptors, although a good starting point, was incomplete. Collecting a large number of known descriptors of psychopathic traits and behaviors, and using statistical analysis techniques, I set out to resolve what were the most common and specific traits and behaviors that distinguish a psychopath from a nonpsychopath.

The result of this work is the Psychopathy Checklist–Revised, or PCL-R, a list of twenty interpersonal, emotional, and lifestyle traits and behaviors. "True" psychopaths have most or all the PCL-R traits, while individuals who have only a few of these traits are not psychopaths. For twenty years now, statistical studies on many criminal populations all over the world have consistently shown the PCL-R to be the gold standard for measuring psychopathy.

Nature? Nurture? Both!

Are psychopathic features the product of nature or nurture? As with most other things human, the answer is that both are involved. A better question is "To what extent do nature and nurture influence the development of the traits and behaviors that define psychopathy?" The answer to this question is becoming much clearer with the application of behavioral genetics to the study of personality traits and behavioral dispositions.

Several recent twin studies provide convincing evidence that genetic factors play at least as important a role in the development of the core features of psychopathy as do environmental factors and forces. Researchers Blonigen, Carlson, Krueger & Patrick stated that the results of their study of 271 adult twin pairs provided "substantial evidence of genetic contributions to variance in the personality construct of psychopathy." Subsequently, researchers Larrson, Andershed & Lichstenstien arrived at a similar conclusion in their study of 1090 adolescent twin pairs: "A genetic factor explains most of the variation in the psychopathic personality." Viding, Blair, Moffitt & Plomin studied 3687 seven-year-old twin pairs and also concluded that "the core symptoms of psychopathy are strongly genetically determined." They reported that the genetic contribution was highest when callous-unemotional traits were combined with antisocial behaviors.

Evidence of this sort does not mean that the pathways to

adult psychopathy are fixed and immutable, but it does indicate that the social environment will have a tough time in overcoming what nature has provided. As noted in *Without Conscience*, the elements needed for the development of psychopathy—such as a profound inability to experience empathy and the complete range of emotions, including fear—are provided in part by nature and possibly by some unknown biological influences on the developing fetus and neonate. As a result, the capacity for developing internal controls and conscience and for making emotional "connections" with others is greatly reduced.

To use a simple analogy, the potter is instrumental in molding pottery from clay (nurture), but the characteristics of the pottery also depend on the sort of clay available (nature).

The most reliable, valid, and widely used instrument for the assessment of psychopathy is the Hare Psychopathy Checklist–Revised (PCL-R). The PCL-R is a clinical rating scale, not a self-report test. The person who is being evaluated does not answer questions, as is the case with other psychological tests. Rather, a qualified psychologist or psychiatrist familiar with the evaluation procedure completes the assessment based on an in-depth interview and a review of information contained in the person's records. Then, for each trait or characteristic, the psychologist or psychiatrist must make a judgment as to whether or not each applies to the person being assessed. For each trait, several criteria and tests must be applied. A technical manual contains extensive definitions and behavioral examples for each of the twenty psychopathic characteristics.

If the rater judges that a person clearly has a given trait, then 2 points are added to the total score; if a trait applies only partially or sometimes, then only 1 point is added to the total. And if a trait just doesn't apply to the person, nothing is added to the total. Because there are twenty traits on the PCL-R, someone can receive a total score from 0 (meaning no psychopathy) to a high of 40 (a perfect match to the prototypical psychopath).

The availability of the PCL-R and the shorter PCL: Screenings Version (PCL: SV, discussed on pages 26–28) has allowed people to conduct extensive research on all aspects of psychopathy, including its neurological bases. As noted earlier, a particular area of interest has been the manner in which psychopaths process emotional material, including emotional words and pictures. The results of several brain scan experiments (using functional magnetic resonance imaging, or f MRI) indicate that psychopaths do *not* show the same patterns of brain responses to verbal and visual emotional material as do nonpsychopathic individuals. Whereas normal people showed a different brain response to emotional words and pictures than to neutral material, psychopaths responded the *same* to each type of material. Psychopaths processed what should be emotional material as if it were neutral in content.

Sometimes answering one question raises others. Why don't psychopaths respond the way others do? Are their brains wired differently? Is their obvious emotional poverty the result of their upbringing? It will take several more years of research to answer some of these questions, but significant improvements in the sophistication of laboratory equipment is helping us move toward a deeper understanding of the psychopath. Many researchers will continue their work well into the twenty-first century.

Since the initial studies on the PCL-R, a large number of researchers have used the instrument to assess criminal psychopaths in many countries and settings. The items have withstood the test of time and scientific scrutiny. Although the PCL-R was developed with offender populations, it also has been used with other groups, including psychiatric patients and the general population. For the latter, however, a more suitable instrument is a derivative of the PCL-R, the Psychopathy Checklist: Screening Version (PCL: SV), developed by Hare and his colleagues. The items in the PCL: SV are listed below, and are scored in the same way as the PCL-R is scored. Total scores on the twelve-item PCL: SV can range from 0 to 24.

We can break down the psychopath's personality into a model made up of four key factors or *domains*. The *interpersonal domain* describes how psychopaths present themselves to others, the *affective domain* includes what they feel or don't feel emotionally, the *lifestyle domain* describes how they live in society, and the *antisocial domain* describes their propensity for antisocial behaviors. *Note that scoring each item requires professional qualifications, adherence to the scoring instructions in the PCL: SV Manual, and access to extensive interview and collateral information.* More extensive descriptions are provided in the book *Without Conscience.*

Domains and Traits of the Psychopath
[from the PCL: SV]

Interpersonal
The person is:
- Superficial
- Grandiose
- Deceitful

Affective
The person:
- Lacks remorse
- Lacks empathy
- Doesn't accept responsibility

Lifestyle
The person:
- Is impulsive
- Lacks goals
- Is irresponsible

Antisocial
The person has a history of:
- Poor behavioral controls
- Adolescent antisocial behavior
- Adult antisocial behavior

What is a high enough PCL-R score to warrant a diagnosis of psychopathy? Most people in the general population would score less than 5 on the PCL-R, whereas the average score for male and female criminals is about 22 and 19, respectively. A cut score of 30 typically is used to identify psychopaths, although some investigators and clinicians use a score of 25 or above for research purposes. About 15 percent of male offenders and about 10 percent of female offenders obtain a score of at least 30.

The PCL: SV has fewer items than the PCL-R, but scores on these two instruments have the same theoretical and practical meaning. Most people in the general population would score less than 3 on the PCL: SV, while the average score for criminals is around 13. A cut score of 18 is typically used for a diagnosis of psychopathy.

Whatever cut score is used, individuals who meet or exceed the score clearly are different from those with lower scores. Whether this difference is in kind or in degree is yet to be firmly established, although the most recent scientific evidence is that the latter is the more likely.

Am I a Psychopath?

A list of psychopathic features frequently evokes concern or a superficial flash of insight. "My God, John is impulsive and irresponsible. Maybe he's a psychopath!" Or, "I'm a risk taker and I sleep around a lot. Holy shit, I'm a psychopath!" Perhaps so, but *only* if a lot more of the relevant characteristics are present.

Think of psychopathy as a multidimensional continuum, much like blood pressure, which can range from dangerously low to dangerously high. We might refer to individuals with really low or high systolic and diastolic blood pressure as hypotensive and hypertensive, respectively. In between these two extremes there is a range of pressures, some considered normal and others reflecting varying degrees of concern, but not yet pathological.

Similarly, the number and severity (density) of psychopathic features ranges from near zero, perhaps sliding into sainthood, to abnormally high, rising into big trouble. We refer to those at the upper end as psychopaths; they have an extremely heavy dose of the interpersonal, affective, lifestyle, and antisocial features that define psychopathy (see pages 26–27).

Most people fall in between these extremes, but primarily toward the lower end. Those in the midrange have a significant number of psychopathic features but they are not psychopaths in the strict sense of the term. Their behavior would depend on the particular mix of features they have. Certainly, many will not be model citizens or very nice people, but others may variously be described as hard-driving, fun-loving, entitled, aggressively ambitious, seriously pragmatic, or difficult.

ACT I, Scene II

OFF AND RUNNING

Dave's first day on the job created much excitement as he was shown around the department and introduced to the staff. There was a buzz about the new person who had been hired away from a larger player in the industry, and who would help them regain some of the lost ground resulting from the problematic new product introduction cycles. Everyone came out to greet Dave, and all who met him immediately liked him. He had personality and good looks, not to mention his strong technical background in the company's major research area, and he projected rock-solid confidence.

After introducing Dave around to most of the department, Frank took him to his new office. "Oh," muttered Dave, a bit disappointed in what he saw. "I thought it would be a little closer to the action," he paused, "and a tad bigger."

"Well, we're growing very rapidly and office space is at a premium," offered Frank, wondering why he was feeling apologetic, "but you'll be moving around soon enough as we occasionally shuffle staff around. In fact, it's quite the joke here."

Dave wasn't amused, but as he turned to face Frank, he threw on a smile and said, "That's great! So, I better settle in and start being productive!"

Frank returned to his office and continued with his schedule of meetings, report writing, and phone calls. He would pick up Dave around 1:30 and take him to lunch in the company cafeteria— actually a high-quality restaurant offering free food to employees. And perhaps, if he could, he would take him over to the executive wing and introduce him to Jack Garrideb, founder and CEO, if he were in and available.

The morning went quickly and Frank immersed himself in his work. Marge, his secretary, startled him when she came to the door about 1:15. "Frank, Victoria from Mr. Garrideb's office called; he'd like you to come over right now," she said, adding before his next question, "she didn't say what it was about." Frank picked up his project book and calendar, and grabbed his suit jacket from behind the door, putting it on as he moved out of his office and down the hall. He decided to look in on Dave as he passed his office to tell him that their lunch might be postponed a bit. Dave wasn't in his office, so Frank continued, his thoughts returning to what projects he had outstanding and what the CEO might need of him on such short notice.

Arriving at the executive suite, which was at the other end of the complex, Frank went to Victoria's desk. "Hi, Vicki, so am I in trouble again?" he joked.

"You know you're never in trouble when it comes to Mr. Garrideb. You're still his favorite," she joked back. Vicki and Frank had started with Garrideb Technologies on the same day, and they had been friends since. The company culture was friendly, relaxed, and informal, but the executive wing was always daunting because of the big-company aura everyone thought they had to project to visitors or potential clients.

Jack Garrideb saw Frank standing at Vicki's desk through his open door and waved him to come in. Frank saw that Jack had someone sitting in his office, but couldn't see much of him in the plush leather chair. "Hey, Frank, I've just been talking to one of yours," said Jack as Dave got up and turned around. "Another good choice! Things in R&D are going to really start rocking if your new associate has anything to do with it!"

Frank was somewhat startled to see Dave in the CEO's office. "Well, Jack, we have to keep up with the marketing guys who keep promising customers products that don't exist yet." He smiled as they shook hands.

"Good luck to you, Dave; you're now working for the best person in the business," said Jack, as Frank and Dave took their leave.

"Nice guy," said Dave as they headed down the hall toward the cafeteria.

Frank's thoughts were already back on the project report he had been writing when Victoria's call interrupted him. "You're lucky that he was in today; he travels too much."

3

What You See May Not Be What You See

Ellyn picked up her small daughter and headed out to work. She locked the apartment door, walked down several flights of stairs, and got out onto the street. The bus dropped her and her daughter off at the brightly lit main square where the evening crowds of tourists and vacationers walked and talked. Her night job depended on these people, and she was looking forward to a good night.

A crowd had formed at the corner of Main and First, blocking her way. Winding through the crowd she saw that a game of three-card monte was in progress. Tourists are warned to avoid this swindle, but there is always someone in the crowd who is sucked in. The game works like this: the dealer has three cards faceup on a small table; one is a king, queen, or jack, and the other two are number cards. He (or sometimes she) flips them over, facedown, moves them around quickly on the tabletop and then stops. The dealer, using a nonstop

and entertaining patter, invites crowd members to bet on which one
of the cards is the face card. If there are no takers, he displays the
cards and starts again. Eventually, some onlooker decides that his or
her eye is quicker than the dealer's hands and places a bet. No one
but the dealer ever wins this game.

After every couple of hands, the onlookers reshuffle and those at
the back get up to the front near the table. Ellyn, still holding her
daughter, made it to the front. The dealer smiled and began talking
directly to her daughter. "You're such a pretty girl; and smart too,
just like your mommy! I bet you're going to go to college someday!"
This playful chatter continued with others near the front when unintentionally a card bounced over and back, briefly revealing its face.
The dealer quickly tried to move them about, but Ellyn and a few
others saw every move.

"I'm in," shouted Ellyn nervously. "I want to bet."

"How much?" asked the dealer tentatively, as the crowd moved
in closer to see what was going on. Ellyn had her rent money with
her, and doubling at least some of it would surely help with the bills.
She thought and thought. "Are you going to bet or not?" shouted the
dealer.

"Yes, yes, a hundred dollars!" Those closest to the action held
their breath. Ellyn didn't look like she had a hundred dollars to her
name, let alone the ability to bet that much on a street game. The
dealer balked—he would have to double her money if she won—but
the crowd spoke up. "Let her play," some shouted. "Yeah, take the
bet!" more joined in. The dealer looked nervous.

"Okay, okay," he said, "show me your money." Ellyn looked a bit
more nervous; she didn't know why she had to show her money since
she was going to win anyway, but the dealer was insistent. "Go
ahead, show him your money," someone said from the crowd behind
her. Reaching into her shirtfront and down into her bra she retrieved
some cash. She pulled the hundred-dollar bill out and held it in front
of her. "Pick your card," he said, and Ellyn did.

It seemed like slow motion, but in reality, the next few moments happened very, very quickly. The dealer flipped the card Ellyn chose and it was the seven of diamonds; he flipped the one next to it and it was the king of clubs. Then someone suddenly yelled "Cops!" from the back of the crowd. The dealer snatched the hundred-dollar bill from Ellyn, quickly folded his card table and disappeared with his accomplices into the moving horde of tourists and visitors. Ellyn just stood there. She was in shock. She had lost. Tears welled up in her eyes. "My rent money!" she whimpered. Some in the crowd left shaking their heads. An elderly woman in an old blue coat tried to comfort Ellyn and patted her little daughter on the head. She took a ten-dollar bill from her purse and gave it to Ellyn. A few others did the same, but these gestures of altruism and goodwill could not make up for all the lost rent money or the shame of having fallen for one of the oldest scams around. This con, as with many others, skillfully uses basic human nature against the unsuspecting target.

The number of people with psychopathic personalities suggests that most of us will come across at least one psychopath during a typical day. However, the ability of clever psychopaths to hide their true nature makes it difficult to tell them from others one might meet on the street. Although we actually observed the events described in the case above on a street corner in a major American city, we cannot, for lack of more information, determine whether the person is a psychopath or just a crook. For all we know, this is a case of a petty criminal (three-card monte is illegal in this city) conning the curious and the gullible into parting with their money. While tourists may find that such "slice of life" experiences make interesting stories to tell friends back home, the fact is that a crime was committed.

Our point is that several abilities—skills, actually—make it difficult to see psychopaths for who they are. First, they are motivated to, and have a talent for, "reading people" and for sizing them up quickly. They identify a person's likes and dislikes, motives, needs, weak spots, and vulnerabilities. We all have "buttons" that can be pushed, and psychopaths, more than most people, are always ready to push them. Second, many psychopaths come across as having excellent oral communication skills. In many cases, these skills are more apparent than real because of their readiness to jump right into a conversation without the social inhibitions that hamper most people. They make use of the fact that for many people the content of the message is less important than the way it is delivered. A confident, aggressive delivery style—often larded with jargon, clichés, and flowery phrases—makes up for the lack of substance and sincerity in their interactions with others. This skill, coupled with the belief that they deserve whatever they can take, allows psychopaths to use effectively what they learn about a person *against* the person as they interact with him or her—they know what to say and how to say it to exert influence. Third, they are masters of impression management; their insight into the psyche of others combined with a superficial—but convincing—verbal fluency allows them to change their personas skillfully as it suits the situation and their game plan. They are known for their ability to don many masks, change "who they are" depending upon the person with whom they are interacting, and make themselves appear likable to their intended victim. Narcissistic people will find psychopaths to be solicitous of their need to get attention; anxious people will find them to be nonthreatening and reassuring; many will find them exciting and fun to be with. Few will suspect that they are dealing with a psychopath who is playing up to their particular personality and vulnerabilities. In the great card game of life, psychopaths know what cards you hold, and they cheat.

Researchers who interact with known psychopaths regularly describe them as social chameleons. Chameleons, of course, have the capacity to assume the coloration of their environment in order to survive. When clinging to either a leaf or branch, they turn green or brown, using their ability to change the color of their skin to blend into their surroundings. Thus, using nature's protection, they can remain invisible to their enemies, yet can sneak up on unsuspecting insects that make up their diet. They are the perfect invisible predator. Like chameleons, psychopaths can hide who they really are and mask their true intentions from their victims for extended periods. The psychopath is a near-perfect invisible human predator.

This is not to say that most people can't be charming, effective, socially facile communicators, and still be honest—of course they can. Many people use impression management and manipulation techniques to influence others to like and trust them, or to get what they want from people—very often subconsciously, but sometimes as the result of training, practice, and planning. However, wanting people to like and respect you (and doing what it takes to achieve this) is not necessarily dishonest or insincere—the need for approval and validation from others is normal. Social manipulation begins to be insincere if you really don't care about the feelings of others or you try to take unfair advantage of others. The difference between the psychopathic approach and the nonpsychopathic approach lies in motivation to take unfair and callous advantage of people. Psychopaths simply do not care if what they say and do hurts people as long as they get what they want, and they are very good at hiding this fact. Given his or her powerful manipulation skills, it is little wonder why seeing a "psychopathic" personality beneath someone's charming, engaging surface is so difficult.

Not all psychopaths are smooth operators, though. Some do not have enough social or communicative skill or education to interact successfully with others, relying instead on threats, coercion, intimidation, and violence to dominate others and to get what they want. Typically, such individuals are manifestly aggressive and rather nasty, and unlikely to charm victims into submission, relying on their bullying approach instead. This book is less about them than about those who are capable of and willing to use their "deadly charm" to con and manipulate others. However, if the charming approach does not work, psychopaths readily can resort to both covert and overt intimidation.

Psychopathy and Narcissism

It is important to note that psychopathy is a personality disorder, and that personality disorders are *not* the same as mental illness. At a basic level, a person with a personality disorder has a limited range of stereotyped "solutions" that he or she applies to most of the problems encountered in life. Those without a personality disorder are able to apply a *variety* of behaviors, depending on what best suits the situation.

Individuals with a personality disorder sometimes have trouble in life because of their limited perspective and somewhat inflexible approach. They have difficulty navigating through a world that does not operate in the one-way fashion they prefer, while those who know them may see them as closed-minded, predictable, and sometimes, unfortunately, annoying.

There are ten personality disorders recognized by psychologists, including *narcissistic personality disorder* and *histrionic personality disorder*, which are important to understand, as they relate to psychopathy.

For example, narcissistic personality disorder involves an excessive need for admiration and a sense of superiority, among other traits. Someone with narcissistic personality disorder is described in the *Diagnostic and Statistical Manual of Mental Disorders*, 4th edition (DSM-IV) as displaying a pervasive pattern of grandiosity (in fantasy or behavior), need for admiration, sense of entitlement, and lack of empathy.

Narcissists think that everything that happens around them, in fact, everything that others say and do, is or should be about *them*. In social situations where this is not the case, they will take action to become the center of attention, such as hogging the conversation or belittling others. Narcissistic people lack other choices in their behavioral repertoire, like paying attention to the needs and wants of others, sharing the floor, and negotiating with others for attention and feedback. Being described as narcissistic is not necessarily a bad thing, according to these individuals, as they see pathological self-admiration as merely a natural reaction to their obvious perfection. After all, "What's not to like about me?" Some narcissists even may complain that their talent and beauty are burdens they must bear.

Narcissists have difficulty learning alternative behaviors; but over time, and with some assistance—as with all personality disorders—they can learn to moderate their behaviors and the negative effect they have on others. The real problem for others is when narcissistic features, especially a sense of entitlement and a lack of empathy, shade into antisocial and destructive behaviors. When this happens, the pattern might be described as aggressive or malignant narcissism, which is *difficult to distinguish from psychopathy*.

Another example is histrionic personality disorder, which has a number of characteristics, the two most salient being emotionality and a need for approval that others may find excessive. These individuals tend to come across as overly dramatic, emotional, and possibly theatrical for the social situation they are in. They sometimes dress and act flirtatiously in an attempt to garner attention. Unlike the narcissist, though, they do not always need to feel superior—they'll accept a supportive role, if available, which can provide them with the psychological support they need.

The number of individuals who can be diagnosed with narcissistic (only 1 percent of the general population) or histrionic (2 to 3 percent) personality disorders is small. In fact, many more individuals appear as "narcissistic" or "histrionic" to those around them than actually have these disorders. In addition, some true psychopaths are mislabeled narcissistic or histrionic because of the self-centered or emotional features they display in public. This makes diagnosis difficult and often confusing for those with limited face-to-face experience with these individuals. Only qualified psychologists or psychiatrists can diagnose a personality disorder, including psychopathy, and differentiate it from others that may look similar.

Note: The above is a simplified explanation of personality disorders. Interested readers are directed to the DSM-IV, used by psychologists and psychiatrists, for a more complete discussion of similarities and differences.

The Manipulative Approach to Life

Many psychopaths are master manipulators and game players; they will use every trick in the book to achieve their goals. The traits and characteristics noted by Hare and Cleckley serve them well and are best understood if explained in the context in which they play out in their daily lives. Understanding how they perform in public can help one begin to catch a glimpse of the real person behind the charming façade and, we hope, will help the reader mount a defense against their clever manipulations.

Let's look at some strategies and tactics used as part of a three-phase process by many psychopaths. Note that this process is a natural outgrowth of their personality and that often it will be more automatic than consciously planned out. First, they assess the value of individuals to their needs, and identify their psychological strengths and weaknesses. Second, they manipulate the individuals (now potential victims) by feeding them carefully crafted messages, while constantly using feedback from them to build and maintain control. Not only is this an effective approach to take with most people, it also allows psychopaths to talk their way around and out of any difficulty quickly and effectively if confronted or challenged. Third, they leave the drained and bewildered victims when they are bored or otherwise through with them.

Within this broad framework, several factors come into play. Here is a more detailed explanation.

When Bad Is Good:
Adopting the Psychopathic Lifestyle

The attitudes and behaviors of individuals with many psychopathic features are systemic, a natural and pervasive part of their general lifestyle. In a sense, they are what they are. However, there are others whose nature is less psychopathic than pragmatic; they adopt some of the trappings of a "psychopathic lifestyle" in order to succeed or excel at their work or profession. They are encouraged in this process by all sorts of pop-psych self-help books that promote a philosophy of aggressive greed, self-entitlement, and "looking out for number one."

In his book *What Would Machiavelli Do?*, Stanley Bing, perhaps tongue in cheek, tells how to *get what you want when you want it whether you deserve it or not. Without fear. Without emotion. Without finger-wagging morality.* The following are some of his exhortations:

- Be coldhearted: *Replace decency and thoughtfulness with insensitivity and hardheartedness.*

- Work hard to become bad: *Most people aren't naturally horrendous . . . but with work we can improve.*

- Be narcissistic: *View others solely as a function of your needs . . . You have enormous selfishness within you . . . Let it out.*

- Be unpredictable: *Very nice. Very mean. Big, big swings. Gigantic pleasure. Towering rage.*

- Be ruthless: For your competitors and those who would bring you down, "*Crush them. Hear their bones break, their windpipes snap.*"

Of course, the more psychopathic one is, the easier it is to follow Bing's road map to amoral personal and corporate success. For most of us, though, social brutality and predation are somewhat more difficult. Even if Bing's book is viewed as a satire, it reads like a blueprint for a psychopath.

ASSESSMENT PHASE

The chance to con and manipulate others is a primary motivator for someone with a psychopathic personality disorder; psychopaths like to play games with people. They often are on the lookout for individuals to swindle or scam, and this first phase of the psychopathic approach involves identifying and assessing targets or prey. Some psychopaths are opportunistic, aggressive predators who will take advantage of almost anyone they meet, while others are more patient, waiting for the perfect, innocent victim to cross their path. In each case, the psychopath is constantly sizing up the potential usefulness of an individual as a source of money, power, sex, or influence. People who have power, celebrity, or high social status are particularly attractive.

In the business world, it is relatively easy to spot those in power—big offices and fancy titles are obvious ways to help us identify who's who in an organization. But do not think that just because you don't have a big office or fancy title that you lack power or assets that a psychopath might find useful. Are you a secretary who controls access to your boss and his or her calendar? Are you a union representative who can smooth over employee conflicts and difficulties? Are you plugged into the grapevine in your company, and do you have access to information that is circulated to everyone in the know? Or maybe you are the person in the mailroom who goes the extra mile to make sure important documents reach their destinations on time? These are examples of *informal* power, an important form of power that is the subject of study in business schools and by organizational psychologists. Your informal power or special authority is a useful asset that corporate psychopaths can use to further their larger, personal objectives.

Besides assessing the potential gain from others, psychopaths assess their emotional weak points and psychological defenses in order to work out a plan of attack. Individual psychopaths do this in different ways and to varying degrees because personal style, experience, and preference play a role in this assessment as well. Some psychopaths enjoy a strong challenge, such as that posed by a confident, well-insulated celebrity or an astute professional with a strong ego. Others prefer to prey on people who are in a weakened or vulnerable state. These might include people who are lonely or in need of emotional support and companionship, the elderly on fixed incomes, the underage and naive, or those who have recently been hurt or victimized by others. Although the usefulness of this latter group may not appear to be obvious from a strictly monetary standpoint, their perceived "ease" of approach makes them attractive to the criminal psychopath who weighs the investment in time and energy.

Chaos: Opportunity Knocks

In August 2005, Hurricane Katrina devastated New Orleans, Louisiana, and large parts of the American Gulf Coast. Although the property damage and the human suffering were staggering, the resulting chaos and confusion provided a unique opportunity for those more concerned with their *own* coldblooded self-interests than with the carnage around them.

At the time, Patrick Meehan, U.S. Attorney for the Eastern District of Pennsylvania, had this to say: "If the lessons of September 11 and the Asian tsunami are learned, some coldhearted, evil scam artists will use this occasion to perpetrate fraud, lining their own pockets at the expense of the hurricane victims." His statement was less prophetic than it was a sober comment on the fact that there are lots of common thugs, criminals, and predators ready to make a buck out of someone else's tragedy. Some of their depredations no doubt were related to poverty, mob mentality, and understandable survival instincts. However, for many opportunistic psychopaths—on the street and in the boardroom—their egregious acts were simply business as usual.

Several psychopathic traits come into play in this phase. While on the surface psychopaths generally want to come across in public as at the top of their game and wear the suit of status, success, and sociability, many are actually playing out a *parasitic* lifestyle. They prefer living off the work of others rather than their own efforts, so being a drifter, moocher, or wastrel is a common lifestyle choice despite declarations to the contrary. In service of this lifestyle, they have no misgivings about asking for and often demanding financial support from other people. Often, the supporter is a family member or friend, but it can easily be a stranger whom they seduce or con into providing food, shelter, and a source of income. It is not unusual, or wrong, for people to rely on the help of others, including public aid, during rough times in their lives, but psychopaths remorselessly use others even when able-bodied and capable of supporting themselves. Not all psychopaths are out of work, of course. But even psychopaths who have jobs like to mooch off others in overt and covert ways; they take from coworkers and employers alike.

Psychopaths *lack empathy* and possibly even the most basic understanding of human feelings. Characteristically, the economic and emotional impact of their selfish behavior on others is irrelevant to them, in part because they believe everyone in this dog-eat-dog world is as greedy and unfeeling as they are. Also, they seem unable to construct an accurate emotional facsimile of others, wrongly concluding that the emotional life of everyone else is as shallow and barren as their own. People do not exist in their mental world except as objects, targets, and obstacles. Psychopaths also *lack feelings of remorse and guilt*, part of the internal moral sense that prevents the rest of us from acting out some of the fantasies we occasionally have about using, manipulating, or hurting others. Some might suggest that psychopaths are such effective predators because they are *not* plagued by doubts and concerns raised by a conscience.

In addition to their parasitic nature and lack of empathy, there is evidence that psychopaths *need considerable novel stimulation* to keep from becoming bored. This need, which recent research suggests may be rooted in their brain physiology, often leads them to search for new and exciting opportunities and to move casually from relationship to relationship. Most people are able to endure tedium and hard work over long periods in order to do significant things in their lives, such as completing a college degree, apprenticing, or working at an entry-level job in hope of a promotion. Psychopaths search for easier routes to the same ends. Many do manage to graduate from college or obtain professional credentials, but in most cases it is less through hard work and dedication than through cheating, getting others to do their work, and generally "working the system." Once on the job, they tend to avoid tasks that become monotonous or difficult, or that need some long-term, serious commitment to complete. They can't imagine how or why anyone, including coworkers, would wait their turn—or work hard—for anything they wanted. Their need for stimulation is reflected in a penchant for high-risk, thrill-seeking behaviors. Many nonpsychopathic people seek the adrenaline rush associated with such behaviors, but unlike psychopaths, they typically do so by evaluating the risks to themselves and to others, and without putting others in harm's way. Sadly for society, the psychopath's need for stimulation shades easily into antisocial and criminal behavior.

"It's in My Genes"

Evolutionary psychology provides another reason for the nomadic lifestyle of many psychopaths: the search for multiple sex partners. Psychopathy is characterized by casual sexual relationships that are devoid of genuine, long-term emotional and personal attachments to partners. Frequent liaisons, the use of sex as a weapon, and the callous treatment of intimates are common features of psychopathic individuals, both male and female.

Recent theory and research in evolutionary psychology suggests that there are genetic reasons for such attitudes and behaviors. In this model, psychopathy is a heritable, adaptive life strategy in which the goal—reflected in the early emergence of aggressive sexuality—is to provide genetic continuity. As indicated in *Without Conscience*, passing on one's gene pool can be accomplished in a number of ways, including the careful nurturance of a small number of offspring. The psychopathic pattern appears to be quite different, but equally (or even more) successful: the production of a large number of children, with little or no emotional and physical investment in their well-being.

This pattern involves the use of a persistent and callous pattern of deception and manipulation to attract potential mates, a readiness to abandon them and their offspring, and the need to move on to fresh mating grounds.

Psychopaths have a great sense of superiority and entitlement, and think nothing of helping themselves to property that belongs to others. Their *grandiose sense of self-importance* leads them to believe that other people exist just to take care of them. Because they see most people as weak, inferior, and easy to deceive, psychopathic con artists will often tell you that their victims deserved what they got. Sometimes their sense of superiority is so great that they will say that they are conferring a *gift* by letting their victims support them. This is obvious in the many cases of cult leaders who are charlatans or outright psychopaths, but can be seen in more subtle cases as well. This condescending air toward others comes across as cocky and egotistical to many observers, but, as we will discuss below, some may find this behavior somewhat charming, even charismatic.

MANIPULATION PHASE

Following identification of individuals who may be useful to them, psychopaths begin to create a shroud of charm and deceit that we have labeled the *psychopathic fiction*. This is the beginning of the manipulation phase.

The first goal here is to gain the trust of the individual through ingratiation and various impression-management techniques. Perhaps one of the most effective skills psychopaths use to get the trust of people is their ability to *charm* them. They often have an engaging manner and make great first impressions on people. Upon this first impression, they may build an elaborate fictitious character, persona, or mask. A psychopath can appear strong, naive, dominant, honest, submissive, trustworthy, worldly, or whatever he or she believes will get others to respond positively to manipulative overtures. Some rely on social stereotypes to help them create a useful façade. For example, they might foster impressions of a suffering artist, a misunderstood spouse, a successful businessperson, a celebrity, a member of a respected profession, or a person with connections to the rich, famous, or infamous.

The French Branch of the Rockefellers

A few years ago, French-born Fabian Ortuno was arrested in the United States after cutting a swath through Long Island's high society by pretending to be a Rockefeller. Although many of his victims wondered about his French accent, they succumbed to his charming ways, and were bilked of large sums of money after investing in a variety of his get-rich schemes.

Once arrested, Ortuno posted bail and promptly disappeared, only to reappear in Vancouver as Christopher Rocancourt, a Formula One racing driver. He was a big hit on the local celebrity ski circuit before he was accused of defrauding a West Vancouver businessman of $200,000. He was arrested but still managed to appear on *60 Minutes,* claiming that he never stole, only borrowed. In Vancouver, he was sentenced to time in custody and extradited to the United States.

Facing a possible twenty-year sentence, he plea bargained and was sentenced to five years in prison. Authorities in several countries wish to question him about a variety of unsolved crimes, including fraud, smuggling, bribery, and perjury.

His wife said, "He only steals with his mind."

Recently released from prison, he has become an author, wealthy, and a celebrity in France, where his ability to con "stupid people" out of their money is much admired. *C'est la vie!*

Some psychopaths lay the charm on too thick, coming across as glib, superficial, and unconvincing. However, the truly talented ones have raised their ability to charm people to that of an art, priding themselves on their ability to present a fictional self to others that is convincing, taken at face value, and difficult to penetrate. Psychopaths do naturally what some politicians, salesmen, and promoters have to work hard to achieve: impress listeners with how they say something. In criminal cases, it is sometimes only after the authorities uncover some heinous crime or masterful deceit that a psychopath's charming mask of sincerity, integrity, and honesty is questioned. In less dramatic cases, it may still take much day-to-day exposure before the façade becomes transparent to a few studious observers, but this rarely happens with most people with whom they interact.

While *lack of empathy and guilt* allows psychopaths to identify their victims in the assessment phase, these traits also help them to con and manipulate shamelessly during the manipulation phase. What contributes significantly to their success in engendering trust in their victims is their almost pathological ability to *lie* with impunity. Unencumbered by social anxieties, fear of being found out, empathy, remorse, or guilt—some of nature's brake pedals for antisocial behavior in humans—psychopaths tell a tale so believable, so entertaining, so creative, that many listeners *instinctively* trust them.

One might think that a long series of lies would eventually become transparent, leading to unmasking the psychopath, but this is rarely the case. The reason most observers do not see through the lies is that many psychopathic lies serve both to allay the doubts or concerns of the victim and to bolster the psychopathic fiction. Their often theatrical, yet convincing stories and entertaining explanations reinforce an environment of trust, acceptance, and genuine delight, leading most people to accept them exactly as whom they appear to be—and almost unconsciously excuse any inconsistencies they might have noted. If challenged or caught in a lie, psychopaths are not embarrassed. They simply change or elaborate on the story line to weave together all the misarranged details into a believable fabric. Well-practiced oral communication skills make this endless stream of disinformation seem believable, sensible, and logical. Some psychopaths are so good at this that they can create a veritable Shangri-la view of their world in the minds of others; a view that they almost seem to believe themselves.

Surprisingly, psychopaths will lie even to people who already know the truth about what they are saying. Amazingly, more often than not, victims will eventually come to doubt their *own* knowledge of the truth and change *their* own views to believe what the psychopath tells them rather than what they know to be true. Such is the power of psychopathic manipulation. In at least one case we have heard, a thief fleeing the law shot at his pursuer. Upon capture, the arresting officer—even though he returned fire—was convinced by the fast-talking suspect that the suspect did not, in fact, have a gun and never shot at the officer! Some psychopaths are proud of this expertise, making fun of their victims' gullibility and often bragging about how they fooled this person and that person. To give the devil his due, this self-praise is justified in many cases.

It is not clear whether psychopaths lie because it is an effective tactic to get what they want, or the act of lying is pleasurable, or both. It could be that psychopaths fail to learn the importance of honesty in their youth, and learn, instead, the utility of lying to get what they want from others. In the typical child, lying and distortion lessen with age, while psychopaths just get better at them. They don't see the value of telling the truth unless it will help get them what they want. The difference between psychopathic lies and those told by others is that the latter typically are less callous, calculated, damaging, and destructive to others. They also are far less pervasive than psychopathic lies. For example, poker players, men trying to talk a woman into having sex, adolescents working their parents over to obtain permission to go to a party, a businessmen trying to close a deal, and a politician trying to get elected or to explain his actions may use a variety of lies to attain their goals. But unlike psychopaths, cynical, facile lying is not an integral, systemic part of their personality, and it does not coexist with the other features that define psychopathy.

Another characteristic of psychopaths is an ability to *avoid taking responsibility* for things that go wrong; instead, they blame others, circumstances, fate, and so forth. They have an impressive supply of excuses for why *they* are not to blame for anything that they have said or done to hurt someone else. Pointing the finger at others serves the dual purposes of reinforcing their own positive image while spreading disparaging information about rivals and detractors. They do this by positioning their blame of others as a display of loyalty to the listener. That is, psychopaths appear to be helping or protecting the individual from harm by passing the blame onto a third party. Blaming the system, the company, or society as a whole for their own behavior is also a common response. In many organizations, coworkers can always be found who distrust the company or are angry about something that happened to them. Psychopaths can use these genuine feelings to generate support for their own position.

Even if those with a psychopathic personality admit to involvement in a crime, they will minimize their role, as well as the negative impact on the victims. Psychopaths may even blame the victims for their own misfortune, offering convincing reasons why they got what they deserved!

As it does in the assessment phase, *lack of empathy, guilt, or remorse* plays an important role during the manipulation phase—by facilitating behavior that is callous and insensitive to the rights and feeling of others. This can lead to the psychological and physical abuse of family, friends, and innocent strangers. Later we will discuss in detail the impact of psychopathic abuse on the victim. The level and intensity of psychopathic intimidation often keeps those who have been abused from coming forward. In psychopathic crimes, abuse can extend far beyond property damage or assault, sometimes intensifying into sadistic attacks on victims.

Hit Them When They're Down

A particularly nasty scenario involves scanning the media for accounts of elderly people who have been victimized by fraudulent scams or schemes, and then approaching them with an offer to help get their money back. In one such incident, a newspaper reported that an eighty-year-old woman had lost her life savings in a venture promoted by a middle-aged woman who had offered to care for her. Following the report, another scamster, posing as a lawyer who specialized in helping victims of fraud, convinced the devastated woman he could get her money back. She borrowed his up-front "recovery fee" of $5,000 from a close friend. You know the rest.

ABANDONMENT PHASE

Once psychopaths have drained all the value from a victim—that is, when the victim is no longer useful—they abandon that victim and move on to someone else. Abandonment is most often abrupt—the psychopath just disappears one day—and it can occur without the current victim even realizing the psychopath has been looking for someone new to use. In crimes such as identity theft, credit card fraud, and construction swindles, the psychopath effectively disappears, typically reappearing with a new identity in another geographic location. The arrival of the Internet has made the psychopathic criminal's life easier, as running and hiding are easily carried out, and targets are plentiful and readily accessible.

Most people feel at least a twinge of guilt or regret, and will want to apologize if they have hurt someone. Psychopaths have only a vague appreciation of these concepts, and sometimes find the idea of guilt or remorse an amusing weakness the rest of us possess—something that they can, of course, take advantage of. Certainly, they are not influenced by the possibility that their behavior may have dire consequences for themselves and others. In part, this is because the past and future are less important to them than is the present. In addition, their own shallow emotions make it difficult for them to appreciate that others might have a much richer emotional life. It also makes it easy for psychopaths to view others as objects or pawns to be moved around at will. Put another way, psychopaths are better at understanding the intellectual or cognitive lives of others than they are at understanding their emotional life. As a consequence, people have value only for what they can provide. Once used, they are discarded. To be able to abandon people in such a callous and harmful manner one must be immune to the feelings of those one hurts. Psychopaths can easily do this because their emotional and social attachments to others are poorly developed; weak at best.

Although psychopaths do not feel the range and depth of emotions experienced by most people, they do understand that others have something called "emotions." Some may even take the time to learn to mimic emotions so they can better manipulate their victims. But they do so at a superficial level, and trained observers can sometimes tell the difference; the real gut-feel behind their playacting is not there. Consider these words by Jack Abbott, a psychopathic killer who was championed by Norman Mailer and released from prison, only to kill again: "There are emotions—a whole spectrum of them—that I know only through words, through reading and in my immature imagination. I can *imagine* I feel these emotions (know, therefore, what they are), but *I do not*."

Practice Makes Perfect

Hare consulted with Nicole Kidman on the movie *Malice*. She wanted to let the audience know, early in the film, that she was not the sweet, warm person she appeared to be. He gave her the following scene: "You're walking down the street and come across an accident at the corner. A young child has been struck by a car and is lying in a pool of blood. You walk up to the accident site, look briefly at the child, and then focus on the grief-stricken mother. After a few minutes of careful scrutiny, you walk back to your apartment, go into the bathroom, stand in front of the mirror, and practice mimicking the facial expressions and body language of the mother."

The emotional poverty of psychopaths and their inability to fully appreciate the emotional life of others have been the subject of considerable neurobiological research, some of it using brain-imaging technology. The results of this research are consistent with the clinical view that psychopaths do not respond to emotional situations and material in the way that the rest of us do. In several functional magnetic resonance imaging (fMRI) brain imaging studies, Hare and his associates found that emotional words and unpleasant pictures did not produce in psychopaths the increases in the activity of brain (limbic) regions normally associated with the processing of emotional material. Instead, activation occurred in regions of the brain involved in the understanding and production of language, as if the psychopaths analyzed the material in linguistic terms. Think of Spock in *Star Trek*. He responds to events that others find arousing, repulsive, or scary with the words *interesting* and *fascinating*. His response is a cognitive or intellectual appraisal of the situation, without the visceral reactions and emotional coloring that others normally experience. Fortunately for those around him, Spock has "built-in" ethical and moral standards, a conscience that functions without the strong emotional components that form a necessary part of our conscience.

Some researchers have commented that psychopaths "know the words but not the music," a statement that accurately captures their cold and empty core. This hollow core serves them well, though, by making them effective human predators. Not only are psychopaths unconcerned about the impact of their own behavior on others—or of possible retribution—they more often than not will *blame* their victim if they are caught or charged with a crime. In fact, it is not uncommon for criminal psychopaths to state that *they* are suffering more in prison than their victims did during the original crime— and they (the psychopaths) deserve some sympathy or special treatment. Other psychopaths may sometimes *say* that they feel remorse for their transgressions, but scrutiny of their behaviors betrays their words as simply lies to get better treatment or an earlier release date. Unfortunately, many co-opt socially supportive belief systems—typically religious beliefs of every kind—declaring that they have found God, repented their sins, and are ready to reenter society.

Praise the Lord

At a judicial conference in Maine, Hare spoke about the ease with which convicted offenders often are able to convince various religious groups, simply by using the right words and phrases, that they too had "found religion." The tactic of the offenders was to tap into the groups' belief that there is good in all of us and that everyone can be redeemed, even though we sometimes temporarily go off track.

After the presentation, a woman came up to Hare, identified herself as a prosecutor, and stated that she was a fundamentalist Christian, as was her husband, a judge. Thinking that he perhaps had offended her, Hare began to explain his comments. The prosecutor interrupted by saying that she was in agreement with what he had said, and that she had heard the same hollow line from many repentant offenders. As described by her, the scenario typically went like this:

Defendant: "I found Christ."

Prosecutor: "Congratulations. You're going to heaven. But first, you're going to jail."

Irresponsibility, another one of the twenty traits that Hare uses to define the psychopath, is not an unusual trait. Many of us make promises we don't keep or enter commitments on which we don't follow through. Typically, though, while we may seem irresponsible in one part of our life, we may be very responsible in others, unlike the psychopath, who is chronically irresponsible in all aspects of life.

Their are many variants on the theme of ignoring responsibility: defaulting on loans, overspending on credit cards, failing to pay bills, neglecting child support, putting others at risk by driving recklessly, and so forth.

The selfish, one-sided, psychopathic approach to life can lead, over a lifetime, to several predictable outcomes. First, psychopaths have *many short-term relationships* over the course of their lives, a direct result of the Assessment-Manipulation-Abandonment process. They may approach many individuals offering "commitment," but then leave when their usefulness has expired. This results in a series of traditional and common-law marriages, short-term live-in relationships, and so forth. They often leave behind a trail of jilted lovers, possibly abused ex-spouses, and unsupported children. Occasionally, this pattern of behavior leads to a reputation as a "player," and some psychopaths will even promote these reputations themselves to build up their status and mystique. Unfortunately, for the psychopaths' partners, these relationships are one-sided, exist without real intimacy, and are often plagued by intimidation, abuse, and violence. Sadly, as many as one in five persistent spouse abusers have psychopathic personalities. Many avoid prison by taking part in court-mandated treatment programs that do them or their partners no good.

Second, psychopaths typically *do not have practicable long-term career or life goals.* Thus, a series of unconnected, randomly selected jobs defines their work history. Despite the lack of a real career, psychopaths will claim all sorts of goals and achievements, and weave a career "history" so convincing that others believe the success, fortune, and achievement they profess to have attained in their lives. In the business world, these fictitious achievements are memorialized in a résumé filled with lies, self-generated letters of commendation, and even fake wall plaques and awards. Even psychopaths who choose a *criminal* career lack clear goals and objectives, getting involved in a wide variety of opportunistic offenses, rather than specializing the way typical career criminals do. This is an outcome of their impulsivity, poor behavioral controls, and low frustration tolerance. That their predatory lifestyle may bother their friends, family, or even fellow criminals is of little importance to them. Depending on the situational demands, though, they can spout or make up what seem like reasonable, attainable goals in order to impress or manipulate others.

ACT II, Scene I

HAIL-FELLOW-WELL-MET

Dave drove around the parking lot looking for a space. He had over-slept and was running late. Normally in and at his desk before Frank arrived, Dave swore to himself and headed for the visitor lot where he knew there would be openings available. Not that there weren't plenty of spaces in the "north forty," the nickname of the parking lot on the far side of the complex, but he hated to walk when he could park much closer. *I should have asked for a reserved spot*, he thought, eyeing Dorothy's new Lexus in the "employee of the month" spot right next to Jack Garrideb's space. He knew Dorothy from her reputation as the hotshot marketing associate. *I should be in marketing*, thought Dave as he pulled into the first available visitor's spot, grabbed his briefcase, and opened the door.

Todd, from site security, was making his rounds. He worked the early morning shift, which suited him just fine. Being a people person, he liked waving and greeting the other employees as they arrived for work, and at a company like Garrideb Technologies, he got great benefits—much more than he would have gotten down the road, working security for some of the other companies in the park. He spotted the red sports car heading for the visitor's lot and decided to investigate. "You're a Garrideb employee, aren't you?" he confronted Dave after noticing his employee decal.

"What? Yes, I'm late for a meeting with the executive committee," Dave said, continuing to get out of his car. "I'm Dave S from research; I have the plans for the new product line," he said, raising his briefcase into the air, "and it wouldn't look good for me or you if I'm late for this meeting."

"Employees park in Lots B, C, and D, sir," Todd reminded Dave. "I'm afraid I'll have to ask you to move your car over to the employee area."

"Listen, Todd," said Dave, eyeing Todd's name from his badge. "I told you, I have a meeting and it's very important."

"Sir, you can't park here," Todd countered sternly. Dave gave him a mean look, closed his car door, and started to walk toward the building entrance. "I'm going to have to ticket you, sir," said Todd, speaking to Dave's back as he moved away.

"Do what you have to do, Todd. I don't care, and I'm certain some important people won't either after I present my material," said Dave loudly as he walked away. "New products pay your salary, Todd, don't forget that!" shouted Dave as he hustled off without turning around.

"Hi, Dave," chimed Debbie, from accounting, who made it a habit to be walking down the hallway toward the lobby every morning, just to bump into Dave. Today, she had walked this route four times and was beginning to wonder if Dave was coming in or not.

"That asshole," muttered Dave under his breath, but loud enough that Debbie could hear him.

"Are you all right?" she inquired, drawing closer and hoping to engage him in conversation. Dave looked up.

"Yeah, I'm okay, just flew in on the red-eye from the coast," said Dave, as he passed her by in the hall. *He's seen me almost every day for three months now, and he's yet to give me more than a "good morning" and a wave!* thought Debbie sadly, as she walked over to the cafeteria to re-refill her cup.

Dave got to his office and threw his briefcase onto the credenza. Grabbing his notebook, he headed for the cafeteria for coffee. "Hi, Marge," he beamed as he passed by her desk. "Is the big guy in today?" he said peering into Frank's office and noting his briefcase wasn't there.

"Off-site executive committee meeting; don't expect any of them back until Wednesday. How was your weekend?" she asked.

"Oh, the usual, I stayed late Friday afternoon to finish that report for Frank; probably the one he's giving to the committee at the off-site." *The meeting I should be presenting at,* he thought.

On the way to the cafeteria, Dave always made it a point to stop by every desk. In his brief three months, he had met and introduced himself to almost every employee. He had his lists. There were the losers, of course. *Guess I met another loser this morning,* he thought, chuckling. But Dave also knew who the winners were, and the wannabes, of course—there were several of them in this fast-growing company.

As he entered the company café, he noticed Dorothy at the coffee urn. *Nice,* he thought, smiling. "So, the employee of the month drinks coffee like the rest of us?" said Dave coming up behind her.

"Oh, hi, yes. I know, the parking spot," Dorothy said, turning. "It's embarrassing, actually. I'd like to think I'm just . . ."

"I'm Dave, pleased to finally meet you."

"Likewise," she said smiling.

"Can I buy you some coffee?" he said jokingly.

"Sure, anytime."

4

Psychopathic Manipulation
HOW DID HE DO THAT?

The group that had formed on the lawn collectively gasped as Ted, their neighbor, was led away in handcuffs by the police. Ted's wife, holding their young daughter, was crying and fumbling in her pocketbook to find the keys to the car. She glanced at the neighbors who looked away out of respect and embarrassment. Ted yelled back to her, "Don't worry, Hon, just a mix-up. Call our lawyer; his number is in my desk, he'll take care of this." Behind Ted and the officer were others carrying file boxes and a computer plus some garbage bags filled with stuff from Ted's house.

"Can you believe it?" whispered Martha quietly to her neighbor, Sarah. "No, I can't," joined Ed, moving closer to the front of the growing crowd to get a better look. Ted was chairperson of the block association that helped to protect the residents from burglars and their children from predators. He attended church when he was in town—his job required a lot of travel. His wife baked cakes to raise money for the building fund and was just a delightful person. No one could fathom what this was all about. "Here comes Ralph; let's see what he found out."

Ralph played softball with some of the people on the police force and checked in with one of his friends who sat in the cruiser blocking the road just in case Ted tried to flee. "Stole lots of money from his company," he said. "Embezzlement, big time. They think he's been doing this for about two years, and it only came out recently. Apparently he was able to hide everything from them."

"Oh my God," gasped a few folks in the group. This was such a quiet neighborhood filled with professionals, many with small children. It didn't make sense that something like this could happen. "It must be some mistake," offered Sarah, "maybe . . ."

"I don't think so," interrupted Ralph. "Apparently, his real name isn't Ted," he looked around and lowered his voice, "and Sheila isn't his only wife."

"Oh my God!" gasped the group collectively.

Psychopaths, Psychopaths Everywhere?

Andrew Cunanan, a restaurant employee in San Diego, had moved to Miami and was trying to enter the social scene when he allegedly met famous designer Gianni Versace at a party. While accounts suggest that Mr. Versace might have snubbed him, this is unlikely, given the gracious, social nature of Versace. For reasons that have never been fully explained, Cunanan, who had already brutally murdered two alleged lovers in San Diego, was able to elude authorities by moving to Miami, despite an arrest warrant, newspaper coverage, and a manhunt. In Miami, he approached Versace, who was returning home after a morning walk, and fatally shot him at point-blank range. Cunanan was discovered hiding out in a houseboat less than three miles from the murder scene. After five hours and as many rounds of tear gas, the SWAT team entered and found Mr. Cunanan's body, an apparent suicide. The tragedy created by this "spree" killer has never been completely explained; there are only questions. Had Cunanan successfully conned his way into Versace's social circle? Was Cunanan a psychopath or "merely" an emotionally disturbed individual whose crimes, though reprehensible, were understandable?

Leading a double life has become big news recently, as improved forensics, coupled with more knowledge about psychopathic manipulation, have increased law enforcement's ability to unmask frauds. On a recent Oprah Winfrey program discussing a book entitled *Blood Brother: 33 Reasons My Brother Scott Peterson Is Guilty* by Anne Bird, Dr. Keith Ablow, a forensic psychiatrist, noted that Scott Peterson, the man found guilty of the brutal murder of his wife and unborn child, fit the profile of a sociopath (see page 19 for the difference between a sociopath and a psychopath). Peterson was able to present the convincing face of a concerned husband, even participating in the search for his missing pregnant wife, all the while planning a future with his (unsuspecting) girlfriend. In home movies, he came across as a normal, fun-loving husband and soon-to-be father. The *real* Scott Peterson, though, can be appreciated by anyone who watched his television interview or listened to the taped phone conversations his girlfriend made once she discovered that he was married and that his wife was mysteriously missing. In these audio and visual documents, he shows no apparent concern, empathy, remorse, or even sadness at his wife's disappearance. Despite (or perhaps because of) a major police investigation, he attempted to leave the country, outfitted with a new hair color and a pocket full of money. Clearly, the evidence amassed by the authorities was sufficient to erase any doubt in the minds of those who counted in the end, as a jury of his peers convicted him of the brutal murder and sentenced him to death.

Is it ever possible to discern the potential for cold-blooded violence before it is too late? As far as we know, neither Andrew Cunanan nor Scott Peterson exhibited any murderous tendencies early on. Were there other signs? Perhaps with more information about their personality and interactions with others over the years, their crimes might become less inexplicable. Even so, psychological "autopsies" are more useful for generating hypotheses about behavioral patterns than they are for providing causal explanations of an event. Furthermore, even if family members, close friends, and associates *had* noticed that all was not right with these individuals, they would not necessarily have appreciated the potential significance of the information, and they might not have known how to act on it. What we can say, however, is that even if we cannot predict specific events, the behavior of psychopathic individuals does not occur out of the blue and seldom is out of character. The problem is that without prolonged and perceptive interactions with these individuals, we typically are not sure what this character is, particularly when it is obscured by a charming physically and socially attractive exterior.

Where Was the Emotional Connection?

Many trial watchers came to see Scott Peterson as a manipulative, charming, pathological liar with a grandiose sense of self and an inability to empathize. "The absence of emotion is a hallmark of a psychopath," forensic psychologist J. Reid Meloy said. "They don't have the internal psychological structure to feel and relate to other people. Sometimes they can imitate it, so they can fool other people, but there will come a point when they can't maintain it." Even passionate, angry, and accusatory outbursts from the family members Peterson was once close to didn't appear to faze him. That fits too, Dr. Meloy said—psychopaths can't form truly intimate bonds with others.

Such an absence of heartfelt emotion "gives the psychopath the ability at times to kill without remorse and to kill for reasons filled with banality," he explained. "Others' emotions of grief and rage and fury are like water off a duck's back."

That apparent lack of emotion raised investigators' suspicions in the first place, police and prosecutors said when they gave their first news conference after the trial began. "His major concerns weren't Laci at the beginning of this case," explained Modesto Detective Al Brocchini. "He is very calm, cool, nonchalant, polite, arrogant. He thinks he's smarter than everybody." Anne Bird, who desperately wanted to believe her half brother was innocent, thought his behavior was strange when he lived with her family during the investigation of Laci's disappearance. "He is the most empty person. Everything he does seems to have been copied from someone else," said Bird, who last visited Peterson at the San Mateo County Jail in January 2005.

Peterson seemed in utter denial as he talked about getting out of prison and leading a quiet, simple life somewhere, she said. "I was wondering if he really understood the extremity of the whole thing. I think he's very bright, but he's kind of soulless. He's very empty. Somehow he's been lost."

Psychopaths need greater stimulation than most other people in order to feel anything, Meloy said—a phenomenon that struck Bird as particularly true in Peterson's case. "The drive from Modesto to Redwood City was a really big deal," she said. "There were blocked-off streets, lights were going, it was really intense. He actually seemed excited about it. I thought, 'This is not something to be proud of. This is your life.'"

Peterson exhibited similar behavior upon his arrival at San Quentin, where he'll most likely spend the rest of his life. After arriving at 4 A.M. on Thursday, he told a guard he was "too jazzed" to sleep. "The most intense emotion he's derived through his whole trial was the excitement he received when he darkened the doors of San Quentin," Meloy said.

Psychopaths are very effective at masking their true selves from those they wish to manipulate and con. Merely having a mental checklist of the traits that define psychopathy does not guarantee success in spotting the psychopath. In fact, it is not uncommon for well-trained researchers in this field of study to be fooled and manipulated by *known* psychopaths they have just met.

Your ability to recognize psychopathic manipulation is increased if you are not seen as valuable or a threat to the psychopath, and therefore of little interest. Psychopaths invest a lot of mental energy in identifying and manipulating their victims, but they don't spend much energy trying to uphold a mask for those with little utility to them; the return on investment is just not there for them. Individuals who are ignored can therefore be in a good position to watch psychopathic individuals manipulate others. With the knowledge of how it is done, they may be able to get glimpses behind the mask.

People learning about psychopaths for the first time sometimes begin to see psychopathic traits in some people that they know. Former bosses, ex-spouses, public officials, teachers, family members, and friends often become suspects if they happen to display behaviors that are on Hare's list of psychopathic traits. Others new to the field will begin to see psychopathic traits in themselves, much like doctors in training who sometimes think they're experiencing the symptoms of the diseases they are studying. Being aware of one's own tendency to attribute psychopathy to those displaying some of its features, including oneself, is important in honing one's skill in spotting the real thing.

Personality: The Three Faces of You

Many books have been written about personality and the complex ways in which it influences our interactions with others. There are theories of how personality develops, how it differs from person to person, and how it reveals itself in one's behavior. However, regardless of the particular theory of personality you follow, there are three common ways that each person's personality can be experienced. All are relevant to understanding psychopathic manipulation, because many psychopaths are astute students of human nature and, unlike most people, *are willing to use what they have learned for their own selfish purposes.* They may not all have textbook learning about personality theory, but they have an intuitive feel that they put to good use. They use their knowledge of personality to control your view of them and ultimately to control you.

To recognize how psychopaths control the opinions others have of them, it is important to understand the differences among three points of view. First, there is the internal or *private* personality—the "me" that we experience inside ourselves. Second, there is the projected or *public* personality, sometimes called the persona—the "me" that we want others to see, the "self" that we present to others when we are in public. And, third, there is the *attributed* personality or *reputation*—the view, based on what we say and do, that *others* form of our personality.

Our *private* or *inner personality* is complex and made up of our thoughts, attitudes, perceptions, judgments, drives, needs, preferences, values, and emotions. Our private self also includes the products of our imagination, including fantasies, hopes, and ambitions, all of which are idealized visions of who we are and who we want to be. In many people, the private self consists of positive traits and characteristics, and we believe that these positive self-perceptions represent who we are. We want others to appreciate these traits, and we can get very upset if someone suggests they are not true. For example, if you believe that you are a loyal, compassionate person, then you would be concerned by anything someone said about you that suggested otherwise.

Our private self also includes personal characteristics we don't like, which, typically, we don't want others to see. While we may try to improve some of these characteristics, we would just prefer to ignore some others altogether. These unpleasant or darker traits include harmful things we do to people, illicit or violent thoughts and fantasies we have, and our general insecurity, greed, and illusions about ourselves and our place in the world. Getting angry and losing control, being excessively rude or annoying to others, acting coarsely to those around us, and being depressed or despondent are examples of things we might do that reflect the darker (but normal) side of our personality. During a typical day, we spend quite a lot of

mental and emotional energy building up and enhancing the positive or bright side of our private self and minimizing or controlling
the dark side. In fact, to preserve our internal emotional balance and
to avoid excessive anxiety, we *need* to believe that our positive self-
evaluations are accurate, and we will invest energy in fighting
doubts as they arise.

The goal for much of the therapy, coaching, and counseling that
people seek is to resolve the internal psychological conflicts between
the bright and dark sides of the personality. Well-developed and researched psychological tests can help shed some light on our hidden
traits. A competent mental health professional can facilitate explor-
ing these parts of the psyche, while providing insights that help us
integrate the parts into a unified whole. As long as our self-image is
mostly positive, and we can accept the less positive side of ourselves
as a normal part of being human, we will value our individual "self"
and conclude that we are okay people. Feeling all right about oneself
comes across as self-confidence and inner strength, two traits valued
in our society.

Your public self, or *persona*, on the other hand, is how you want
those around you to see "you." Your persona is a subset of your private self—a carefully edited version, to be sure, of your private personality that you reveal to others in order to influence how they see
(and judge) you. Anyone who has ever tried to make a positive impression on another—perhaps on a date or during a job interview—
understands how difficult it can be to maximize the positives and
minimize the negatives of your personality. Despite our best efforts
to control what we reveal to others, we do unintentionally reveal private personality traits to others on occasion, but, overall, our persona
reflects the personality we want others to see.

This brings us to the third view of personality; how *others* view
and describe *us*. This is the *reputation* others assign to us based on
what they see, hear, and experience when interacting with us. Unfortunately, despite our best efforts to present a positive persona, people
will form their own opinions, both correct and mistaken, based on

what we do, how we look, the clothes we choose to wear, and whether they agree with our values and beliefs as filtered through their *own* biases, stereotypes, likes, and dislikes. The filters other people use to evaluate us can, to varying degrees, distort the picture folks get of who we really are.

The problem is that all of us form first impressions of others very quickly, perhaps during the first seconds of meeting someone for the first time. Once formed, people solidify their first impressions by filtering out new information that contradicts their early impressions, and preferentially let in information that is supportive. The people we like right off become even more likable, and those we don't care for remain so. For example, you may feel an affinity for those of a similar religion or political party and generalize this to other aspects of their makeup. Feeling affinity for someone makes us more accepting of the things we like about him or her, and more forgiving of those things that we might dislike. Consistency between a person's words and deeds also plays an important role in reinforcing his or her reputation. Consistency leads us to see people as honest— even if we don't totally agree with their views—while inconsistencies we notice may leave us wondering about them. All of these filtered perceptions can cause problems, of course, *if we misjudged the persona of a person when forming a first impression.*

To summarize our model of personality so far: We have a *private* self made up of positive traits we value and want others to appreciate, and a collection of negative traits and characteristics we prefer to keep to ourselves. When we interact with others, we present a carefully crafted *persona* or public self comprised of a selection of traits and characteristics from our private self that we want others to see. Sometimes we may exaggerate a few of our positives just to make an impression or to exert influence on others. Occasionally, material from our private, dark side slips into the public view without our being aware; at other times, we may be aware of traits that slip through, and we feel embarrassed or guilty. Finally, our *reputation* is the "personality" by which others come to know us. Ideally, our reputations accurately reflect the psychological traits we want to show, but, in fact, observers filter what we present through their personal biases, prejudices, and preconceptions. This may cause them to form an incorrect impression of our personality.

Using What You Have

If they happen to be intelligent, "well bred," and physically attractive, psychopaths can have a devastating impact on the people they meet.

For example, Caroline is a very attractive and intelligent thirty-year-old British woman. Her father was a barrister and her mother a successful stage actress. Caroline went to several of the best schools but seldom stayed at any one of them for very long. She got into some minor difficulties on occasion—for example, she was unable to account for some missing money during her volunteer work for a charitable organization—but was always bailed out by her parents. She moved in fashionable circles, where she had many brief affairs.

For several years, Caroline was involved with a pseudo-religious cult, and her "direct line to the saints" helped her to manipulate elderly people into "buying their own little piece of heaven." Later, she met an international smuggler and this led to her first prison term, a three-year sentence for diamond smuggling. She is a delightful conversationalist, exuding an engaging charm and wit that keeps you captivated for hours. Her description of her current circumstances and the events that led up to it has an almost romantic quality. Caroline likes the fast life and loves excitement. For the past four years, she has been combining those interests as a diamond smuggler, making regular runs between Johannesburg, New York, Tel Aviv, and Amsterdam, and packing thousands of dollars' worth of diamonds on each trip.

Caroline's unusual occupation—simply the latest in a long string of successful scams and cons—rewarded her in two ways: it provided her with a substantial income to support her lavish

lifestyle, and simultaneously was a constant source of excitement. Caroline stated that walking through an airport with thousands of dollars' worth of smuggled diamonds was a tremendous
thrill, "an incomparable rush." When she was first caught, by a
married customs agent, she was able to convince him not to turn
her in and ended up having a brief affair with him. She later
turned him in as part of a plea bargain when she was caught a
second time. Although he lost his family, his job, and his reputation, she was unmoved: "He had a good time; now the party's
over."

Her only regret was that her days as a runner were probably
over now that Interpol knew about her. She had vague plans to
become a stockbroker or a real estate agent. Meanwhile, she
was working on a scheme to be deported, in hopes that it will
lead to a reduced sentence. In a letter to a British official about
this matter, Caroline suggested that his wife or girlfriend might
like a "little sparkling something on her finger," and that she
could easily arrange this for him.

Your reputation may not coincide with the public self you are
trying to project, or the internal personality you personally experience. In an ideal world, all three views of the personality would line
up. We would be happy with our private self, feel comfortable revealing it through our persona, and feel safe in the knowledge that those
with whom we interact come to know us for who we truly are. But
the world is not such a perfect place and people are not perfect be-
ings. The best that we can hope for in most social situations is that
our persona reflects the things we want to share with others, and that
observers are open-minded enough that their attributions about us
and our resulting reputation are accurate.

Sales representatives, human resources staff, and other professionals who spend much time interacting with people become good
at judging personality traits and characteristics. Psychologists and
psychiatrists, of course, are trained in doing personality assessments

and can usually see a bit more of the underlying personality dynamics. So do poker players looking for "tells" leaked by other players. But to their credit, psychopaths have the deserved reputation of being good judges of the personalities of others—perhaps because they work hard at it—and have the uncanny ability to project the most effective persona, depending on the situation, to get what they want. How do they do it? To psychopaths, your face, words, and body language are your autobiography, printed in large type.

Let the Games Begin: Forging the Psychopathic Bond

Foremost on the psychopath's agenda during the assessment phase is deciding your utility or value, followed by figuring out the inner workings of your personality. While this assessment progresses, the psychopath begins to focus efforts on building a close, personal relationship on which later manipulations will rest. As noted above, one need not be rich and powerful to attract the attention of a psychopath on the make; almost everyone has some sort of utility for an enterprising psychopath.

As interaction with you proceeds, the psychopath carefully assesses your persona. Your persona gives the psychopath a picture of the traits and characteristics you value in yourself. Your persona may also reveal, to an astute observer, insecurities or weaknesses you wish to minimize or hide from view. As an ardent student of human behavior, the psychopath will then gently test the inner strengths and needs that are part of your private self and eventually build a personal relationship with you by communicating (through words and deeds) four important messages.

The first message is that the psychopath likes and values the strengths and talents presented by your persona. In other words, *the psychopath positively reinforces your self-presentation,* saying, in effect, *I like who you are.* Reinforcing someone's persona is a simple, yet powerful, influence technique, especially if communicated in a convincing—that is, charming—manner. Unfortunately, many people we deal with in our personal and professional lives are so self-absorbed and narcissistic that they rarely see our persona because of the preoccupation they have with their own. Finding someone who pays attention to us, who appreciates or actually "sees" us, is refreshing; it validates who we are and makes us feel special. The psychopath quickly fulfills this need.

The Puppetmaster

In describing his role in the murder of his friend's father and the attempted murder of his friend's mother and sister, an offender had this to say:

A friend of mine came in and we started talking, getting to know each other. Well, I started to get to know *him* better. Because the more he told me about himself, the more leverage I had. The more I know about the guy, the more I know what buttons to push. So, I started pushing those buttons. He had a lot of unresolved issues from his childhood, so I tried to get to the root of the problem and started to get him to feel very angry, very hostile toward his family. I said, "They have money. Why don't you take some? I'll help you spend it because I'm your friend." We got together and it escalated and I encouraged the escalation. I don't know if in the back of my mind I truly believed what the capabilities were, but I didn't care. So it started to become a plan. I just keep fueling the fire, the more fuel I added to the fire the bigger payoff for me. And plus that sense of control, power. I was the *puppetmaster* pulling the strings.

We invest considerable mental energy in presenting our persona every time we interact with someone. But behind our outward presentation, and sometimes mixed in with it, are aspects of our private self, both positive and negative, that we like to *keep* private. We rarely want to share parts of our private self with business associates and acquaintances; we reserve this for close friends and serious relationships. However, as a motivated student of human nature, the psychopath, on meeting us for the first time, can often surmise some of the issues or concerns that exist in our private self. Using this information, the psychopath crafts a simulated persona—a mask—that mirrors or complements these characteristics. Subtly, through clever banter, the psychopath begins to share bits of personal information, seemingly letting down his or her guard with us. These conversations resonate with you because someone is sharing personal details that reflect values, beliefs, and issues *similar to your own*. The psychopath's second message is *I am just like you.*

Meeting someone who shares the same values, beliefs, and life experiences is not very common, so it is wonderful when it does occur. It is easy to open up to someone like this, and soon we are sharing more and more of our inner thoughts and feelings. To our great pleasure, we want to believe that this person *understands* us at a much deeper level than anyone else we have met. Having parts of your private self understood and accepted by someone means you can relax, let down your guard, and begin to trust that *this* person is different—he or she may like you for who you *really* are, behind your own mask or persona. Happily and with relief, you conclude that the psychopath will not pose a psychological threat; in effect, the psychopath's third message is: *Your secrets are safe with me.* Safety or security is one of our most basic psychophysical needs; the psychopath willingly fulfills this need.

Giving Them What They Want

Like many writers, John Steinbeck understood the ways in which psychopaths—in this case, a female—can use sex-role tools. This excerpt is drawn from his description of Cathy Ames, who would marry to become Cathy Trask, the madam in Stein-beck's novel *East of Eden*.

Cathy learned when she was very young that sexuality with all its attendant yearnings and pains, jealousies and taboos, is the most disturbing impulse humans have. And in that day it was even more disturbing than it is now, be-cause the subject was unmentionable and unmentioned. Everyone concealed that little hell in himself, while pub-licly pretending it did not exist—and when he was caught up in it he was completely helpless. Cathy learned that by manipulation and use of this one part of people she could gain and keep power over nearly anyone. It was at once a weapon and a threat. It was irresistible. And since the blind helplessness seems never to have fallen on Cathy, it is probable that she had very little of the impulse herself and indeed felt a contempt for those who did. And when you think of it in one way, she was right.

When the psychopath convinces us that he or she understands and accepts our weaknesses and personal flaws, then we begin to be-lieve in the potential of the relationship to go further; we believe this person will be a true friend. True friends, of course, share information—often intimate information—about themselves with each other. Relationships develop and mature as people share more and more of their private lives with their partners, including their in-ner desires, hopes, and dreams. Some of it is personal, other topics are mundane, but all of it is relevant to manufacturing a picture that fulfills our deep psychological needs and expectations. The psy-chopath is all too ready and willing to fulfill these needs. Because a psychopath—our new true friend—is an excellent communicator; he or she easily picks out topics that are important to us and reflects sympathetic points of view, sometimes complete with enthusiasm or "emotion" to reinforce the spoken words. The psychopath uses glib verbal and social skills to build a firm reputation in your mind—one that includes strengths you wish you had and weaknesses you understand. This psychological bond capitalizes on your inner personality, holding out the promise of greater depth and possibly intimacy, and offering a relationship that is special, unique, equal—forever. This is not easy to carry out, but the psychopath exerts notable effort communicating that he or she is *exactly* the person you have been looking for in a friend, partner, or new hire. The psychopath's fourth message is: *I am the perfect friend . . . lover . . . partner . . . for you.*

Once this is accomplished, the psychopathic bond—your fate—is sealed. Later interactions merely reinforce the foundation formed during this early part of the manipulation process.

What makes the psychopath-victim relationship any different from a real bond formed between two people who meet each other and find that they have a lot in common? For one, the persona of the psychopath—the "personality" the person is bonding with—does not really exist. It was built on lies, carefully woven together to entrap you. It is a mask, one of many, custom-made by the psychopath to fit your particular psychological needs and expectations. It does not reflect the true personality—the psychopathic personality—that lies beneath. It is a convenient fabrication.

Second, these relationships are not based on informed choice. The psychopath chooses you and then moves in. Outsiders, without the benefit of intimate conversation, may see what is really going on, but we tend to discount these observations, and may spend energy convincing our friends that this person is special.

Third, because it is faked, it won't last like genuine relationships. While genuine relationships change over time—love may turn to hate, marriages end in divorce—the initial starting point was based on real data, as it was known at the time. People change over time, and sometimes grow apart. The psychopath, though, will not invest more than minimal energy in maintaining the relationship unless you can offer something *really* special, which is not usually the case. Hence, when the relationship ends, you may be left wondering what just happened.

Fourth, the relationship is one-sided because the psychopath has an ulterior—some would say "evil"—and, at the very least, selfish motive. This victimization goes far beyond trying to take advantage of someone on a date or during a simple business transaction. The victimization is predatory in nature; it often leads to severe financial, physical, or emotional harm for the individual. Healthy, real relationships are built on mutual respect and trust; they are based on sharing honest thoughts and feeling. The mistaken belief that the psychopathic bond has any of these characteristics is the reason it is so successful.

In summary, the psychopath's psychological game involves analyzing the individual's expectations and desires, and then reflecting them in a psychological mask that is so convincing the person bonds with him or her. This bonding can take place very quickly, even during the space of one cross-country airplane ride. There are two payoffs: the psychopath wins the immediate game by gaining the person's trust, and the victim, now in the grip of the psychopath's power, will soon give up whatever the psychopath requests or demands.

We have reviewed many cases of individuals involved with psychopaths. Those who have been in long-term relationships with psychopaths often describe them as the supreme psychologist or mind reader. The more they interacted with the psychopath, the more they felt drawn in or mesmerized by the façade. Many referred to their psychopathic partners as their "soul mates" and reported how much they believed they had in common with the psychopath. It is even more disturbing to hear some victims' reports—once they have been cut loose during the abandonment phase—that they *miss* the relationship and want the psychopath *back* in their lives. It is very difficult for many to believe the relationship never really existed. The whole process is particularly insidious and difficult to get over if the psychopath is physically and personally attractive. How to avoid being ensnared in this one-sided relationship will be discussed later.

ACT II, Scene II

PLUCKING THE APPLE

Dorothy sat hunched over her laptop studying the recent report from the focus groups on the new project. She liked what she read and smiled to herself. Garrideb had always supported "skunk works" by their top employees, and Dorothy's recent promotion gave her the authority to proceed. She had shown her boss that she could get all of her regular work done with time to spare to work on her own ideas.

The sun had long set and the cleaning staff had all left the building. She enjoyed her work and putting in long hours did not bother her. Engrossed in her thoughts, she had not noticed what time it was.

"Burning the midnight oil again," came a voice from the doorway.

"Oh," she jumped, turning around, "Dave, you startled me!"

"Sorry, just passing through and saw your light on," he said, approaching. "Must be something good, judging by your concentration."

"Oh, just something I'm playing with," she said, nervously shuffling some papers on her desk.

"Personal business? On company time?" he joked.

"Hardly. More like company business on personal time," she smiled back playfully.

"And I thought I was the only one overworked here," he said, leaning over her desk to take a look at her computer screen.

"Sorry, can't look," she said, standing up to block Dave's view.

"Excuse me," he said, pretending to pout and backing off. "I thought you trusted me! We've known each other for a month now—and I always buy you coffee in the morning."

"The coffee is free, Dave. You're going to have to do better than that," she quipped. Dorothy and Dave had gotten to know each other pretty well since he first approached her in the cafeteria. The morning coffees had turned to the occasional lunch, and they had drinks together once after a company function. They shared stories about the company and laughed about some of the more colorful staff, but nothing out of the ordinary or inappropriate. Dorothy's focus was always on her work and career, and her dad's advice about mixing business with pleasure was etched in her mind. Not that she didn't find Dave attractive—all the women did—but she really didn't know much about his personal life, and felt that she should never cross that line.

"Do you really think they're going to support you on this?" he asked probingly.

"Well, Jerry said he would consider anything I come up with as long as I have the data."

"Yes, but Jerry's not the decision maker here," countered Dave.

"Well, who is, you?" she laughed.

"Frank's really the one you have to convince. He's the roadblock here, you know. He only likes ideas he comes up with, and regardless of what marketing says, unless development approves it, it's history. Jerry just doesn't have the in with the big boys like Frank. Frank will quash it the first chance he gets."

"I think he'll like my idea," she said, feeling a bit defensive, "and Jerry will make a good pitch for it."

"I would line up a few more ducks before I float anything to Jerry," Dave suggested in a paternalistic tone Dorothy had heard that Dave sometimes used with others.

"So I guess Frank hasn't liked any of your ideas yet," she said pointedly. "You've been here a long time by Garrideb standards; what's your track record?"

"Boy, you get feisty at times, don't you," said Dave, diffusing the growing tension in the room.

"Sorry, it's just that I've been working on this for over a month now, and I don't want to think that politics is going to stand in the way."

"This is a big company now, Dorothy. There's going to be politics. And," he said interrupting her before she could respond, "you're not very comfortable with things political, I'd say."

"We're not all big shots like you, Dave. I'll get this through on my own."

"I'm just suggesting that sometimes it's wise to work with others. One hand washes the other, you know."

"Please," she said dragging the word into two syllables and rolling her eyes. "I know, you're going to make me an offer I can't refuse, right?" she said, turning back to her computer screen.

"Well, maybe . . ."

5

Enter the Psychopath, Stage Left

Lawrence took the collection plates down the stairs to the church basement. He poured the money onto the table in the kitchen and the committee members began separating the bills and coins into piles for counting and depositing in the safe. The normally talkative members of the collections committee always grew silent as they counted. When everyone finished, the committee members rotated two positions to the left around the table in the church's kitchen and they recounted the piles of bills and coins for accuracy. The totals, written on small notes, were collected and handed to the new church treasurer, who made the entries into the ledger.

As the group rolled the coins into paper wrappers, the treasurer added up the numbers. "This is a good week; there's enough to cover the mortgage payment and utilities, plus some left over for the restoration fund."

"Amen," sighed the others. This had been a rough month for the parish. Many were shocked about what had happened, but all had come to the painful realization that they had been taken in by one of their own.

The detectives had explained to the congregation during a parish meeting that they were victims of what experts call an "affinity" fraud—a deception in which a person uses the appearance of shared personal beliefs and values to con a group into investing in phony business deals. Sam had been that person. He had joined the church nine months earlier and had become an active parishioner. He was bright, well liked, and, above all else, trusted. So much so that several members had invested their own money in some business deals he had going. These "opportunities" seemed safe and profitable. The early dividends were sizable—and had been for some time, judging by the high-quality clothes Sam wore, the luxury car he drove, and the big house he owned across town.

Sam's approach was always the same, according to the detectives. He would move into town, join a church or temple with a large congregation and several donation-funded community outreach programs, and then become increasingly active as a volunteer. Newcomers always attract attention and stimulate curiosity, and Sam's seemingly endless energy, unwavering sincerity, and positive outlook led many parishioners to seek him out for friendship. Conversations would naturally turn toward how he made a living, and Sam would share his story. In so many words, Sam explained that he was once a high-flying investment banker who realized the shallowness of his chosen profession only after his young wife and infant daughter died in a horrible car accident. His resulting bout with depression, alcohol, and pills finally led him to understand the Creator had something more in store for his life. Sam quit his job and moved out of his fancy penthouse apartment to fulfill his newly found purpose. Because he continued to do well with his investments, he didn't have to work, but could dedicate his life to helping others, and give back to the community in the name and spirit of his lost family.

Eventually, folks from the parish approached Sam, seeking personal financial advice. Some invested in the programs he managed, and after the dividends started coming in, many more followed. His obvious skill at managing money made him a natural candidate for church treasurer. Soon the congregation voted to invest money from the building fund and the after-school tutoring program in Sam's programs. They had grown tired of no-interest savings accounts and high-interest loans eating away at their weekly intake from parishioners. Sam's generosity and willingness to help others was the opposite of all that was bad about the banking industry. Financially, things could not get better.

But then, one day, Sam disappeared. He didn't show up for services, and no one had heard from him for a week. When the mortgage company called to say the last payment check had bounced, people grew concerned. Discovery of the emptied bank account and safe-deposit box led them to call the local police. Few suspected that theirs was the fourth religious group he had targeted during the past three years.

Sam, now living in a different state, clicked the computer mouse on the latest headline about "Sammy the Slimeball" ripping off innocent churchgoers. Sam kept up on the progress the police were making—or not making—in tracking him down by reading the press coverage on the Internet. "We want to thank our generous neighbors, especially those of differing religious beliefs in our community, for their spiritual support and financial contributions in our time of need. Our children's education program and food for the elderly programs have continued with their help, and our treasury restoration fund is growing," reported John, the new treasurer.

Sam smiled as he put on his tie, picked up his suit jacket, and headed out for Friday services.

Psychopaths often are cunning, master manipulators, able to influence individuals into fulfilling their own selfish ends. They hide their true motivations and project carefully formed personas to capitalize on the needs, expectations, and naïveté of individuals useful to them. When finished with their victims, they move on.

When trying to manipulate several people simultaneously, particularly in a group of peers, there is the risk that someone will suspect the truth and raise doubts about their aims, possibly jeopardizing their plans. Therefore, many psychopaths focus their efforts on one person at a time because it takes a lot of effort to maintain multiple façades in a group, each one custom-designed for the intended individual, especially if the stories involve complex lies and deceit. Some psychopaths, however, enjoy the challenge of running several different deceits concurrently while assuring that their victims never share information with other potential targets, or better yet, never even meet one another.

Unless caught and prosecuted for breaking the law, psychopaths suffer little consequence for the physical, emotional, psychological, and financial abuses they leave behind. The sad fact is that few victims—coworkers, partners, and spouses—report them to the authorities (or to their friends, for that matter) because of the shame they feel for being conned. Even in large firms, such as banks and brokerage houses, frauds and scams sometimes are not reported for fear of damaging the reputation of the firm. Psychopaths know and use this to their advantage. Others are too intimidated by fears of reprisal or litigation to speak up, being thankful that the psychopath simply is no longer in their life but has moved on to some other unfortunate person or firm.

Administrators and staff in prisons and psychiatric hospitals are painfully aware of how psychopaths operate in groups. In these structured settings, it takes little time for psychopaths to figure out the two main participants in the power structure—inmates versus guards and patients versus doctors or staff. Given this knowledge, they effectively make use of the group dynamics and role expectations of the different players. For example, some psychopaths successfully manipulate prison officials to get themselves transferred to a forensic hospital, where they enjoy more freedoms. By manipulating psychological test scores—some psychopaths are as test wise as many psychologists and psychiatrists—they can convince staff that they are "crazy" and don't belong in prison. Once in the hospital, they manage to manipulate and control other patients. Some manipulate the forensic hospital staff to be transferred *out* of the hospital back to a prison setting using similar maneuvers ("I'm not crazy like the others").

"On Sunday he prayed on his knees. On Monday he preyed on his fellow man."

—Caption from the *Vancouver Sun*,
May 20, 2000

Bryan Richards wheedled his way into a religious community by convincing its members that he was "one of them." He is a member of a line of distasteful predators who attached themselves to religious, ethnic, cultural, or special-purpose groups in which the members share common interests and typically are very trusting of others who profess to share their beliefs. Many Christian groups, for example, readily open their hearts to any newcomer; especially those who profess to have "found Christ." Unfortunately, these groups often also open their wallets, unwitting players in what is known as affinity fraud.

As described by Douglas Todd and Rick Ouston in the *Vancouver Sun*, Bryan Richards, whose real name is Richard Bryan Minard, is a smooth-talking, woman-chasing, Net-scamming evangelist who blew into a small Canadian town with a convincing line that he was a Christian, just like the members of the unsuspecting group he had targeted. "Don't despair. God's always there."

He ran a local low-wattage radio station and described himself as "the rock jock who spins for Jesus." He also ran numerous scams, including selling members time-shares in resorts he didn't own and vacation packages he never paid for, and pirating music

for his 30-minute "Christian Power Hour" program. He also ran a
Christian dating service, had numerous girlfriends, and "chased
the unmarried women." He attempted, and often achieved, "instant intimacy" by spinning a bewildering line of tall tales that
many found exciting and fascinating. His checks bounced.

As one of his victims said, "My feeling right now is that if [he]
weren't on this earth, it would be a better place."

Affinity groups—religious, political, or social groups in which all
members share common values or beliefs—are particularly attractive
to psychopaths because of the collective trust that members of these
groups have in one another. Those who perpetrate affinity and similar frauds rely on the common belief system of the group members
for cover. Common belief systems allow people who may be very
different in many other aspects of their lives to find common ground
for social interaction. As long as the psychopath can accurately es-
pouse these beliefs while in the presence of group members, the true
motives are less likely to be discovered. Religious belief groups, open
to new members joining their group from all lifestyles, readily assume that those who join them hold similar beliefs and values, and
tend to focus on professed beliefs and values and to forgive past
transgressions. These noble qualities, unfortunately, make them easier targets for manipulation by unscrupulous fraudsters. While most
people join affinity groups to associate with those who share their
values, beliefs, and interests, psychopaths join to take advantage of
them by hiding within a well-defined set of personal expectations.

Heaven on Earth?

The poetic phrase, "fleecing the lamb," was used as the title
of a book exposing the flagrant lack of ethics and regulation involved in the shameless promotion of highly speculative—and
almost certainly worthless—investments. But with its implied

reference to the willing subordination of the flock, the phrase has even more biting relevance when applied to religious congregants and cult members turning over their earthly possessions and their exclusive loyalty to a charismatic leader.

Jim Jones, the fundamentalist San Francisco preacher whose followers, in the hundreds, ultimately killed themselves at his bidding, remains our most horrific example, but examples of other hustlers posing as paternal and spiritually enlightened clerics abound. Turn on your television to some cable channels to see God's blessings, as directed through His earthly representative, being shamelessly sold for money—cleverly hidden among many legitimate religious programs. The phony evangelist portrayed by Burt Lancaster in the 1960 movie *Elmer Gantry*, would have thought he was in con paradise if he too could have delivered his pitch to millions of people at one time.

The vulnerability of needy believers has been well known for centuries, and few would dispute the probability that around a campfire some time in the prehistoric past, certain of our more persuasive ancestors were offering security against the demons of the dark and the promise of an afterlife in exchange for a place in the cave, a juicy portion of the kill, and the warm company of women. All too often, the modern counterpart of this charismatic spiritual leader is a charlatan, a cynical manipulator capitalizing on an opportunity almost too good to be true: a trusting audience ready—eager—to be entertained by, and to follow the exhortations of, any self-proclaimed emissary of God who happens to come along. How else to explain the attraction of the Bhagwan Shree Rajneesh, the giggling 1980s cult leader with scores of Rolls-Royce automobiles and hundreds of needy followers? "Surrender to me, and I will transform you. That is my promise," a mantra that resonated with all too many lost souls before the cult collapsed amid rumors of skullduggery and attempted murder.

This type of fraud is disturbing because of the ease with which a social predator infiltrates, cons, and manipulates affinity groups. It also is a testament to the power of impression management and to the tendency of many to be more influenced by style than substance. However, not all members of a given affinity group are so gullible. Indeed, informal observation of a number of such groups suggests that something like the one-third rule may apply. For example, when a latter-day Elmer Gantry, such as Bryan Richards, makes his move on an unsuspecting religious group, perhaps a third of its members will see him as convincing or charismatic, a third will be suspicious ("he makes my skin crawl"), and a third will reserve judgment. The interesting part is that when the scams, deceptions, and depredations are revealed, many of the initial opinions remain *unchanged*. Those who were impressed at first still believe they were right and that there must be a mistake or misunderstanding. Those who were suspicious at first now feel vindicated ("I knew he was bad news"). And the remaining third still are on the fence ("what happened?").

"I Felt Like I Was Lunch"

In *Without Conscience,* Hare noted that many people feel uncomfortable in the presence of a psychopath, whom he described as a social predator. Although most people can't quite put their finger on what bothers them, many comment that they were bothered by "a predatory stare and empty eyes."

In a recent study, researchers J. Reid Meloy and M. J. Meloy studied the reactions of mental health and criminal justice professionals concerning their "physical reactions" while interviewing psychopathic offenders or patients. The reactions were varied and included sensations and feelings that were gastrointestinal (queasy stomach, feeling of illness), muscular (shaky feeling, weakness), cardiovascular (pounding heart), pulmonary (shortness of breath), perceptual (watchful, couldn't look in the eyes), and dermatological (skin crawled, goosebumps). Many reported feelings of general anxiety, being ill at ease, repulsion, fascination, and stimulation. Some reported that they wished to flee the scene or that they felt as if they were about to become lunch.

The authors suggested that their findings could be interpreted as suggestive evidence of a primitive, autonomic, and fearful response to a predator. They described the psychopath as an intraspecies predator.

Getting Down to Business

Business organizations pose the next level of challenge for the psychopath. They are different from affinity groups, forensic hospitals, or prisons in their purpose, complexity, and structure. Although they can potentially present severe constraints to psychopaths wishing to misuse coworkers, managers, or the company itself, they do offer tremendous opportunity.

To start, business organizations have a fundamentally different reason for existence than other groups. They are designed to combine the labor of many people into a product or service to be sold for financial gain. For example, a local bakery will employ bakers to produce the pies, cakes, and breads; an office manager who orders supplies, hires the help, and handles the bookkeeping; and salespeople who will describe the various pastries and breads, hand out samples, pack the customers' selections, and handle the cash. Although it is not out of the question that some psychopaths work in a small neighborhood bakery, most tend to take on jobs in companies where they can take advantage of others, make a big killing, *and* hide as well. A neighborhood bakery, usually run by family members, wouldn't offer them the opportunities they require, at least not as long as it remains small and tightly controlled.

For example, the bakery might evolve into a major, national player in the baked goods industry. Initially, the owners may decide to open a second shop across town. They will need to staff this one and train the new help in their business processes. They may hire a maintenance person to keep the increased number of ovens and other

kitchen appliances running, a phone operator to handle telephone orders, and specialty bakers who can create new and different treats to
help differentiate this bakery's product from competitors'. Eventually,
the owners may decide to buy or lease trucks so they can deliver large
orders to commercial customers, hire a full-time accountant to do the
books, bring on cleaning staff, a marketing team, and so forth. The
bakery's success, as with any business venture, relies on several important factors: how good is its product, how are its customer relations,
and how well does it manage the operations? Managing all this
growth is not easy. To the degree that all the people, all the functions,
and all the equipment work together and cooperate toward the same
end, the business will run smoothly and evolve to meet increasingly
complex business demands. In a perfect world, everything *would*
run smoothly, but as most readers understand from their own work
experience, this is rarely the case. Without additional organizational
development, our hypothetical family-run business would grow un-
controlled, quickly running off the track.

Historically, increased size and business complexity brought with
it, out of necessity, *bureaucracy*, a term many small business owners
dread, but a model of business that evolved to address the needs of
growth. Bureaucracy typically involves a lot of rules and regulations in
the form of systems, processes, and procedures. The recipe for sour-
dough bread, which used to reside in the mind of the baker, is now
captured in a "batch sheet" or similar formulation. The original own-
er's insistence on "using only high-quality ingredients" is now called
"following good manufacturing practices." While this standardization
of things is necessary for success, it does cause a lot of stress.

The Corporation as Psychopath

The Corporation is an award-winning documentary that uses
extensive file footage and interviews with a number of well-
known commentators and experts to evaluate the moral and so-

cial behaviors of the corporate world. The documentary uses a selected set of examples of corporate misbehaviors, as well as a brief clip of a longer interview with Hare, to make and bolster its position that the corporation meets the diagnostic criteria for psychopathy.

As a promotional release for the documentary put it: *"Diagnosis: the institutional embodiment of laissez-faire capitalism fully meets the diagnostic criteria of a psychopath."* Although the producers of the documentary stated that they used the term *psychopath* merely as a metaphor for the most egregious corporate entities, it is apparent that they had in mind corporations in general. The short excerpt from the interview with Hare did not convey his view that although the attitudes, philosophies, and behaviors of a *given* corporation (as a legal entity) might be considered psychopathic, at least as an academic exercise, such a "diagnosis" hardly would apply to all, or even most, corporations.

To refer to *the* corporation as psychopathic because of the behaviors of a carefully selected group of companies is like using the traits and behaviors of the most serious high-risk criminals to conclude that *the* criminal (that is, every criminal) is a psychopath. If the PCL-R, its derivative, the PCL: SV, or the B-Scan (see page 230) *were* to be applied to a random set of corporations, some might qualify for a diagnosis of psychopathy, but most would not.

We doubt that psychopathic individuals would be very successful in a highly structured traditional bureaucracy, for several important reasons. First, psychopaths are generalized rule breakers; rules and regulations mean little to them. The sheer number of policies, procedures, and laws governing how companies must act, as well as the fact that managers and supervisors are charged with enforcing them, makes them inhospitable to those prone to psychopathic behavior. They would not last long in a traditional, textbook bureaucracy. It is unlikely that they would even consider working for one, unless they knew the boss and could get away with getting a paycheck without actually producing any work.

Second, we know that psychopaths are not team players. They are far too selfish to work with others toward common goals. Recall that psychopaths manipulate individuals by presenting a mask custom-tailored to the occasion. Successful manipulation relies on three important conditions: (1) the psychopath needs one-on-one access to the individual, (2) the relationship that is fostered must be kept private, and (3) there can be no means to bring deviant behavior to the attention of management. In bureaucratic organizations, where much of the work is done in teams, it would be difficult to gain such restricted access to useful individuals and for clandestine manipulation and serious counterproductive behavior to go unnoticed. All employees are *expected* to be productive and focused on achieving objectives while on the job. All are expected to be honest, decent employees and not be abusive toward their colleagues. Given that prosocial behaviors and attitudes are *required* in most employment situations but difficult for those with a psychopathic personality to maintain in any consistent way, how could they survive?

Third, psychopaths have little genuine interest in the short- or long-term goals and objectives of the organization. Any suggestion that their efforts should take into account the good of the company would be foreign to them. They are much more likely to be motivated and guided by relatively immediate needs and gratifications—a quick score—than by the possibility of uncertain future goals and rewards, particularly if they require dedication, hard work, and personal sacrifice.

Fourth, traditional business organizations do not offer an easy means to hide. Counterproductive work behaviors that are visible to others and reported to management are often dealt with through human resource policies, such as codes of conduct and rules and procedures to handle complaints about sexual harassment, bullying, and other forms of unacceptable behavior. Internal auditors typically investigate suspicions of fraud, theft, or other forms of deceit. If proven true, these may eventually lead to legal action by the organization against the employee. Often, termination and a negative employment reference result.

Finally, psychopaths don't share the same work ethic of most other workers, who typically believe in an honest day's work for an honest day's pay, who take pride in doing a good job, and who value long-term employment. It is difficult to imagine that a psychopath would work diligently from 9 to 5 in the hope of becoming manager in five or six years. This is not to suggest that psychopaths never work in routine, dead-end jobs or in trades or professions that would seem to require training and experience. Many do, but it is very likely that their qualifications are questionable; their performance self-serving, unreliable, and untrustworthy; and their actions even illegal. Think of high-pressure sales representatives, predatory repair people, "pump and dump" stock promoters, Internet scamsters, fraudulent counselors, and shady professionals of all sorts, to name but a few.

But what about the so-called *corporate* psychopath? How does he or she survive and thrive in a big company? The fact is that many organizations are prime feeding grounds for psychopaths with an entrepreneurial bent and the requisite personal attributes and social skills to fool many people. Like all predators, psychopaths go where the action is, which to them means positions, occupations, professions, and organizations that afford them the opportunity to obtain power, control, status, and possessions, and to engage in exploitative interpersonal relationships.

Despite the problems and challenges associated with joining a large business, there is much to be gained, and psychopaths, like most of us, assess the risks against the potential reward. There is the opportunity to make a lot of money, to gain status and power, and all the perquisites that go with them. The psychopaths' ability to take advantage of a company—commit fraud, steal, abuse coworkers, make a big salary—while being in its employ, requires more sophistication than the simple social manipulation they present out in public. For the corporate psychopath, this is the ultimate challenge.

We know that individuals with psychopathic personalities are prone to lying, rule breaking, and deceit. To be successful in an organization, they would have to operate covertly, that is, *under the radar*, cognizant of the policies, rules, regulations, and official codes of conduct, but able to circumvent them for a significant amount of time. They would have to manipulate many coworkers and managers into believing their lies, while *neutralizing* the negative impact of any coworkers who discovered (and threatened to uncover) their lies and deceit. To manipulate coworkers, compliance systems, and management observations consistently would be very difficult, possibly beyond the ability of all but the most talented and persistent. Few psychopaths would have the wherewithal to try it, and those who did would fail quickly. *Or so it once was thought.*

Organizational Manipulation

To understand the success of the corporate psychopath, we must realize that textbook bureaucracies rarely exist and in modern times seldom survive. Instead, organizational structures, processes, and culture are always evolving and developing toward an ideal whose picture is, at best, unclear and ever changing. This constant change and uncertainty causes stress for most employees and managers, but opens the door for the psychopath.

Babiak has shown that psychopaths may have little difficulty influencing others even on the job, where their manipulations may attract more attention. This is best understood in the context of a case. During a long-term consulting assignment, many years ago, Babiak had the experience of working with a psychopath without knowing it at the time.

> *I was asked to work with a project team that was experiencing a decline in its overall productivity and a significant increase in conflict. Some team members had even asked to be transferred to other projects, despite the prestige associated with working on*

this high-performing team. When questioned by management, the team leader and some members said they did not know what was causing the difficulty. A team-building program was launched for the team members in an attempt to isolate the problems and help the team regain its previous high-performance levels.

Interviews with team members, observations from coworkers in other departments and other management, and review of relevant human resources documents provided a preliminary picture of what was happening. Many members of the team felt that one of its members was the primary cause of its problems, but were afraid to come forward. They reported to me, privately, that this individual circumvented team processes and procedures, caused conflict, acted rudely in meetings, and did more to derail progress than to promote it. He often showed up late to meetings, and when he finally would arrive, he hadn't completed the tasks he was assigned, routinely blaming others for his failures. Some suggested that he bullied, even threatened, team members who did not agree with him. At every turn, he undercut the leader's role on the team, who also happened to be his boss.

Some other members of the team felt differently, though. They told me that he was a solid performer whose ideas were both creative and innovative. This group of supporters said that he was a true leader and contributed toward the team's objectives. A few members of the management committee even commented that they thought this person had the potential for promotion into a management position someday. Depending on whom you were speaking with, you would get a different picture of this person. It was as if these groups of coworkers were describing two different people instead of one. The behaviors of this individual and the different reactions of the various team members—that is, the split between supporters and detractors—suggested that something more than mere office politics and interpersonal conflict was going on behind the scenes. But what?

A subsequent review of this person's record by the personnel department revealed that he had lied on his résumé and did not have the essential experience or education that he claimed to have. The security department also discovered that he routinely took home company supplies of significant monetary value for personal use; the auditing department also found several suspicious inconsistencies in his expense account. The division between the supporters' view and the detractors' view became even wider as more and more information was forthcoming.

Local management reviewed much of this information, but, unfortunately, before any action could be taken, senior management reorganized the departments involved, and the team was disbanded. The team leader was moved to another location and the individual who was at the center of the controversy was given a promotion—into his boss's job—and a leadership role in the department.

I considered this case for a long time after the business relationship ended but was unable to satisfactorily explain all the discrepancies (only some examples reported here). One day, while rereading a copy of Cleckley's book, I realized that the controversial team member might have a psychopathic personality. My field notes and documents were filled with examples of behaviors similar to those mentioned by Cleckley and studied by Hare. Perhaps psychopathy would explain most of the conflicting observations made by so many people so close to the individual. Using the information available, I completed the Psychopathy Checklist: Screening Version (PCL: SV) on this person, just as an experiment. The results were startling.

This individual came out very close to the PCL: SV cut score for psychopathy—a score much higher than that expected even for most serious offenders. The PCL: SV also yields four subscores (see page 27) that reflect psychopathic features in four areas: Interpersonal, Affective, Lifestyle, and Antisocial. Known criminal psychopaths tend to score high on all four, *while those like the reader score low on each one. The individual who caused such controversy on the team scored high on the first two factors and moderately on the other two. This profile indicated that he was grandiose, manipulative, deceptive, and lacking in empathy and concern for others, but also that he was less impulsive or overtly antisocial than most psychopaths. He had not broken the law or seriously victimized others, at least as far as we knew.*

During the next few years, several individuals working in other businesses were brought to my attention by employees who felt that they had been victimized by coworkers. Business executives and human resources professionals, following public speaking engagements and education sessions about psychopathy, also shared war stories about individuals whose behaviors had caused some difficulties at their companies. In some cases, I had enough information to complete the PCL: SV on them. Some exhibited the same profile as the individual noted above, but some did not—they were merely problematic employees engaged in counterproductive or deviant work behavior for reasons unrelated to psychopathic personality.

Female Psychopaths

"Why aren't there any female psychopaths," an interviewer asked one of the authors. The fact that she could ask such a question reflects a curious wrinkle on sexism: the view, held by many people, that relatively few female psychopaths exist in society—or even prisons—and that those who do exist differ in fundamental ways from their male counterparts.

The issue is clouded by sex-role biases in the diagnosis of the disorder. Thus, when a female and a male each exhibit a psychopathic pattern of core personality traits—grandiose, egocentric, selfish, irresponsible, manipulative, deceitful, emotionally shallow, callous, and lacking in empathy, remorse, and guilt—a clinician will often diagnose the male as a psychopath (or antisocial personality disorder) and the female as something else, usually histrionic or narcissistic personality disorder (see page 40). In each case, the clinician's diagnosis is influenced by expectations of how psychopaths should behave. That is, the clinician expects psychopaths to be tough, dominant, and aggressive, and a woman who does not project these characteristics therefore is not a psychopath. What the clinician fails to understand is that the behaviors of male and female psychopaths, like those of most other people, are shaped by the sex-role stereotypes cultivated by society. The same underlying personality structure may find different behavioral and social expression.

Although the process of socialization fails to embed in the psyche of psychopaths the network of inner controls we refer to collectively as *conscience*, it nevertheless makes them aware of society's expectations about sex roles, about what is expected of them as men and women. More than most people, they effectively use these expectations as potent tools for manipulation. So a female psychopath might make full use of the passive, warm, nurturing, and dependent sex-role stereotype in order to get what she wants out of others, just as a male psychopath might use a macho image, intimidation, and aggression to achieve satisfaction of his desires.

Female psychopaths effectively use society's expectations about female behavior to their own advantage. But, more than most women, they also are able to break out of the traditional sex-role stereotypes, to go beyond conventional boundaries. This is readily apparent among female offenders, where the prevalence of psychopaths is almost as high as it is among male offenders. The variety and severity of criminal acts performed by these women, as well as their capacity for cold-blooded violence, are similar to those committed by their male counterparts.

Sex-role stereotypes about the behavior of women are changing rapidly. In a sense, the public is just catching up with a reality that long has been recognized by writers and those in the entertainment business. Female psychopaths frequently are well portrayed in fiction, true-crime books, television, and movies.

Over the years, we were able to collect more information on how some of these individuals—industrial or corporate psychopaths—interacted with coworkers and management over extended periods. Gradually, a consistent pattern emerged, a pattern eerily similar to the parasitic lifestyle described in chapter 3. Based on all our observations, it is now clear that a small number of individuals with psychopathic personality features can be found in some business organizations. Some highly motivated individuals with psychopathic personalities (as assessed by the Hare PCL-R or PCL: SV) were able to enter an organization, evaluate strengths and weaknesses in its culture (processes, communication networks, corporate politics), use and abuse coworkers, "deal with" opposition, and climb the corporate ladder. How they did it, and more important, why they were so successful, took a number of studies and a bit of time to fully understand and answer. When cases were compared side by side, some similarities were noted, with almost every industrial or corporate psychopath following a similar career progression. These individuals were able to enter the corporation, adapt to its culture, and manipulate coworkers and executives, as described in detail below and in the next chapter.

Entering the Corporation

The initial challenge for any psychopath trying to join a company is, of course, to be hired. Like psychopaths who easily enter people's personal lives, corporate psychopaths are able to join organizations more easily than one might expect. This is because the standard techniques used to screen out underqualified individuals are well known and little match for the psychopath's lying and manipulative skills.

The typical selection process involves reviewing the résumés of job candidates for the knowledge, skills, abilities, and attitudes needed to do a good job. On the surface, the process seems quite straightforward, but it involves a lot of planning and effort and is not foolproof. For midlevel and lower-level jobs, lists of requirements can be gleaned by watching current employees who exhibit outstanding performance records. However, when the job is new and there are no incumbents, supervisors and human resources professionals create the lists based on research from other, similar companies. Once there is a clear sense of what is wanted in the job applicant, then each candidate can be evaluated through detailed probing and questioning by interviewers.

This process is especially effective for technical jobs or those that can be quantified such as those found in research and development. But as one moves up the corporate ladder into jobs with greater scope and less clear responsibilities, the task becomes more difficult. "Strategic planning," "critical thinking," "freedom to act," "leadership," and other variables must be added to the list—and these are much more difficult to quantify. This makes selecting the most qualified job candidate difficult, and "gut feel" or "chemistry" begins to take on more of a role in decision making about who is the best candidate for the job. This is most evident during face-to-face interviewing, *exactly* the place where the psychopath shines. The less clearly defined—or higher level—the job, the easier it is for a psychopath to be hired.

It is common knowledge among executive recruiters that 15 percent or more of the résumés they receive contain distortions or outright lies. Psychopaths, whose personalities are *defined* by chronic lying, among other things, are quite adept at creating written documentation—résumés, letters of recommendation, citations, and awards—out of whole cloth. They can fabricate a work history custom-tailored to the job requirements, and back it up with phony references, job samples, and appropriate jargon.

Psychopaths have an advantage in person as well as on paper. They can talk a good game during the interview, coming across as smooth, talented, bright, sensitive, self-confident, and assertive. Their storytelling abilities reinforce their résumé "data," and the whole package they present can be quite compelling. Unfortunately, if hiring decisions are based on easily faked résumés and unstructured interviews by untrained interviewers—where expertise is evaluated based on the ability to convince the interviewer you know what you're talking about—the company runs the risk of hiring someone who is a fraud.

A further complicating factor is that the hiring process has many objectives beyond merely adding new employees or replacing those who have left. It is very common, especially in rapidly growing companies, to hire people based primarily on *perceptions* of their management potential or future contributions to the company. That is, some people are hired because they might fit the requirements for the next job up or beyond, not necessarily for the one for which they originally applied. As noted above, higher-level jobs tend to be more broadly defined, and specific technical skills and abilities are not as relevant or critical to assess. Unfortunately, it is easy for the unsuspecting interviewer to believe that a psychopathic candidate, because of his or her convincing communications style, may have leadership potential beyond the technical knowledge, skills, and abilities listed on the résumé. A clever psychopath can present such a well-rounded picture of a perfect job candidate that even seasoned interviewers can be caught up in the excitement of convincing the individual to join the company.

The role of charm in persuading the interviewer that one possesses the characteristics most often sought in new employees cannot be overstated. When we question managers about the traits they look for in high-level employees, they often state they want individuals who are bright, conscientious, honest, and socially skilled. Unfortunately, these *same* traits were ascribed to the corporate psychopaths we studied by those who liked and supported them. Interestingly, these are also the characteristics victims report seeing in con men and women, before they realized that they had been scammed or deceived.

Much of an organization's success or failure depends on its human assets: what knowledge, skills, and attitudes they bring to their work; how well they understand and are understood by the company;

and how well they get along with each other. The selection process is very important to the ultimate success of the company, but it is not always easy to find individuals who are a good match for the company and its objectives. Likewise, it is not easy to identify individuals who will grow and prosper with the company over time, as opposed to those who enter bearing a different, more selfish agenda. Personality is an important factor in employee selection, but some personalities can be quite deceptive and extremely persuasive.

The subsequent steps are described in detail in the next chapter.

ACT III, Scene I

PANIC TIME

Frank left the meeting exhausted but happy that it was only 7 P.M. on a Friday night. Most days he left the office much later. "Another important meeting, Mr. Frank?" asked Marissa, the night cleaning crew supervisor.

"Yes, always meetings. But this one was useful; we actually got some things done." Marissa smiled and Frank continued down the hall toward his office. He flipped on the light and saw the folder Dave had left for him in the center of his blotter. Opening it, Frank saw the report Dave wrote, the printout of the slides Dave had prepared, and the disk with the files. Excellent, he thought as he put the folder in his briefcase, added some other files from his desk, and then closed it up. Turning to the door, Frank sighed and thankfully headed home to a great dinner with the family, a Saturday at the zoo with the kids, and a Sunday flight to the meeting where he would make his presentation.

The aroma of pancakes and eggs filled the kitchen as Frank served up breakfast for the family. Frank enjoyed this Sunday morning ritual with the kids and often went to church with them, but today he had an afternoon flight and needed to finalize his presentation. Most of it was done; he just had to integrate Dave's data and then he could get on with the packing. Sally herded the kids into the car and drove off for church, lunch with Grandma, and back home in time to see Frank off on his trip.

Silence, thought Frank, smiling, as he carried his coffee into the den. Frank was scheduled to speak to the executive board's strategic planning meeting on Monday morning. Last-minute details were worked out with the other presenters during the Friday meeting; he was confident that the board would support his new product proposals—they always had in the past. And this time he had Dave's research, which would augment his presentation.

Frank opened Dave's folder and began reading the report and looking at the charts. Frank read and read. He studied the charts. He sipped coffee. He opened the folder to see if he had forgotten to take out part of the report. Growing concerned, Frank reloaded the disk and searched for more files. There was nothing else; he had all the material there on his desk. Frank started getting nervous and then angry. "This is crap!" he said aloud as he picked up the phone and dialed Dave's home number. The phone rang and rang. There was no answer, and there was no answering machine. *How could anyone* not *have an answering machine these days?* he thought angrily. Rummaging through his briefcase, he found his phone book and dialed Dave's cell phone number. The call went straight into voice mail. Getting control of himself, Frank firmly and clearly told Dave that he didn't have the full report and asked Dave to get back to him as soon as possible with the numbers he needed.

Frank reread the material, and it dawned on him how familiar it was. His anger slowly turned to fear as he realized where he had read this material before. This was from an article he had read in an industry magazine a few weeks back—an article written about their chief competitor. He turned his briefcase upside down on the floor. There among his stuff was the magazine. He flipped through it to the article. "Oh, my God!" exclaimed Frank as he realized that Dave had taken paragraphs from the article and retyped them into his report. The charts were the same, except he had changed the product labels and the legend to say Garrideb Technologies, and had increased the figures 12 percent across the board. There were no new data, no real projections, and no new product presentation!

Frank realized what he had to do. He logged onto the corporate computer and began searching through databases. He knew he still had the flip charts in the closet from the off-site planning meeting that he had run himself before he handed the project over to Dave. He furiously e-mailed requests for information to his staff, hoping that they, being the compulsive folks he knew them to be, were at home working, as well. Finally, he called his travel agent and got her to change his flight to the later one that night. He would miss the cocktail party and dinner, but there was no other way. He had to finish his presentation—his reputation and career depended on it.

Frank's cab pulled up in front of the hotel. He got out, declined help with his bags from the bellhop, and quickly headed for the registration desk to check in. Turning toward the elevators, Frank spotted John, his boss, walking through the lobby bar. Before he could duck into the elevator, John waved him down. "Frank, Frank, glad you made it. We were worried; how are things at home?"

"Oh, John, fine. I just had to change flights because of a family thing. Sally's mother called . . ."

"No problem, Frank, I understand. Look, I really love your presentation. I think it's a winner. You've really knocked the ball out of the park this time," said John enthusiastically, patting Frank on the back and pulling him back into the bar.

"You do?" asked Frank, not knowing what presentation John was talking about.

"Yes, the ideas are so fresh; just what we need to pull us out of this slump and rebuild the board's confidence in us," said John as he ordered two martinis. "You know, you're pretty sly, Frank. You never mentioned any of this to me on Friday—wanted to surprise me at breakfast before the meeting?"

"Well," squeaked Frank, wondering what was really going on. "John? Which version of my presentation did I send you?"

"Oh, I just assumed it was the final one," said John as the bartender put down their drinks, and John signaled him to start a tab. "I got it from Dave, earlier this evening."

Frank reached for the glass and downed half his martini before he said: "Dave?"

"Yes, he called and told me you had some issue at home and weren't sure you would make it to the meeting. So he went ahead and sent the latest version, knowing you were preoccupied." John paused. "You know, he's really got the right stuff, hasn't he?"

"I . . . I," stuttered Frank.

"And you, putting in a whole slide thanking Dave and the team for their input. A bit much, Frank—the picture I mean—but a nice thought nonetheless." Frank finished his drink and smiled weakly.

"You look like you've had a rough day, Frank. Would you like another?"

6

Pawns, Patrons, and Patsies
ROLES IN THE PSYCHOPATH'S DRAMA

"There'll be two of us," said Ron to the hostess who greeted him at the door.

"Okay, follow me," she said, picking up two menus and indicating for Ron to follow her. "Is this okay?" she asked.

"This is great," said Ron, smiling, as he took a seat facing the door and placed the plastic grocery bag under the table next to his feet. The hostess positioned the menus on the table and removed the extra tableware, leaving two place settings on the table.

"Gloria will be with you shortly," she said, smiling. "Can I get you a drink while you're waiting?"

"Two martinis, one dirty and one extra dry," said Ron, not looking up from the wine list. Ron was the best salesperson the company had ever seen. He was a master of the face-to-face sale and had gotten customers who had had long-term relationships with competitors to switch to his company. Ron had a carefree lifestyle, enjoying many perks at work such as a company-leased luxury car (significantly above the standard allowed for a field salesperson at his level) and an expense account for entertaining clients. Everyone seemed to look the other way when Ron's expense reports came in for processing. Occasionally, the liquor bills, visits to gentlemen's clubs, and other obviously out-of-the-ordinary things were questioned, but with his boss's signature on the reports, there was little the accounting department could do, other than roll their eyes and joke about how the West Coast handled business dealings. The few times Ron's boss Joe, the regional sales manager, pushed back, Ron simply talked his way around it, promising a big sale down the road. Ron was very persuasive and knew how to play Joe very well.

Joe arrived shortly, a bit out of breath, and found Ron perusing the menu.

"Hey, Ron, you're looking great—sorry I'm late. Traffic, as usual," said Joe, extending his hand.

"Joe, good to see you," responded Ron, rising up briefly to offer Joe a firm handshake. "There's a New York strip special today; hope you're hungry."

"More thirsty than hungry," he started to say, just as the server returned with the drinks. Ron indicated which drink was Joe's and waved the server off.

"To another great month," Ron said loudly, raising his glass. They both sipped their drinks and got down to business. Ron pulled out his latest call report and handed it to Joe. Despite the lack of sales for this month, Ron had made a significant effort "beating the bushes," meeting almost daily with potentially large clients. Without looking, Joe took the report. "And here's my expense report," said Ron, handing it to him with a pen on top. Joe pretended to read it, merely glancing actually, as he signed the report. "Thanks, Joe," said Ron, reaching under the table for the bag and sliding it across the floor toward Joe.

Ron waved to the server, indicating that they needed two more drinks as they continued discussing baseball scores, the weather, and Joe's grandchildren. Sipping his second martini, Joe said, "Ron, I have some news for you."

"Oh?" questioned Ron, motioning to the server.

"Ron, I've decided to take my retirement; I'll be leaving the company at the end of this month."

"Joe, that's great. Congratulations! What made you decide?" asked Ron.

"Well, they've offered me a package, and with the kids now out of college, my wife and I decided to sell our house and move up to the lake. The stress is getting to be too much for me, as you know, and I guess they realized it, too."

"So, when are they going to move on your replacement?" hinted Ron with a smile. Ron knew that Joe had repeatedly recommended him for a promotion based on his performance reviews, and given this development, he eagerly anticipated Joe's telling him he got the promotion.

"That's just it, Ron," started Joe slowly. "They're not telling me. I've heard rumors that they want to use the regional job as a developmental position for someone on the plan. They may rotate someone in from one of the other regions."

"What!" exclaimed Ron, his face starting to get red. "What do you mean, someone from the other regions? I'm the best there is, I know the territory, I deserve the promotion; you put me in as your replacement, right? Doesn't that count for anything?"

"Yes, I know. Of course, I put you on the plan—every year when they ask, I tell them you're ready to move up now, but they—"

"That's unacceptable!" charged Ron. "Who's making this decision?"

"Personnel, of course."

"You know, they have no clue what this job entails. Who are *they* to do this? What does Sam say?" Ron asked pointedly about Joe's boss, the VP of sales.

"I had it out with Sam, Ron, arguing for you to get the job;

honest, I did. But Sam hasn't been able to convince the selection committee. They're hung up on the sales figures as well as some of the other stuff."

"Listen, Joe, let me call your wife. I'll explain to her that your stress is—"

"Ron," interrupted Joe, "my wife didn't make this decision; I did." Joe looked down and then up into Ron's eyes, saying, "Well, they made the decision for me. It's the best for all of us."

"I can't believe they forced you out after all these years."

"Times change, and I guess I have to, too. They're offering to pay for a program, as part of the deal, to help with my problem."

"You don't have any problem, Joe," said Ron.

"Thanks, Ron, but both you and I know I do," said Joe, lowering his voice. "I think they have my best interest at heart. Few people get this kind of support when they go. They really want me to straighten myself out. The server arrived to take their order, and Ron picked out a special wine to celebrate Joe's retirement.

The rest of the afternoon was loud and raucous, as all the previous monthly lunch meetings between them. On the surface, Ron appeared happy for Joe and talked about visiting him and his wife up at the lake, fishing, and barbecuing. In his mind, however, he was planning his next move.

After lunch, they shook hands and exchanged a big bear hug. "I'll process these," said Joe, picking up the paperwork.

"Don't forget the package," reminded Ron, indicating the grocery bag under the table.

"I won't be needing that anymore; thanks, though, you've always understood. I'll miss working with you."

Ron entered his corporate-paid apartment. "Damn," he swore, falling into the easy chair in the living room. He picked up his cell phone and began dialing. This would be a long night on the phone; time to call in some favors and get some dirt on Jack, his rival for the promotion.

Jack got the promotion into the regional manager position, and was now Ron's boss. A methodical, focused, and detail-oriented person, Jack spent considerable time reviewing each salesperson's performance record and then planned to meet personally with each member of the sales team to establish objectives, meeting schedules, and new performance measures.

Ron had also done his homework: his friends in personnel gave him the lowdown on Jack's performance record (stellar); his friends in accounting gave him insight into Jack's spending habits (which paled against his own); and even his peers in Jack's old region gave him insights into his personal style and family details. As Jack moved through the region meeting individually with the salespeople, Ron followed up with calls to his colleagues to find out what Jack was saying. When Jack arrived for his meeting with him, Ron was ready.

While the others complied with the new procedures willingly, those who knew him waited to see how Ron would respond. Ron's reputation in the company as a "raconteur" had always been a cause of concern among the sales management committee. He had learned from his old boss Joe, an old-school "belly-to-belly" salesperson, how to gain customers and close deals using personal influence and personal charisma, but this style was growing less effective with the Internet's arrival and a new breed of sophisticated, hard-driving competitors. Sam, the VP, had inherited the Ron and Joe team a few years earlier. Knowing that Joe was close to retirement age, he tolerated his style, but he never liked the fact that Joe protected Ron, covering for him when he missed targets and approving expenditures that exceeded corporate guidelines. With Joe gone, Ron's style was fair game, and Jack was going to take care of the problem.

Jack and Ron met for a lunch meeting in Ron's territory. Ron started with the sweet approach, trying to butter Jack up with a congratulatory bottle of wine, small talk about Jack's kids' soccer games, and stacks of positive performance reviews, miscellaneous charts, and letters of thanks from big customers (and long-term friends).

Jack was not so easily swayed. When Jack began explaining how he wanted to manage the region and presented Ron with his new requirements, Ron started pushing back, eventually raising his voice enough to get the attention of other diners in the fine restaurant. He argued that he didn't need any more controls than those previously imposed by Joe, and promised to deliver whatever Jack needed to make him look good in the eyes of top management. Jack had heard that Ron would sometimes get loud in order to get his way, so he decided to hear him out, but then come back firmly. Ron's arguments eventually turned into veiled threats of turning the other salespeople against Jack, legal action, and possible damage to Jack's career.

This guy's nuts, thought Jack as Ron continued his arguments, almost ranting and raving. Sensing that Ron was about to end the meeting and walk out, Jack said, "Look, Ron, I appreciate all you have done, but the industry has changed. We're no longer in the catbird seat with our products, and this region—your region—is the weakest link."

"Then you—they—should have fired Joe years ago!" said Ron, finally. "I've been covering for him since I got here. Do you know what it's like working for . . ." Ron caught himself, paused, and then continued, his voice cracking slightly, "someone who's never around when you need him to close a deal, can't get any advice worth listening to, forced to always cover for him. I've been all alone here, Jack, fighting for the company and this is how they reward me—with more procedures, more demands, more grief!"

Although Joe's personal problem had been an open secret in the region, others outside the region did not know, so Jack was taken aback by this revelation. His gut reaction was that this was an inappropriate topic for them to discuss, but Ron's persistence and obvious frustration began to get to him. He listened more carefully to Ron's difficulties in dealing with Joe, trying to apply some of the management techniques he had learned. He stroked Ron's ego and reflected his understanding of Ron's dilemma. By the end of the conversation—once Ron had calmed down—Jack promised to help

Ron reorient his sales approach to what the company now needed, and take into consideration all that he had been through.

The conversation ended on a positive note and Jack felt he had accomplished his task. His objective for the meeting had been to turn Ron around or else take the necessary steps to get rid of him. Jack now felt that he could build a relationship with Ron and things would improve. They agreed to meet again in a month and parted with a handshake.

Ron entered his apartment and threw off his jacket and tie. Nestling in his sofa, he grabbed his cell phone and dialed. *This will be easy*, he thought, smiling to himself.

A Kid in a Candy Store

Once the hiring process is complete, new hires undergo an orientation and socialization process that often includes training in job competencies, exposure to key corporate messages, and indoctrination into cultural values of the company. This is a time of excitement and happiness for most new employees, as the chance to learn and grow in a new job is very motivating. It is also an exciting time for the individual with a psychopathic personality, but for different reasons altogether.

First, the psychopaths' simple one-to-one manipulative approach to life (discussed in chapter 4) that governs many of their outside relationships is particularly effective in organizational settings. Several characteristics of business life facilitate the application of these techniques. First, there is an assumption made by employees and managers that coworkers who have made it through the hiring process, especially if the company uses rigorous selection criteria, are honest people with personal integrity. Honesty and integrity are a "given" in most organizations, rarely *tested* on any but the most superficial levels.

The assumption that fellow organizational members are similarly predisposed toward honesty hangs in the background, coloring the perspective of coworkers and managers, who would never suspect that
one of their own colleagues could have ulterior motives. This trusting
environment may not rise to the level of that experienced in religious
or other affinity groups, but certainly is sufficient for psychopathic
manipulation to be successful in companies. As a result, the psychopath blends in well—a good "kid" like his or her peers.

The Psychopath in the Next Cubicle

A compilation of *Dilbert* comic strips has the title, *What Do
You Call a Sociopath in the Next Cubicle?*
Answer: A coworker.
A catchy title, but misleading. The comic strips depict a wide
range of workplace characters, including at least one ". . . flam-
ing @SShole, one interminable bore . . . one person who needs a
metronome to breathe . . . and the guy who uses his speaker-
phone in the cubicle." Some may be sociopaths, or even psychopaths (see page 19), but most are probably ordinary people
trying to function and survive in a competitive environment.
However, if the person in the next cubicle (a metaphor for any
workplace associate) really *is* a psychopath, you may not be
aware of what lies behind the mask. Perhaps the most dramatic
examples of working next to a psychopath without realizing it
come from the serial murder literature. Consider that author Ann
Rule worked in the cubicle next to Ted Bundy while he was doing
his nasty business. Or think of the workers who saw nothing unto-
ward about the behavior of John Gacy (businessman and part-time
clown who murdered young gay men, burying their bodies under
his house), Dennis Rader (Cub Scout leader, active church member,
ordinance enforcement and animal control officer for his town,
who became infamous as the BTK—Bind-Torture-Kill—killer), or
Gary Ridgeway (industrial truck painter who murdered at least
forty-eight people and is now known as the Green River Killer).

The cold-blooded actions of these killers, and the stunning "emotional disconnect" between these actions and the feelings and rights of the victims, effectively were hidden from view in most social interactions.

The attitudes and behaviors of the corporate psychopath in the next cubicle are much less extreme than those of serial killers, and presumably *much easier to disguise.*

Second, organizations actively seek out people who are able to get along with others and possess the traits that make them easy to get along with in return. Readers will easily recognize, based on their own work experience, that this makes good business sense, as agreeable people tend to be easier to work with in general; "getting along" makes work life a lot more enjoyable, and cooperation leads to greater productivity with minimal conflict. The psychological labels sometimes used for these personality traits include "need-affiliation," "agreeableness," and "socialization," among others. Many organizations test for these during their selection process, but even if not done through formal testing, there is usually an attempt to glean information about these and similar characteristics during the interviewing process. On the surface, however, people with psychopathic personalities can and do easily come across as friendly and agreeable—they get along with the other "kids" at work or play. It is only beneath the surface, well hidden from view, that darker tendencies lie.

Third, most people who join an organization do so because they *want* to work in order to make a living; the work ethic is ingrained in them from their earliest years. While "work" can take on many different forms, the basic concept involves exchanging goal-oriented efforts for money or reward; essentially, an exchange takes place between employee and employer that satisfies the needs of both. There may be misunderstandings or disagreements about *amount* of effort expended, *how well* the goals were accomplished, and *level* of reward, but the basic model is pretty much part and parcel of any employment relationship. Having a sense of entitlement and being parasitic, however, psychopaths do not adhere to this fair-exchange model of work, wanting instead large rewards for mediocre effort or poor performance. Their work ethic is geared more to making themselves look good than to doing a decent job. This attitude is concealed, of course, from their employers and coworkers.

The Psychopathic Fiction

We know that psychopaths are self-centered, manipulative, and irresponsible, and that they are unlikely to give an employer an honest day's work, so how do they mask these traits once they're hired and expected to interact with others on a daily basis? The answer lies in their ability to create a fictional story about themselves that fulfills the global requirement and expectations of the company and its members. Once the fiction is firmly established in the collective mind of the group, it is easy to hide negative, counterproductive traits. A company's standards are not too difficult to discover, as companies openly share descriptions of ideal members, and encourage adherence to these descriptions, through performance objectives, mission statements, standards of performance, codes of conduct, value statements, and other such communications. Companies also publicly reward those who are good corporate citizens with bonuses, promotions, "employee of the month" awards, and similar forms of recognition. By acknowledging the contributions and successes of its members, a company (or any social group for that matter) hopes to inspire the same productive behaviors and values in others. This is a good thing for everyone as profitable companies create job security, and job security increases the ability of employees to buy goods and services, raise a family, and pursue other socially desirable outcomes.

However, astute psychopaths or fraudsters are capable of mimicking those in the company who are perceived to be good performers and high potentials without actually being one. In this sense, the persona they readily adopt is more a reflection of the demands of the situation than an indication of who they really are. Recall that the chameleon may mimic a leaf but does not turn into one. The resemblance is strictly on the surface and designed (instinctually in the lizard, cognitively in psychopaths) to offer protection while "hunting" and scanning for chances to take advantage of the situation.

While masking one's true intentions through role-playing may be easy in social intercourse, it is a much harder task to maintain the façade over the course of full-time employment, which involves interacting in close quarters with a large number of coworkers on a daily basis. The first step toward success is to build one-on-one relationships with important individuals in the company who will ultimately, often unwittingly, provide protection and cover for the intended plan of action. The sometimes rather elaborate charade or "psychopathic fiction" that is ultimately woven throughout the organization also fulfills the psychopath's needs for game playing, thrill seeking, and control; thus, it is doubly rewarding to someone so motivated.

In the previous chapter, we suggested how easily those with many psychopathic features could enter organizations. Once inside (that is, employed), psychopaths revert to their natural three-phase behavior pattern—assessment, manipulation, and abandonment. How they apply these to the work environment is covered in the next sections, where we outline how they create and maintain the fictional tale of the "ideal employee and future leader."

Assessing the Organization and Its Members

The process starts harmlessly enough. Once they join the company, psychopaths try to meet as many people in the company as they can, spreading positive first impressions and collecting as much information as possible. While meeting and greeting organization members,

they study their coworkers' organizational roles and almost instinctively assess their short- and long-range utility or value. A person's
value is based on where he or she fits into the organizational hierarchy (sometimes referred to as *position power*), technical abilities (*expert power*), access to information (*knowledge power*), and whether he
or she controls staff, money, and other assets (*resource power*).

There should be little surprise that the natural predatory manipulation used by psychopaths to con people in public can be applied
to business settings. What may be surprising is how easily this can be
accomplished. Corporate cons use the early months of employment
to study, understand, and ultimately penetrate organizational barri-
ers. They identify key players, analyze personalities of potentially
useful coworkers, and study the interaction and communications
patterns among workers. They quickly begin to understand and then
integrate the culture of the organization into their outward style and
approach.

BUILDING A POWER BASE

When considering how people influence each other to get things
done in organizations it is always important to consider the role of
power. There are many kinds of power used in an organization, some
more obvious than others. One important type is called *informal*
power, which is the ability to influence what is going on without being given the official ability or authority to do so. While every employee has some asset (knowledge, skills, and abilities), informal
leaders typically have more ability to influence the operations of the
organization. Seasoned managers know who the informal leaders are
in their organization, and engage them in their own efforts to manage the entire group. Almost instinctively, fraudsters find these individuals and build strong relationships with them with the intent of
using them to their advantage.

In addition, there are others with power and influence that are
more formal. Individuals with position power are of significant inter-

est to the corporate con. Getting close to those in power positions is not an easy task, however, as they tend to be very busy, they may travel a lot, and they have many others surrounding them who also want their time and attention. An industrious psychopath, though, manages these obstacles with ease, capitalizing on any opportunity, however contrived, to make contact and gain exposure.

The nature of organizational life actually *facilitates* the process of making contact with formal and informal leaders in the form of a typical "honeymoon period." This period, which can last up to a few months, is a time when new employees are expected to learn about their jobs and the organization, and are given considerable leeway to do so. Being on the early part of the learning curve insulates new employees from organizational criticism as they move about freely, learning the ins and outs of the organization's culture. Relying on organizational naiveté during this period, a clever and motivated employee can approach individuals in power whom others with more seniority are too timid to approach or have learned to avoid, often for political or personal reasons.

Starting literally in the elevators and hallways, and landing eventually in their offices, the corporate cons begin to introduce themselves to key managers and executives, brazenly disregarding the chain of command others respect. By the time the honeymoon period ends, they have established a strong, positive presence and identity in the minds of key players that will come in handy later on.

A talented corporate fraudster easily comes across to executives as an ambitious, enthusiastic player; competence and loyalty, two critical business values, are assumed. To coworkers and peers, he or she comes across as a likable person, perhaps a bit narcissistic or manipulative, but friendly, open, and honest nonetheless. Whether one is an informal leader, a power holder, or a regular employee, it's quite refreshing to meet a charismatic new employee who expresses a desire to become an accepted member of the team or displays respect and admiration.

Psychopaths are not the only new employees who try to understand and make use of the sociopolitical structure of the company, of course; almost all new employees do. However, psychopaths do so with very little intent of actually delivering a work product to the company commensurate with the salary they receive. Also, their emotional poverty does not support allegiance or loyalty to the company or their coworkers, although they can speak the necessary words to indicate intense loyalty to the firm. Their personas might be compared to the enthusiasm of a kid in a candy store.

The Dark Triad

Among the personalities that present problems for society in general and for the corporate world in particular are *narcissism*, *Machiavellianism*, and *psychopathy* (including its less severe variant, *subclinical psychopathy*), sometimes referred to collectively as the *dark triad*.

As described by researchers Nathanson, Paulhus, and Williams, "Those high in narcissism are characterized by grandiosity, entitlement, and a sense of superiority over others. . . . Such individuals are arrogant, self-centered, and consistently self-enhancing. . . . Individuals high in Machiavellianism are characterized by cynicism and the manipulation of others. . . . these individuals exploit a wide range of duplicitous tactics to achieve their self-interested goals. . . . Those high in subclinical psychopathy are characterized by cold emotion, interpersonal manipulation, impulsive thrill-seeking, and a tendency to engage in antisocial behavior. . . . Even those who have avoided being arrested tend to engage in dangerous and often illegal behaviors with little concern for the consequences."

In a series of studies, Paulhus and his colleagues have shown that of the members of the dark triad it is *subclinical psychopathy* that is most strongly related to a variety of socially deviant behaviors, including cheating, plagiarism, self-reports of misbehavior, bullying, and drug use. [In this case, subclinical psychopathy is measured by the *Self-Report Psychopathy-III Scale* (SRP-III; Paulhus, Hemphill & Hare, in press).] This is not surprising, given that psychopathy combines some of the features of narcissism and Machiavellianism with aggressive and antisocial tendencies. We might refer to psychopathy as the *mean* side of the dark triad.

SUPPORTING ROLES—THE PAWNS AND PATRONS

If psychopaths are the writers, directors, and stars in the psychopathic fiction, then it is important that those around them be cast in supportive roles. The first goal in creating the psychopathic fiction is to convince others of their honesty, integrity, and sincerity. Concurrently, they focus on the identification and manipulation of potential "pawns," or those individuals who have something the fraudster wants. There can be many pawns in an organization, all being identified for the specific resources they can potentially provide, such as information, money, expertise, staffing, influence, contacts, and so forth.

Later down the road, when psychopaths need a resource, they will manipulate the pawns to get it or simply ask directly. Asking for favors of "friends" and never actually repaying is a surprisingly common technique used. Many pawns are so enamored by the persona of the psychopathic fraudster that they give him or her whatever is needed, however inappropriate or outrageous the request.

Eventually, psychopaths are able to convince a large number of people that they are their best friends, trusted confidants, loyal coworkers, and all-around good people with whom to associate. They are able to create a fiction and maintain it in day-to-day interaction. Competence and loyalty, two important organizational traits, go unquestioned. With the kind of "evidence" they provide (through charm, charisma, and dissimulation), it is no surprise when they blame any concerns or negative perceptions raised by others on envy of their popularity, a simple misunderstanding, or the failure to know them well enough.

Among the supporters, we also often found in our research a small group of high-level individuals with only limited experience with their psychopathic subordinate, but who accepted the persona presented to them. Despite the limited exposure, each interaction had been so well orchestrated and left such positive impressions that these higher-level supporters began to advocate for the subordinate. Believing him or her to be loyal, competent, and extremely success-ful, they began to accentuate the positive and eliminate the negative. In fact, some would use their positions of power to defend the sub-ordinate's reputation from the criticisms of his or her peers or other executives.

This phenomenon was puzzling at first. Why would seemingly astute businesspeople take such a strong position in favor of a lower-level employee when they admittedly had only occasional interaction with him or her? We believe that the fictional "ideal employee and future leader" persona was so convincing that many members of the management team were readily charmed. Something out of the ordi-nary was going on here. For reasons only later to be uncovered, a group of high-level individuals began to act as "patrons" of the psy-chopaths. Patrons are influential executives who take talented em-ployees "under their wing" and help them progress through the organization. Once this patronage is established, it is difficult to overcome. With a patron on their side, psychopaths could do almost no wrong. Powerful organizational patrons (unwittingly) protect and defend psychopaths from the criticism of others. These individuals would eventually provide a strong voice in support of the psy-chopaths' career advancement.

Guided by their assessment of the personality traits and poten-tial utility of coworkers, psychopaths establish networks of per-sonal and, when possible, intimate relationships, all supporting the fictional persona of the ideal coworker and future leader. During this assessment phase, the pieces are being placed on the playing board, and the pawns (those the psychopath will manipulate) and the patrons (those who will unwittingly protect the psychopath) are identified. This is the time for gathering information and for initial positioning. The personal relationships established during this phase provide the psychopath with tools that will prove useful in later phases.

It should be noted that many talented and well-motivated employees attempt to make positive impressions on those around them. Only a small proportion deceive and manipulate to such an extent that the integrity of the organization is in danger of being compromised. At this point in the process, however, it is exceedingly difficult, if not impossible, to tell the difference between normal impression management and predatory deception.

Although we have labeled this a distinct phase, assessment is in fact an ongoing process, occurring whenever psychopaths meet someone new. Many modern organizations experience continual change among staff members, and new relationship networks and business issues emerge. This provides psychopaths with the continual opportunity to assess the pawn-patron potential of new players as they join the company or take on new roles. This constant change (often frustrating to the rest of us) adds interest, challenge, and new opportunities for psychopaths to perpetrate their fiction—a motivating factor not unlike that experienced by con men and women when dealing with people in open society.

LOW-UTILITY OBSERVERS

Not everyone that psychopaths meet interests them. There are plenty of coworkers and managers who have little to offer in the way of influence, assets, or potential support. Being ignored, these individuals are in a good position to see what is actually going on. They may realize that the psychopath is not who he or she pretends to be, and may even witness the manipulation of others. This, however, takes time and extensive interaction; and most people mind their own

business, not taking careful note of others' revealing interactions—
assuming they even know what to look for.

Manipulating Management and Coworkers

The manipulation stage forms the great bulk of the daily organizational existence of psychopaths. During this phase, they manipulate
others toward their own end. The goal of their game is to set up a
scam within the organization's structure that can fulfill their need for
excitement, advancement, and power—all without concern about
harmful outcomes to others. Typically, thrill seeking and game playing are satisfied by the fast-paced manipulation of coworkers, executives, vendors, or customers. Winning almost always involves
financial and power rewards, such as a steady paycheck for work
rarely completed, and promotions into increasing levels of authority.
It can also include derailing the careers of coworkers up to and including their unjust termination.

For example, Dan, a corporate con, used Chuck's informal power
in the organization. Chuck was a very likable person with a stellar
reputation as a solid citizen in the company; he was often described
as a straight arrow and a high-potential individual contributor. His
integrity was unassailable and his work performance was above expectations; his decisions about his work (and sometimes that of others) were rarely challenged. Recognizing Chuck's potential, Dan
went to great lengths to build a bond with him. Eventually, this bond
grew to the point where Chuck felt a special kinship toward Dan;
what Chuck lacked in extroversion and leadership potential, he saw
in Dan. Dan was the person he wished he could be. In fact, several
coworkers referred to Chuck as Dan's shadow because they always
seemed to hang out together. Others referred to him as Dan's "soul
mate." Chuck's association with Dan and his descriptions of him to
his coworkers lent a lot of credence to Dan's persona as the competent, loyal, talented employee, much like Chuck.

On occasion, Chuck would explain away Dan's temper as an expression of his artistic, creative bent. What others saw as rudeness and hostility, Chuck saw as Dan's standing up for what he believed in. In addition to defending him to the others, what made Chuck particularly useful to Dan was the fact that Chuck was an acknowledged expert at his own job (as well as the jobs of many others). As it turned out, Chuck was the key to Dan's success, working extra hours to help his "friend" do his job. No one realized that he was actually doing Dan's work for him while Dan was out politicking and manipulating others.

When trying to understand and explain their successful manipulation in organizations, we first thought that the psychopaths were merely ingratiating themselves with those at the top of the organization and with the most power, while abusing peers and subordinates at the lower levels. This is not an unusual tactic in organizations. However, the more we learned about these individuals, the less our observations could be explained by simple ingratiation techniques—most executives and coworkers were too smart to fall for this approach for very long. The relationships between our subjects and their supporters turned out to be more complex than this.

Two factors were important: the extensive use of clever impression management techniques, and the use of secrecy. Using a variety of influence tactics, the psychopaths manipulated their network of one-on-one personal bonds to gather information they could use to advance their own careers, derail the careers of rivals, or enlist technical support when the company made demands on them (to actually do their jobs). Specifically, their game plans involved *manipulating communication networks* to *enhance their own reputation*, to *disparage others*, and to *create conflicts and rivalries* among organization members, thereby keeping them from sharing information that might uncover the deceit. They also *spread disinformation* in the interest of protecting their scam and furthering their own careers. Being exceedingly clever and secretive, they were able to cloak their association with the disinformation, leading others to

believe that they were innocent of manipulation. Secrecy is a key to
a corporate con's success.

Impression Management, Deception, and Lies

Impression management, deception, and lying are integral
and necessary parts of social interactions. In some
occupations—poker, politics, advertising, and so forth—they are
key job requirements.

Nonetheless, most poker players, politicians, advertisers, and
other "situational" deceivers would find it more difficult to convince their mothers or wives of their sincerity in matters unrelated to their jobs. That is, their prowess at lying is specific to
their "work."

In contrast, the deceptions of psychopaths are generalized
and pervasive, part of a natural stratagem that ranges from cool
indifference to the truth to malevolent intent to deceive and
control.

Secrecy also helped corporate cons to reinforce the bonds they
built with others. Telling someone a secret, even if you know that he
or she will share it with others, implies a level of trust that cannot
help but raise expectations of friendship and respect. Chuck admired
Dan and wanted to emulate his outgoing, assertive nature, but would
never want others to know this. Being accepted as his friend allowed
him intimate access to Dan's behaviors and (apparently private)
thoughts, and might, he reasoned, help some of these traits to rub
off on him. Secretly helping Dan complete assignments was a small
price to pay and not any different from sharing his homework with
high school and fraternity brothers years before. He also knew that
Dan would never reveal his inner desires and would take care of him
down the road, especially when Dan was selected to attend management seminars given by the company—a luxury Chuck could not experience. They were a natural fit.

MASTER PSYCHOLOGISTS?

Many psychopaths appear to be masters at understanding human psychology and at finding and exploiting the weaknesses and vulnerabilities of others. It is unclear whether this reflects an inherent talent or whether they simply work harder than the rest of us at searching for buttons to press. In any case, their strongest challenges no doubt are individuals with strong personality traits such as narcissism, assertiveness, and dominance. These individuals are particularly important to psychopaths because they also tend to be in the higher levels of power. Although they may share some of the psychopath's traits (that is, strong ego, sense of entitlement), they lack the psychopath's cold-blooded efficiency.

Unfortunately, no group is more surprised to learn that they have been psychologically manipulated than those who believe they are smarter and stronger than others, no matter how true this may be. Narcissistic managers, in particular, tend to rise to management positions in organizations in disproportionately large numbers. Being particularly self-absorbed, they are known to use (and abuse) their subordinates and play up to their superiors to assure their own personal career success. (See pages 40–41 for similarities and differences between narcissists and psychopaths.) We have spoken with a number of narcissistic managers who *also* felt victimized by corporate cons: much to their own surprise—and not easy for them to admit—they were outclassed and outgunned. Additionally, and this really plays into the hands of the corporate con, individuals with strong personalities, such as narcissism, are far less likely than most to seek assistance, guidance, or even personal feedback until it is too late, making them attractive long-term targets.

As noted above, psychopaths identify and use *informal* leaders to support their quest for status and power. Individuals with informal power exist in every organization and play a major role in keeping the organization's day-to-day operations afloat. Consider Mary, a staff assistant for a major company. She was a delightful person, had a wealth of information about the organization, and as we learned from several others, was a major conduit of the office grapevine. Her cubicle was a regular stop for Doug on his daily rounds of the company. A simple "Hi, Mary! How was your weekend?" from Doug, followed by a leisurely discussion of life's events, would often lead to his sharing "secret" information with Mary about critical organizational issues, key managers, and potential changes. Enthralled with this amount of trust and attention from someone higher up, Mary in turn kept Doug informed of the behind-the-scenes information she had obtained from others.

Understanding that in every organizational rumor there is a kernel of truth, Doug was adept at singling out potentially useful information and storing it in his memory for future use. Given the right opportunity, Doug would "trade up" these bits of information by approaching key individuals and hinting that he was aware of key organizational issues and decisions. Believing that Doug was on the inside track, they felt comfortable about revealing additional pieces of information, which Doug mentally cataloged for future use.

Meanwhile, Mary spread positive, glowing stories about Doug throughout the organization, testifying to his integrity, sincerity, and generosity. "He's going places, I've heard, and I know it's true," she volunteered to anyone who would listen. She would then tell tales of how Doug was being given important projects to work on, how he helped others with their jobs without taking any credit for himself, how some senior executives confided in him because they trusted him, and how he was on the inside track of what was going to happen in the future. These and other messages were relayed throughout the organization long before Doug's name made it to the corporate succession plan. Who was the original source of the stories? Doug, of course.

Besides being manipulated into covering for psychopaths, some coworkers actually carry their workload in exchange for things that are not readily apparent to observers at the time. For example, all Chuck needed was a little attention and praise for his work, a need Dan managed to fulfill quite effectively. Mary needed a good source of reliable information, and Doug knew how to play her like a fiddle.

DETRACTORS

THE EXTRAS

We did find coworkers, peers, and executives who saw through some of the manipulation and deceit. One group, the extras—those who were not actively being manipulated—worked with or near the psychopaths and noticed inconsistencies, lies, and distortions of the truth. They were able, on some level, to see behind the mask; they were not taken in by the psychopathic fiction. Unfortunately, few brought their concerns to the "victims" or to management. Reasons for this silence most often included "I'm minding my own business"; "No one would listen to me"; and "It's not my place to intervene." In rare cases, some expressed an "If they're dumb enough to fall for this, they deserve what they get" attitude. Others stated that the individual was far too influential for them to cross; these observers preferred to stay out of the line of fire.

During confidential research interviews, we heard stories that helped us understand the psychopathic maneuvers that took place. Members of the observer group volunteered numerous references to deceitful behaviors (under promise of confidentiality): "He's a liar and a manipulator. It's amazing he's so successful, but then, maybe not, considering how business is these days" was the conclusion of some peers. Psychopathic workers very often were identified as the source of departmental conflicts, in many cases, purposely setting people up in conflict with each other. "She tells some people one story, and then a totally different story to others. Sometimes she'll tell one person that 'so-and-so said this about you' and then do the same thing with the other," said one exasperated peer. "It's so high school."

As we suspected, many in this group initially liked their manipulative coworkers, but learned to distrust them over time. "He's rude, selfish, unreliable, and irresponsible," said one coworker, "but there was a time, when he first started, that I liked him a lot." "I knew her stories were exaggerations," offered another coworker, "in fact, many times outright false, but I never wanted—I think *none* of us wanted—to call her on her lies. For a time she was entertaining. I can't laugh at her antics now; at best I think she's a sad case." After a pause, this coworker continued, "but that is giving her a lot more credit than she deserves—she's a snake."

THE ORGANIZATIONAL POLICE

Some individuals have policing roles in organizations; jobs designed to maintain order and control. They may work in human resources, security, auditing, and quality control, among other functions. They are necessary to the smooth running of any organization, but they pose a threat to corporate cons, who try to avoid them as long as they can. Should someone in a policing role suspect that something is amiss, his or her job is to confront the person and/or expose the behavior to higher management. Many of these policing individuals have excellent critical thinking and investigative skills and are charged with a special responsibility, typically fostered by professional and personal ethics and moral values.

Although few in number, and rarely interacting on a daily basis with the psychopath, these staff members were particularly astute when it came to their suspicions. "This guy is no good," said the auditor who reviewed expense reports. "I don't trust her; she's too good to be true," said the employment supervisor who conducted one of the initial interviews. "Bad vibes," said the security manager. "I'm going to watch him for a while."

In corporate settings, people in these functions are sometimes referred to as the *organizational police*. While many may cringe when referred to by that name, their role, much like their municipal police counterparts, is to protect the organization and its members. We believe that by being on the lookout for deceitful and possibly illegal behavior, such as lying, cheating, bullying, and stealing, these individuals have the ability to uncover psychopathic manipulation early on. Unfortunately, in at least some of the cases we reviewed, the organizational police were unable to effect much improvement. Beyond making known their observations, collecting information on violations of company policy, and raising issues about "questionable" interpersonal behavior, some could not influence management decisions regarding the well-established fraudster. Without top management support, organizational police are often unable to uncover and handle the corporate psychopath's subcriminal behavior.

Corporate Fraud in the Boardroom

PricewaterhouseCoopers (PWC) reported that in 2003, 37 percent of 3,600 companies in 50 countries had suffered from fraudulent acts, with an average company loss of more that $2 million. The actual average loss likely was much higher because of failures to detect or report frauds, or a tendency to write them off as a commercial loss. *One quarter* of the frauds were committed by *senior managers* and *executives* with a sophisticated understanding of the company's internal controls and risk management procedures.

In spite of the public outrage at the recent spate of high-profile scandals in the corporate world, things are not getting any better. In 2004, the percentage of companies in the PWC global survey that experienced fraud rose from 37 to 44 and then to 45 in 2005.

PWC suggests that corporations should be on the watch for the executive who:

• Engages in activities indicative of a lack of integrity

• Is prone to engage in speculative ventures or accept unusually high business risks

• Displays a poor attitude toward compliance with regulatory or legislative obligations

• Is evasive, uncooperative, or abusive of the audit team

• Lacks a *proven* track record

DISCREPANT VIEWS

The most striking thing about these and other cases was the mixed reactions of the corporate cons' coworkers. In every case, we found a strong discrepancy in the perceptions between those who viewed their actions in a very positive, favorable light and those who saw them in a negative light. We wondered how a fictional persona could be maintained in an environment that included negative perceptions and doubt. Eventually, it became obvious that the psychopaths were effectively balancing the discrepant views of their coworkers, and relying on consistent charm, occasional intimidation, the basic trusting nature of people, and frequent organizational changes to maintain their fictional personas in the eyes of those who mattered most.

To summarize up to this point, unsuspecting coworkers quickly form impressions of psychopaths based on their personal interactions and the details they learn from others. For most, the initial impression is positive and these individuals either like the person or take a neutral position (but see page 92). One might expect that the impressions of a charming personality would spread throughout the company and take hold of virtually all its members. We found, and indicated above, that two separate and distinct camps evolve with opposing views of the psychopath's value to the organization. The supporters (labeled pawns and patrons) felt that they were valuable contributors to the success of the organization; they described them as team players and solid corporate citizens. Detractors (labeled extras and organizational police in the psychopathic drama), however, reported all manner of underhanded, deceitful, manipulative behaviors by the same individuals. We know that this was possible because their view of these individuals was not colored by the charming façade. The organizational police who raised the red flag had been trained to look for and uncover deceitful behavior and often did so—but were not always listened to. Finally, the extras, because they lacked any organizational influence, posed little threat, and had no perceived value to the psychopaths, were not as carefully finessed.

Certainly, it is not unusual for individuals to be liked by some and disliked by others. This is as true at work as it is at home or school. But in an organization, there is usually a majority point of view based on a specific, identifiable organizational issue such as a turf battle, and a minority view based on a personal issue such as envy. Normal political battling rarely surfaces in so clear and intense a form as it does with a psychopath. Clearly, the detractors despised these individuals, and the supporters almost worshipped them. It was as if employees were describing two entirely different people. In a great number of these situations, it seemed that the psychopath could switch from warm and friendly to cold, distant, and almost hostile depending on with whom they were interacting.

Abandonment and Confrontation

Exposure to the other side of the psychopathic personality increases in proportion to the decline in the utility of the pawns. As the psychopath no longer has a need to maintain the façade for these individuals, psychopaths will generally abandon those whose utility is spent. But abandonment does not always lead to realization that one has been used or conned. For example, blindness to this reality might be reflected in the perceptions of an investor who still believes in the good intentions of an exposed scamster, despite having lost his life savings. How might this play out in organizational life?

In organizations, pawns are eventually abandoned, in both the social sense—the psychopath no longer associates with them—and the psychological sense—the friendship generated as part of the psychopathic bond turns cold. But because the psychopath is now working in an organization and cannot run away from the scene of the crime, abandonment becomes more obvious to those affected, as well as to those around them. This dramatic shift from friendly coworker to cold, dispassionate stranger is a consistent element of psychopathic behavior, and affects victims in predictable ways—ways that may work to the benefit of the psychopath.

This "dark side" of a previously charming coworker comes as a shock to those used as pawns. When faced with this "new" side of the psychopath, they frequently question their own behavior first, blaming themselves for the changes they are now sensing in the psychopath. "What did I do?" is a common self-doubt. Although these pawns may not yet understand what has happened, they begin to see glimmers of the true psychopathic personality—a realization we are told is "chilling."

Eventually, pawns conclude that they have been patsies. They feel cheated, defiled, and often incredulous that the person they liked and trusted betrayed that trust. And, we found, it was not always over major things that the truth became known to them. It was sometimes only a small incident that changed their perception enough so that the true nature of the "snake" in their midst became evident. But embarrassment and shame often keep them from coming forward.

Organization members who were willing to discuss with us their interactions with their abusive, manipulating coworkers reported feeling abandoned when the latter moved their attention to others. They also reported experiencing the most common victim response: *silence* due to shame at being conned. Like so many other victims, they wanted to keep their shame secret. This response, of course, plays into the hands of the psychopath who is protected by the tendency toward silence and secrecy.

Interestingly, while most victims reported feeling ashamed at being conned, and therefore reluctant to speak about their experiences, a few also felt disappointment when the psychopath in their company moved his or her attentions to others in the organization. It was almost as if they had lost something they valued—a close friend—when the psychopath stopped using them.

CONFRONTATION

In organizational settings, the manipulation skills of psychopaths are challenged by the constant need to manage the growing discrepancy in the views of them by a large number of fellow employees. We believe that a breakdown begins to occur when the psychopath's web of deceit and manipulation becomes unwieldy and too many people have had glimpses of their dark side. Eventually, someone tries to do something about it. A former pawn might challenge or confront the individual, and perhaps even try to bring the situation to the attention of higher-ups. Unfortunately, by this time the psychopath is well positioned through the influence networks already established with others in the power hierarchy. The tables are turned because the credibility of the complaining employee has already been "managed" and undermined. The employee wonders what has happened. As potential rivals and detractors are neutralized, the psychopath is free to continue operations unchallenged.

This has an intimidating effect on bystanders in two ways. Those working with the employee who was defeated see the demoralizing effects up close and conclude it is not worth fighting the psychopath. Others may assume that the psychopath has been selected for future leadership roles and can do no wrong, and is therefore immune to attack. Unfortunately, they have come to believe that this person is not to be challenged and is protected by upper management. Some might conclude that the management team is not as astute as once thought, and rather than signal to upper management that there is a deceitful person on board, they adopt a wait-and-see attitude. The increase in cautious inaction among coworkers is another subtle but powerful effect that psychopathic behavior has on the organization. By creating a niche safe from the attacks of rivals, the psychopath can maintain his or her operations for a lengthy amount of time.

It now seemed clear that the corporate psychopaths we studied started out being liked by all who met them because they were able to make and maintain excellent first impressions. But then over time, some coworkers began to realize what was going on and turned against them. Given this scenario, one might predict that eventually the psychopaths would fail, that they would be uncovered, or that they would offend the wrong person and be removed from the organization before great psychological and financial harm was done. But this did not happen. Most of them are still enjoying successful careers in their original organizations. The few exceptions left their companies for larger jobs in other companies—some of them competitors—who most likely were sold a greater "bill of goods" than the original organizations in which we found these people. Unfortunately, some unnamed victims were reorganized out of their jobs, had their careers derailed, or left their companies in disgust.

The natural phases of psychopathic behavior—assessment, manipulation, and abandonment (see pages 43–54)—are common in society as psychopaths move from victim to victim. We added an initial phase to capture the process they use to gain entry into the organization, and now we will add a subsequent phase, which we label *ascension*.

Ascension Phase

As a direct result of their manipulation skills, corporate cons are able to build careers that lead them to increasingly higher-level positions in the organization. This need not be the CEO's job, of course, as not all psychopaths aspire to that position. But one position that often is immediately attractive is the one occupied by their patron.

Once the psychopath's manipulation network has expanded to include the whole power structure of the organization, and all key players are in his or her corner, the ascension can take place. Almost simultaneously, and seemingly overnight to the victim, the entire power structure shifts its support to the psychopath who moves up into the now deposed patron's position. The risks of this actually occurring are even greater in organizations undergoing chaotic change, as business fortunes can rise and fall almost overnight, providing the necessary rationale for reorganization. We will discuss this more fully in chapter 7.

The psychopathic drama continues to unfold as high-power and high-status individuals, the patrons, who protect the psychopath from doubts and accusations of other organization members, and who facilitate fast promotions, advanced assignments, and job rotations, find themselves betrayed. Sadly, the patron becomes a patsy, losing organizational status and often his or her job to the psychopath, who has been lobbying for the promotion all along.

ACT III, Scene II

AN HONEST MISTAKE?

"Was I copied on that e-mail from Dave?" asked Frank, as he downed the second martini and grabbed his coat.

"I think you were, Frank. But, why don't you check tonight, and if the file hasn't come through, call me and I'll forward it along," offered John, as they headed for the elevator.

Frank got off the elevator on his floor of the hotel and pulled out his key card. He jammed the card into the lock twice before the hotel room door opened. He pushed his way in, dropped his suitcase near the door, and threw his computer case onto the bed. He quickly pulled his laptop out of the case, hit the start button as he opened the screen, and walked over to the desk in search of an Internet port. Placing the laptop down, he took the wire and made the connection. It would be a few minutes before his system was up, so he fished some dollar bills out of his coat pocket, grabbed the ice bucket, and left the room, heading for the vending area. The humming sounds of the ice machine drew him down the hall and around the corner, where he found the ice machine. He knew he would be up late; caffeine was a necessity to combat the two martinis he had had with John earlier at the bar. Soon he had two sodas and a bucket of ice in his hands, and was on his way back to his room. *There better be an e-mail from Dave*, he thought to himself, getting angrier and starting to walk more quickly.

Line after line of e-mail scrolled up his screen. Most of it was junk. But then finally he saw it, an e-mail from Dave. "Okay, let's see what this is," he muttered to himself as he opened Dave's e-mail. There was an attachment, a positive sign—the first in several long hours. Frank read the message:

> *Frank: I got your phone message; didn't understand what you were talking about. I left the disk on your desk Friday afternoon. Anyway, I went to the office and found the disk on the floor in your office. Figured you ran out with the folder, but the disk must've fallen out. Here it is. I also sent a copy to John in case you didn't make it; you sounded upset.*

"Left the disk in my office?" said Frank aloud. Like a person frantically trying to find a set of lost keys, Frank played back his steps from last Friday evening repeatedly in his mind. ". . . fell on the floor?" Frank was puzzled, but he had to stay focused. It was getting late and he still had to prepare for the next day's meeting. He clicked on the e-mail attachment and it opened to the first slide of the presentation. He slowly clicked his way through the presentation, stopping here and there to read the text. At the first chart, he lingered for quite a while and studied the figures. Frank opened the original file that he had picked up in his office and searched for the same chart. Or was it the same? No, the charts were different, very different. In fact, except for some introductory material and graphics, the entire presentation was different from the one he had picked up from his desk late Friday. Frank's mind was oscillating between attempts to answer the question, *What the hell happened?*, and attempts to focus on what he was going to say during the meeting tomorrow.

Taking another gulp of soda, Frank continued to review the new presentation. He liked what he read. Eventually, a deep sense of calm overtook him. *This is good; this is really good*, Frank thought, smiling.

Having finished reviewing the presentation and writing notes for his talk, Frank packed up his computer and got ready for bed. *The committee is really going to like this*, he thought, getting under the covers and turning out the light, *Dave came through*.

The quiet in his mind did not last long. *But, how could I have left it in the office? I put everything I found in my briefcase.* Frank started doing the deep-breathing exercises he had learned in the stress management course. *No wonder John was pleased, this is really a creative, well-thought-out plan*, Frank sighed, smiling again, as he tried to refocus on the positives. *Good thing I ran into John in the lobby and he raved about it. I may not have learned about it until the morning—what a nightmare—if Dave hadn't found the disk in my office.* Or had he?

Frank's eyes opened, paranoia starting to get the better of him.

7

Darkness and Chaos
THE PSYCHOPATH'S FRIENDS

Ginny sat in her office reviewing the interview schedule for the day. She pulled Al's material out of the stack and flipped through the folder. She sighed as she read the file. *Another one of these,* she thought, anticipating the boredom she'd feel during the conversation. *But maybe he'll surprise me.*

The receptionist rang Ginny and informed her that Al was in the waiting room. Ginny went to get him, files in hand, and led him back to her office through the maze of cubicles, copiers, and conference rooms.

"Did you find the building okay?" she asked, smiling.

"Hard to miss, actually," Al said, with a slight sarcastic tone as he looked around the department layout.

They got to Ginny's office and she gestured toward a chair for Al. He glanced around, obviously disappointed at the small size of the space, the stacks of paper and files, and the low-cost metal furniture. Al hadn't seen anything like this for years; as VP of finance for Acme Tech, he had grown accustomed to oak, mahogany, and teak. "Nice office," he said, faking a smile.

Ginny reviewed the information Al had provided on the forms. As she worked her way through his employment history, she asked pointed questions about the responsibilities he had in various jobs, the types of things he could do, and his interactions with others. She also asked about his family and upbringing. "We were dirt poor," Al said proudly, "and I worked my way through college and supported my mom and younger sisters, as well. I had to become the man of the house very early because my father was a drunkard and left us high and dry." Ginny took careful notes as Al spoke, occasionally referring to her prepared set of questions.

"What kind of work are you doing now?" she inquired.

"I'm doing a bit of consulting, not much, actually, I'm looking for the right fit."

"What kind of job would be the best fit for you, then?" she asked, checking a few boxes on her worksheet and writing in some comments.

"Vice President–Finance," Al started to say, but paused when he saw Ginny stop writing in midword. "What? That's the job I had at Acme Tech—why should I settle for less? I have a lot of financial experience; I have a long record of accomplishment, as you can see on my résumé. A company would be very smart to hire someone with my experience. I just had a turn of bad luck; not really my fault, as you know reading my cover letter. There were some bad actors on the executive team at Acme; they put the blame on me because I had been tough on them. I was clearly the strongest leader the company had had in a long while, so they framed me."

Ginny continued making notes and asked a few more questions. "So you can be a tough boss?"

Al was ready for this question. It was his time to make his pitch: "You bet I can be tough—like getting my staff to work long hours and go the extra mile for the good of the company!" he said, beaming. "But, I'm not tough on everyone. Some people don't respond to tough love, you know—they need to be coddled. I do that too," he said, nodding. "A leader needs flexibility—I was nice to the big guys and, when it suited my agenda, hard on the little people. Little people like strong leaders; it makes them feel comfortable."

Ginny glanced at the clock on the wall over Al's head. Seeing this, Al continued, speaking very quickly, "I have the style, the smarts, and the looks to carry off any VP job. I worked hard all my career and wasn't afraid to confront the competition. If you want to be successful, you have to be ambitious," Al said, leaning forward and gesturing, "and stab the competition in the back, right? I showed them I could run with the wolves and not falter if I met someone who stood in my way. I made hard decisions others didn't like, and then wasn't afraid to use their disagreements to uncover their disloyalty to the company." Al leaned back in his chair, paused, and said, "I always supported the company; I talked up company goals, objectives, mission, and vision and whatever the hell else they thought was important. I was always a team player, as well. I kept the important ones in the loop and proved my loyalty repeatedly. It paid off because I got the promotions, the big salary, the nice offices, cars, and all that stuff. It's hard for me to admit"—Al paused, dramatically— "but they were fooling me all along and I never knew it. I never realized they were really a bunch of crooks and they were using me—I was the fall guy."

Ginny interrupted Al and began to close the meeting. "Here is your copy of the consent form and a copy of the judgment. You're expected to pay restitution in regular installments. We'll work out the specific schedule during our next meeting. You'll need to look for a job and bring me a list of companies you've applied to, with phone numbers I can call to verify. We'll meet every week, here in my office, until you are settled, and then biweekly. I've signed you up for counseling and they will meet with you once we're through here. You'll meet with them weekly in a group setting, and take some course work on managing your finances and anger management, as well. They will report to me how you're doing. Do you have any questions?"

"No," Al said, feigning a humble smile. "I know what I have to do and, trust me, I'll pay everything back. My goal is to regain my integrity. Thank you for helping me and seeing my side of things."

Ginny rose as the counselor arrived at the appointed time. "Hello," he said to Al, "come with me. I'll introduce you to some of the others."

As Al left with the counselor, Ginny finished her notes. She added a few more observations, completed the assessment, and closed the file, placing it on top of one of the many piles surrounding her desk. *No surprise about his personality*, she thought.

As she walked to the reception area to pick up her next client, she ran into a fellow probation officer. "How was your morning?" her colleague asked.

"You know, these white-collar guys are the worst," she said. "They get their hand slapped, never do time, brag about it, blame everyone but themselves, and then, once they land another job, do it all over again. What an attitude; give me a car thief any day over these guys—at least they're honest."

Psychological Employment Contract

Historically, people have joined large organizations because of the many benefits afforded them. Businesses, the military, and governments offer chances to build a career in one's area of competence; they provide access to financial and technical resources individuals rarely acquire on their own, and, for those so motivated, there is the opportunity for advancement. The "psychological contract" implied by employment in older (1940s–1970s)-style organizations could include a long, profitable career; job security; good benefits; and employment for life. The "gold watch" received upon retirement was one of several symbols promised those who worked hard, did a quality job, and did not steal or lie. The implication that one could stay employed as long as the company could sell its product had a powerful effect in building employee loyalty. The psychological contract afforded individuals the feelings of security, trust, and respect they expected, and provided companies the well-trained and experienced workforce they needed to compete successfully.

Loyalty and competence were the foundations of a strong bond between employees and their employers for many years. Both organization and individual profited from this model because of the stability it offered, and because of the focused energy, talent, expertise, and experience available to address day-to-day business issues and minor marketplace fluctuations. The reality was not always so rosy, of course, but in general, this model of stability worked, especially during times of high demand, intense profitability, and limited competition, when manufacturing, engineering, and basic service industries were at their peak.

Employee surveys collected during this period showed that job satisfaction was influenced more by the chance to interact productively with others than by money. While money was, and is, always important, it was rarely first on the list—in fact, money tended to be rated somewhere in the middle, often lower than social interaction, job security, "the chance to do meaningful work," and "appreciation from the boss."

Management theories popular at this time focused on building and enhancing individual self-esteem, listening and responding to ideas from employees, and capitalizing on human needs, such as security, social interaction, career advancement, and *self-actualization*, a term that captured the psychological need to achieve one's own potential in life. During the late 1970s, teamwork replaced traditional command-and-control hierarchies as employees were entrusted with decisions affecting their own work, and group decisions about needed business improvements often took precedence. As organizations grew and developed more sophistication, they tended to integrate systems and processes into their culture—such as quality circles and participative management—that linked the most important elements of employee satisfaction to company profits.

Normal Change

During the normal course of business operations changes occur regularly, although not always as predictably as one would like. Change was relatively slow but steady during this period and technological changes could be effectively met with management and employee education and training. For example, financial changes, measured in terms of fluctuations in profit and loss, might lead to educating employees on cost structures, and then initiating cost containment, reengineering, and gain-sharing programs to address unfavorable (negative) variances from budget. The financial impact of other changes was more difficult to quantify, especially those affecting the structure of the organization, such as "centralization" or "decentralization" of functions, changes in reporting relationships, the size of staff, and the mix of talents required to keep the business profitable. The processes used to create and sell products also changed as technological innovations took the form of new or upgraded equipment emerging from advances in science and engineering. The employees who comprised the organization routinely changed, although not dramatically—3 to 5 percent turnover was considered normal—due to attrition, hiring, and retirement. Major business changes sometimes required replacing employees with those better educated in the latest technology, but given enough lead time and supporting programs (such as retraining and outplacement assistance), the transitions could be made smoothly.

Despite much of the change during this early period, many organizations and most people were able to adapt quite effectively, and the psychological contract, although stretched, helped in this effort.

How We Respond to Change Matters

People respond to changes in many different ways, and how we, as individuals, perceive change often determines how we react to it. In general, any change to the status quo—a new situation, unexpected event, or unmet expectation—is initially met with apprehension and frustration, and is experienced as negative unless accompanied by adequate forewarning and additional, reassuring, information.

Imagine that your company has decided to reorganize and you are told that you will be getting a new boss and you will be asked to perform a new job. How would you feel? You could find yourself going through several emotions. Basic psychology tells us that when our actions toward the things we want (technically called *goal-directed behavior*) are blocked, interrupted, or delayed, we experience *frustration*. The feeling of frustration drives a variety of subsequent behaviors, which differ from person to person depending on his or her personality and situational factors. The most prevalent response to frustration, though, is anger or *aggression* toward those who are changing our plans or getting in our way—yelling and complaining are socially approved ways to express frustration, but overt physical aggression is not unheard of. Other reactions to frustration include the tendency to *avoid* those who are frustrating us (for example, by calling in sick); the desire to *escape* the frustrating situation (for example, by fantasizing about leaving the company); "regressive" behaviors, such as feeling *hopeless* and wanting to cry; and physiological and psychological *stress*. These initial frustration reactions are quite natural, perhaps hard-wired into the makeup of most of us. Unfortunately, none of these gut reactions *really* help us deal with the change that caused our frustration in the first place. Instead, they take energy that could be applied to the changed situation (in this example, learning about our new boss and job) rather than dissipating it in somewhat unproductive activities (in this example, anger, complaining, and calling in sick).

However, once we get over the initial frustration we can get back on track, start to think of the situation as a problem to be solved (rather than a personal attack) and return our focus to the real goal (in this example, getting along with our new boss and doing a good job). During this time, through problem solving and decision making (technically called the *increased striving* stage), we try to understand what has really happened to us and assess whether and how we can learn to live with it. We analyze and evaluate just how "bad" the situation is and begin to strategize our way out, around, or over the barrier that we now see blocking our path.

Once we figure this out, we can take well-thought-out action and work toward reestablishing our connection to the original goal that was taken away from us. Should this fail—and it may—we are at least better prepared to seek a reasonable substitute. These "try harder," "get back into the game," "never give up" feelings and behaviors can be very productive, certainly more so than the frustration we initially felt.

During major organizational change, virtually all affected employees experience frustration at the same time and go through these stages, although at different rates and degrees. Managing the collective emotional state of an organization is not an easy job; inexperienced managers and executives may not even know that it exists, labeling discontent with the changes at hand as simply resistance and skepticism. In fact, resistance is a reasonably good indication of frustration, while skepticism is a good indication that individuals have moved into the problem-solving and decision-making (increased striving) stage. Executives who wish to manage change need to help employees move from the resistance stage, through the skepticism stage, and into the support stage.

A good sign that people have entered the skeptic state is their raising questions about the proposed changes and beginning to look for a rationale that makes sense to them before they can begin to feel comfortable again. Before they lend their support, many skeptics need to be convinced that the proposed changes are good for them *and* the long-term survival of the company. Some may offer alternative strategies for dealing with the business issues at hand, once they understand them. They want to be included in the process—a sign to them that they are valued and respected as individuals.

With increased communication from the organization, some individuals will have their skepticism addressed to their satisfaction, and they will become supporters. Supporters are those who ultimately like and agree with the change being proposed, and are willing to exert effort to support it; to them the change is good. Other individuals will find their earlier fears confirmed and decide that they cannot go along with the changes. Some may decide that the changes are not in their best interests and choose to take their talents elsewhere: they may leave the organization or seek a transfer to another department.

One key to overcoming frustration is information. The amount of accurate information you have about the change, in particular, the potential impact of the change on you—answers to the question, "What's in it for me?"—can and will affect how long you remain frustrated. Honest and accurate information is the antidote to concerns and fears brought on by impending change. Seeking information is a natural response to disruptions to the status quo; it is an attempt to reestablish stability in a seemingly unstable world.

Managing Change Is a Leader's Job

Managing change is a difficult business, perhaps one of the greatest tests of effective leadership. It requires the right blend of human resource management and tactical business and financial skills, as well as an excellent sense of timing. Seasoned leaders familiar with normal reactions to changes in the workplace take the necessary action to bring as many individuals on board as soon as possible. The questions and concerns of skeptics are addressed openly, and potential leavers are sometimes offered incentives to remain on staff during the transition, especially if they have knowledge, skills, and abilities that will be required by the organization in the future. Unfortunately, there are always some less enlightened leaders who turn a blind eye toward the concerns of affected individuals. Perhaps they believe in their own power to "edict" change, do not care about who leaves and who stays, or are unable to confront the frustration and powerlessness they *themselves* feel.

Change professionals, sometimes called organizational development specialists, can help executives manage the many facets of change and help the organization maintain as much stability as possible while the change takes place. This is often done by sharing information in a timely manner, enhancing communications among staff, job retraining, and, when the change necessitates downsizing, instituting useful outplacement services. Not surprisingly, many people will go along with and support changes brought on by competition, declining sales, increased business costs, or other business factors if they are let in on the process and their fears are addressed early on in the process. If the organization's culture has been one of open communication and trust in management's ability to manage the business, the task of change is easier, and the number of supporters will reach the critical mass needed to assure success.

Change Is a Fact of Life

If things never changed in our lives, we would be quite bored. From the moment of our birth, things around us are changing. As individuals, we are changing—physically, emotionally, and intellectually—and as members of various social groups we are faced with change: siblings may be added to our family, parents grow old and eventually die, friends come and go, familiar faces in the neighborhood change, buildings and roads are built where beautiful forests once grew, and companies go in and out of business. Rulers and governments may also change. In an "ideal world," periods of change will alternate with periods of stability and calm. Focus will shift back and forth between worrying about the future and getting back to the job we were hired to do.

One might think that with all the changes we have experienced in life we would be quite good at handling change and would have been prepared for the business changes of the 1980s and 1990s. Unfortunately, for many people this was not the case. The rate of change in business—and many other aspects of life—accelerated dramatically during the 1980s and the 1990s; the changes came too quickly and there were too many of them at once. There seemed to be no calm between the storms, and little time to deal with today's frustration before being hit again. Without time to regroup, extreme stress and fatigue begin to overwhelm the organization and its members; frustration turns to fear, and fear to panic.

New technologies began to advance faster than many organizations' ability to keep pace. The demand for better-quality and lower-cost products increased beyond the ability to cut costs and still meet demand. Government controls increased in some areas and decreased in others. Advances in computerization, in particular, have accelerated the rate of technological change affecting organizations and have led to dramatic social changes among the workforce as well. Some of this change has had a positive effect. The Internet has opened a whole new world of exploration and study. Commerce in the computer age has advanced to the point where people can shop or do their banking at home at any time of night or day, and small entrepreneurial companies have grown in number as markets opened up that were once thought out of reach. Education—on just about everything—is now available to a greater number of individuals around the globe.

There have also been negative effects of this rapid change. A tremendous burden has been put on large organizations, forcing them to reinvent themselves quickly in order to remain competitive. As almost a defensive maneuver, some large corporations have needed to merge, acquire other companies, or downsize their own staff just to maintain their financial position. A larger number of people were put out of work than in previous times. While many seasoned businesses downsize, knowing that the human impact is often dramatic and the business decision is sometimes precarious, others do so out of fear, placing the human impact lower on the list of issues to be managed. A few companies merge simply for short-term financial gain with little understanding of, or concern for, the fact that their decisions dramatically affect the people who work for them and the *long-term* viability of their companies.

Clearly, major changes can be successfully implemented if they take place over a reasonable amount of time and the frustrations they create are effectively managed. They can breathe new life into a stagnant situation, reenergize everyone to work toward a new vision of the future, and create opportunities where none existed before. But during the unstable period of the 1980s and 1990s, too many things changed, seemingly all at once, with little time to build supporting policies, procedures, and systems before the next changes came about. In contrast to old-style bureaucratic organizations that were built on stability, consistency, and predictability, the new *transitional* organizations were forced to give up these "luxuries," having to become more fluid in the face of an unstable, inconsistent, and unpredictable future. In order to survive, many management processes had to be dismantled because they were no longer effective (or efficient), and supporting them with time and energy could no longer be justified. Organizations got "flatter" as middle management positions were eliminated in an effort to streamline decision making. Support services were outsourced or moved entirely out of the region to save time and money and reduce the number of headaches. This degree of change did not allow leaders to maintain the same commitments to long-term employment as their predecessors. A dwindling workforce was being asked to do more with less, or else join their colleagues who lost their jobs. At some point along the way, the concept of the "psychological contract" was challenged, and it eventually gave way to a world where the employee-employer relationship was seen as a *transitory* one rather than a long-term partnership. This dramatically affected executives, managers, and employees emotionally, psychologically, and socially—causing even the most confident people to feel that they had lost control of their lives.

Are We There Yet?

The rate of technological change has been rapid since the turn of the twentieth century and is growing exponentially every minute. You need only consider how outdated your new computer is barely one month after you take it out of the box. Or the fact that the length of time between the Wright brothers' lifting off at Kitty Hawk and Neil Armstrong's first step onto the moon was only sixty-six years—barely one lifetime! When business or industry upheaval overtakes the organization's ability to respond effectively, a state of chaos is created. Few of us are ready to handle chaotic change effectively, and evolution has not been very helpful, moving at its own slow pace. When thrust into chaotically changing situations, we experience intense feelings of frustration, stress, loss of control, and anxiety.

Now imagine that rapid change becomes the *rule* rather than the exception. Yesterday's change is changing today, and will change again tomorrow; there is seemingly no light at the end of the tunnel. Companies that once focused on determining the ideal vision of the "future" organization (and planning the necessary steps to get there) now find themselves in a *constant* state of transitioning. Furthermore, not everything changes at the same rate, and interrelated elements become unglued, adding confusion to an already unstable time. Organizations in a constant state of transitioning are characterized by unclear, outdated, unenforceable, or nonexistent work rules and policies; inconsistent risk taking; greater tolerance for controversial, perhaps even abusive, behaviors; and antiquated measurement systems and communication networks. At best, the ideal future states of these organizations are fuzzy.

The leader's job becomes increasingly complex but far less well defined during these times of change—itself a frustrating thing. Traditional strategic planning, organizing, and motivating skills are of limited use. While a good deal of this change is perceived to be necessary for the company's survival, can executives, managers, or employees survive as well?

Who Succeeds?

Who succeeds in this environment, in this new culture of change? Most management experts agree that in order to survive the chaos, employees, managers, and executives must adopt constant change as a work style and lifestyle—the management term for this is *embrace* change. They must become faster thinkers, more assertive and persuasive. They must become much more creative, capable of designing, developing, building, and selling new products and services to meet ever-changing demands in a world of fierce competition and highly selective buyers. They must learn to feel comfortable making faster decisions with less information, and recover from mistakes more quickly. They must be willing to live with the consequences, even if they risk failure. They must take control of their own careers by reassessing their talents and skills and then repackaging them for the new marketplace. While our parents and grandparents worked for one or two companies for their entire lives, we must be ready to move through six or seven.

(Organizations that survive chaotic times are those whose employees not only grow comfortable with uncertainty, but can build systems, processes, and structures capable of anticipating it and flexible enough to respond to it (that is, change again, as necessary). In order to do this, successfully transitioning companies need fewer superfluous rules (which hold back progress) and clearer mission-critical rules (which keep the business on track). They need a much more meaningful set of guiding principles that managers can use to make informed decisions when new problems and unique situations arise. A good example is the business decision made by the Johnson & Johnson Company, whose executives turned to their founding principles for guidance during the Tylenol tragedy. Their decision— to remove all Tylenol products from the shelves so no additional consumers could be placed in harm's way—cost a lot of money, loss of market share, and disruption to the company's operations, but the costs paled against the consequences that were avoided. Those who recall this event may remember that the entire nation was caught in the grip of fear, and other related industries, in particular the product packaging industry, were also affected. J&J, when faced with an unprecedented situation, made a dramatic decision that turned out to be correct, and it is continually held up in management seminars as an example of excellent leadership during a time of uncertainty. Having clear, shared values and sticking to them unwaveringly is the key; we will say more about this in a subsequent chapter)

Enter Those with Entrepreneurial Spirit

At the top of our "success list" would be individuals with *entrepreneurial* spirit, those who enjoy change and the challenges it brings and the opportunities it affords. Entrepreneurs, whether in business or science, seem to have very high tolerance for frustration. The definition of an entrepreneur, according to Webster's dictionary, is "one who organizes a business undertaking, assuming the risk for the sake of the profit." Contrary to popular belief, not all entrepreneurs start their own companies. In fact, there is evidence that many entrepreneurial types can be very effective working within big companies, particularly those that are willing to make some accommodations for their needs. Entrepreneurial types require access to resources, a continuous stream of challenges to do new and exciting things, personal recognition for success, feedback about failures, and, most of all, freedom to act. While these accommodations are difficult for old-style bureaucracies to offer, the transitioning organization—forced to make changes to its business model, anyway—is in an ideal position to adopt these new approaches. By replacing the long-abandoned employment-for-life psychological contract with the new entrepreneurial psychological contract, transitioning organizations are better able to gain the flexibility needed to survive chaos. This requires treating employees as individual contributors, responsible for their own career advancement, and rewarding them with large salaries for innovative, fast-paced problem solving—as well as the chance to continue to work on new, exciting projects. The symbiosis of employees with entrepreneurial talents and the transitioning organization can lead to the constant reinventing, rebuilding, and reenergizing that both need for survival and growth. If well managed (using new management techniques, of course, not old ones), the results can be impressive.

Unfortunately, this business model is far easier to theorize about than to actually implement. There are several reasons for this, all of them very human. First, it is very difficult to convince current executives, managers, and employees that they should give up their need for safety and security—no longer part of the contract—in exchange for a model in which their skills and abilities may not be worth anything tomorrow, and the company feels no obligation to retain them. Second, it is difficult to regain employee loyalty, especially once the organization has breached the employment-for-life psychological contract and substituted an entrepreneurial psychological contract. Management credibility, one of the foundations of employee loyalty, is also open to question—"How come they let the company get into this situation?" and "Didn't they see this coming?" are recurring challenges those in control must constantly face from the workforce if they expect to attract and retain talented entrepreneurs. Third, those with power and authority rarely give it up willingly, even in service of the greater good of the organization. (President George Washington is one of the few great leaders who rejected "kingship" and refused to continue as president once he felt his job was done.) These individuals may feel threatened by the erosion of their own positions, and can sabotage the transition by virtue of their sense of entitlement. Fourth, organizations may look to new employees, often much younger and less experienced, in order to find those with entrepreneurial spirit. This is often easier than converting those already on board because of the opportunities the new hires see and seek. Current individuals may not want to support the new entrepreneurial employees, who seem to be getting more attention than they ever got themselves. At the very least, this may create envy among the current staff, especially when asked to give up precious resources (such as money and staff) they may have fought long and hard to acquire. Fifth, all of this assumes that companies can find individuals who *truly* possess entrepreneurial talents in the marketplace, a task far more difficult than expected—for the competition for them is fierce.

Hiring, retraining, or promoting the right people has never been easy; it is a constant struggle to find candidates who can fit in, even in stable times. During transitioning, the job requirements of an entrepreneur, themselves vague, make the process even more prone to wrong decisions.

But I'm Not as Bad as the Others

A former top executive who had reported directly to the president of a large company had received stellar performance reviews and was considered a role model at the company. Yet he was fired, along with several other executives, after fraudulently billing the company for millions of dollars of unauthorized spending.

In his wrongful dismissal suit brought against the company, the former executive contended that he may have violated the company's integrity code, but that his behavior was not as bad as that of other miscreants who were treated less harshly by the company. The judge rejected this argument on the grounds that a good work record doesn't mean that blatant dishonesty should go unpunished.

The Pretenders

Would someone with a psychopathic personality, turned off by earning an honest living in general, even be interested in joining one of these transitioning companies? Unfortunately, the answer we found is yes, as organizations have become more psychopath friendly in recent years. Rapid business growth, increased downsizing, frequent reorganizations, mergers, acquisitions, and joint ventures have inadvertently increased the number of attractive employment opportunities for individuals with psychopathic personalities—without the need for them to correct or change their psychopathic attitudes and behaviors.

What is it about these new organizations that make them so attractive to psychopaths? First, these "entrepreneurial pretenders" find change personally stimulating. Their thrill-seeking nature draws them to situations where a lot is happening and happening quickly. Second, being consummate rule breakers, they find the increased freedom to act to their liking. These pretenders capitalize on the lessened reliance on rules and policies and the increased need for freeform decision making that characterize organizations in a chaotic state. Third, as opportunists, they take advantage of others in ways that are not always obvious. In particular, the opportunity to get a leadership or management position is extremely attractive because these positions offer the psychopaths a chance to exert power and control over people and resources, they tend not to require involvement in the details, and they command larger-than-average salaries. Because a leader's ability to get people to do things is often of more importance than his or her technical capabilities to perform work tasks, pretenders lacking in real work expertise are not disadvantaged; their talents are assumed and their phony or exaggerated backgrounds often accepted at face value.

Entrepreneurial or Just Plain Crooked?

In 2005, the Canadian government was rocked by a patron-age scandal involving several hundred million dollars that were funneled by the party in power to advertising agencies. A judicial report on the scandal roundly criticized the party and the ad agencies, who had provided kickbacks for use by the party.

Recently, the Canadian Ethics Commissioner startled the country by stating that the affair could be viewed either as a "tri-umph of theft" or as a "triumph of entrepreneurship," depending on "how you look at these things." He also opined, "I don't be-lieve we have a bunch of criminals who are trying to get away with something. But what we've got is a bunch of people who are trying to do exactly the right thing who sometimes do the wrong thing." The ad agencies that were recipients of the government's largesse were merely examples of a good businessman who "smells blood and says, 'Jeez, this is not an opportunity that will ever come twice in a lifetime.' "

Such ethical relativism is part of the reason psychopathic and other unprincipled "entrepreneurs" find it so easy to line their pockets with the unwitting contributions of those whose ethical standards are more fixed.

In an early 2006 election, the scandal-ridden political party was voted out of power.

While leadership may seem like an easy job to a psychopath, re-quiring little more than the application of his or her natural conning and manipulation skills, in reality it involves much more talent, skill, and experience. But the constantly changing state of the business works in their favor, clouding the difference between "good" and "bad" leadership, allowing pretenders to move about the organization through rapid promotions and transfers faster than the results of their behaviors can be measured, evaluated, and handled, thus eluding exposure. Short-term results, or what may look like results, can be deceiving, especially if cleverly presented, and can provide enough cover until the next promotion. This is especially true when the performance measurement systems themselves are in a state of flux or perhaps nonexistent. Psychopathic pretenders can thrive on and hide within the chaos of transitioning organizations.

Would an organization in need of strong leadership hire a pretender? Not willingly, of course, but because a pretender can seem like an ideal leadership development candidate to a company seeking entrepreneurial leadership, this mistake can happen quite easily. Likewise, the corporate psychopath on staff, having already created a persona of the ideal employee in the minds of executives and employees alike, can easily morph into a high-energy, visionary entrepreneur. Once this label is affixed, conning or bullying others can seem like an effective management style, especially when many in the organization are still paralyzed by the chaotic change surrounding them, caught in their personal frustrations, and unable or unwilling to accept the new business model. In contrast to the rest of the organization's members, the corporate psychopath looks like a knight on a white horse, cool, calm, and confident. The fact that the psychopaths' efforts rarely result in long-term business improvements is clouded by their self-serving bravado and the mystique that follows them.

When dramatic organizational change is added to the normal levels of job insecurity, personality clashes, and political battling, the resulting *chaotic milieu* provides both the necessary stimulation and sufficient "cover" for psychopathic behavior.

Secrecy

There is another aspect of organizational life—whether business, military, religious, or government—that facilitates the entry, manipulation, and deceit of the pretender: secrecy. Secrecy is a part of organizational life. The need for secrecy is quite understandable and is sometimes built into the organization's procedures, as in the case of protecting trade secrets from competitors or keeping detailed financials confidential during premerger negotiations. Some secrecy is defensive in nature, as when a decision is made that will negatively affect some individuals, and the resulting action needs to take place before there is forewarning, as is often the case with terminations. Or an employee may not expose a coworker's indiscretions out of fear of reprisal, thus colluding in the secret keeping. Some secrecy is inadvertent, though, such as when events happen faster than the organization's communication mechanisms can respond. As a result, people are left in the dark and unable to do their jobs properly. In these cases, those in the know may not intend to keep secrets; they simply do not have the opportunity or time to share the information with others.

During times of chaotic change, when more information is better than less, secrecy tends to *increase* for the aforementioned reasons as well as perhaps other reasons. Regardless of the appropriateness of the secrecy, the impact is often to *increase the levels of distrust* among employees, *reduce the levels of management credibility or perceived trustworthiness* in the eyes of those kept in the dark, and to *increase mistakes* made due to lack of timely, accurate information.

Developing Integrity

There are few organizations in the Western world that could survive with the allegations of mismanagement, scandal, and corruption that permeate the United Nations. For many delegates, officials, and employees, particularly those from developing nations, the UN is little more than an enormous watering hole.

Concerned about its shabby image, the UN recently developed a multiple-choice "ethics quiz" for its employees. The "correct" answers were obvious to everyone [*Is it all right to steal from your employer? (A) Yes, (B) No, (C) Only if you don't get caught*].

The quiz was not designed to determine the ethical sense of UN employees or to weed out the ethically inept, but to raise their level of integrity. How taking a transparent test could improve integrity is unclear. There has been no mention of how management and other officials did on the test.

Secrecy is the pretender's friend. The success of psychopathic manipulation, especially in large groups of people, depends on maintaining a cloak of secrecy about what is really going on. A *culture* of secrecy in an organization makes it much easier for pretenders to hide and much harder for management to catch them in their lies, to accurately rate their performance, or to see the abuse they heap on coworkers. To the degree that transitioning organizations increase their level of secrecy, they run the risk of providing cover to pretenders who have entered their ranks.

ACT III, Scene III

LET'S DO LUNCH

Try as she might, Dorothy couldn't get the ringing out of her ear. Her eyes opened, and she realized she was in her bed at home and the phone was ringing.

"Hello," she said sleepily, opening her eyes slightly to see the clock radio.

"Who is this? Dave? It's eight o'clock in the morning, Dave. And it's Sunday," she recalled falling back on her pillows, the phone next to her ear. "What's going on?

"Yes, you woke me up," she groaned. "I was out last night. I didn't get in until 2 A.M.

"Of course, I'm alone," she said, absentmindedly. "Jeez, Dave. Mind your own business.

"What?" she asked, not understanding what Dave was saying. "Can't this wait until tomorrow?"

Dave began his story.

"What does the executive committee meeting have to do with me?" she questioned, sitting up. "Why should I—"

Dave cut her off. He explained that Frank was in a bind because he didn't have a presentation for the upcoming meeting. John, Frank's boss, was disappointed in his ideas for the upcoming year and wanted a whole new presentation by Monday. Frank called Dave, desperately needing his help. Dave saw this as the perfect opportunity for Dorothy to get her material in front of those who counted.

As Dave's words slowly sank in, she got out of bed. "You want *what?*" she said, heading to the kitchen to put on some coffee. "Let me get this straight: John's pissed at Frank because Frank's new product idea sucks, and you want me to give you my stuff so you could give it to John? Am I getting this right, Dave?"

Dave continued.

"I'm not interested, Dave," interrupted Dorothy. "My boss hasn't even seen my project. Why should I give it to you for Frank or John or whoever?"

Dave explained his plan further.

"Oh, *sure* you're going to put my name on it," she said, rolling her eyes. "I wasn't born yesterday; I know how you operate." Dorothy watched the coffee drip as Dave persisted in telling her that this was her best chance to get her ideas in front of the executive committee and with both Frank's and John's support.

"I really don't relish the thought of your giving my presentation to the committee, no matter how 'opportune' the time," she said, getting a clean cup from the cupboard.

Dave explained further.

"You're not giving the presentation? Then, who is?"

"*Frank* is going to give my presentation—as his own?"

"As *ours*, yours and, mine, then? Mm-hmm."

"Why would Frank want to present my project ideas—sight unseen, I might add—to his boss, just because you ask him to?"

Dave responded.

"It must be nice to be so trusted by your boss, Dave. I'm really not interested," she said, pouring her coffee and taking a sip.

"Yes, Dave, I'm your friend," she said, not believing Dave would be using this tactic. "And, you're my friend. And the *only* reason you called—not for Frank or John or the good of the company—is to help out your friend Dorothy."

Dave interrupted again, telling her that she could be the hero, and Frank would be indebted. Frank would never challenge any of her future ideas, and she may even get a promotion as a result of the exposure of her work to the executive committee.

Dorothy took another sip of coffee and thought. "How do I know I can trust you, Dave?" she asked, intrigued in spite of herself.

"Together? We'll put the presentation together—together, you and I. I get to put my name on it. You'll tell Frank the idea was mine."

Dave responded to each of her concerns, reassuring her at every step. Dave responded to her voice, but sang to her heart.

"Yes, I have my computer at home. Why, what are you thinking? You want to come here? Today? To work on . . . in your dreams, Dave," she said exasperatedly.

Dave continued. No, he wasn't going to hit on her. No, he wasn't going to tell everyone he had been to her apartment. Yes, he would bring lunch.

"Hmmmm," sighed Dorothy. "I'll tell you what, Dave. You can come over and we will work on this together. But, if I change my mind *anytime* while we're working, the deal's off. Got it?"

8

I'm Not a Psychopath, I Just Talk and Act Like One

Smith charged down the hall toward his office. Marching past the staff without a glance, he reached the door and barked for his secretary to have Jones come to his office immediately. His face getting red, Smith threw the files in his hands down onto the desk and dropped into his big chair with a huff.

Minutes later Jones arrived, half knowing what to expect, but not knowing why. There were stories about Smith's calling staff members into his office to read them the riot act after a senior management meeting, but since Jones's projects were not on the agenda, this couldn't be the reason for the summoning. So far all her interactions with Smith had been cordial; there was no reason to suspect a change.

Smith's secretary greeted Jones and led the way to the office door. Smith motioned Jones to enter and the door was closed behind them. The secretary went back to her desk and resumed typing on her computer. She glanced at the staff member sitting at the desk to her left and the staff member to her right and sighed. Everyone knew what was about to happen.

The "scoldings," as the support staff called them, occurred roughly once a week, usually on Friday afternoons after the morning senior management meeting. Smith was never happy after these meetings, but no one was sure why, as the minutes were kept quite secret. Obviously, someone was chewing him out at these meetings and he felt the need to take it out on members of his staff; how else could the staff explain it?

Jones was a very likable person. She was the newest addition to the staff and had come to the firm with outstanding references and portfolio. She was always nice to everyone, with a cheerful disposition and an even temperament. She had survived almost three months without being called to Smith's office—an unofficial record by all accounts.

The secretaries jumped in unison when the first binder hit the trash can. Throwing projects into the trash was one of the dramatic things Smith did to accentuate his disappointment, disapproval, and disgust with the work product. The effect is powerful at the time, especially with the professional staff who take great pride in their binders and presentations. Soon the voices started to penetrate the air—loud voices: first Smith's and then Jones's, then back and forth, then a bit of quiet, then more loudness. It was always hard to hear the exact words through the walls, but occasionally one or two would slip through. Sometimes curse words, but not this time.

Smith had studied Jones long enough to know that foul language wouldn't work on her; he was shrewd—he had to wear her down with intellect. He had to convince her that her work was less than optimal or even rather poor. He would threaten her with reassignment, demotion, or termination, but would leave the door open for her to redeem herself down the road. He *would* convince her, of course, of all these things, as no one left Smith's office until he or she was convinced. Jones could not pretend to be convinced—she would actually have to *be* convinced—and she would, eventually. And, she would be *thankful* for Smith's help and guidance. Jones would fall into line as her coworkers and predecessors; Smith counted on it.

Smith prided himself on his ability to break people down and then build them up again—but not too far up, just enough to keep them on a leash. He needed to control people and couldn't stand it when someone had a thought, an idea, an insight that he, "the boss," should have had. He hated to be wrong, as well—and, of course, in his own mind, never was. At least this was the theory some of the staff members had developed about Smith. Others were more humorous: some hypothesized about his being dropped on his head by the doctor who delivered him, having been raised by wolves, left in a field by aliens, or bitten by a mad dog in his youth. Humor helped make the situation tolerable but didn't always heal the psychological wounds. It was much harder for some than others to come to terms with Smith's behavior.

His attacks were not confined to the office. Those on his staff— almost half of the company—were fair game just walking the halls, working in meetings, or sitting in their cubicles. When Smith entered a department, a veil of tension seemed to spread through the atmosphere; heads went down and people acted busier than they really were. It was even money that he would strike: rage rising in an instant, followed by an equally rapid return to calm and a smile. But sometimes he just made the rounds of the offices smiling, wishing people well, asking about their kids' soccer practice, and just being nice. It was so disconcerting. The new staff were always taken in by this approach and often concluded that Smith was a warm, caring, easy-to-talk-to boss. No one dared warn them, however, about what lay behind the smiling exterior, for no one was sure who might be one of Smith's spies.

What really irked everyone was the fact that sometimes Smith was right. His ideas sometimes really were better than the staff's, and sometimes he did know more than they did. Nevertheless, all would agree, there were other, less venomous ways to communicate that didn't involve the destruction of the egos of staff or morale of those trying to do a good job for the company.

Jones seemed to have a solid ego, not overly inflated like some or shrinking like others, quite healthy by most accounts, and she was definitely working her hardest to do a good job. The secretaries wondered how Jones would handle it.

A few more crashes, yelling and shouting, and desk pounding were heard coming through the wall. Then silence. The secretaries lowered their heads to their desks and computer screens as they heard the door open. Jones emerged, standing as tall as she could, but clearly taken aback by what had just transpired. She headed down the hall quickly, clasping her folders to her chest.

As if on cue, the secretaries rose in unison. They each, taking their handbags, headed down the hall toward the women's room. Smith's secretary indicated to the wide-eyed part-timer to watch the phones and handle any visitors. "It'll be okay," she said, realizing that the young person didn't really want to be left alone in the office.

At the door to the restroom, they stopped but did not go in. Jones was far senior to them, and their relationships were strictly professional. After a few knowing looks, the two junior secretaries returned to their desks. Today, Smith's secretary would stand guard and not let anyone interfere with Jones's privacy.

Following training programs and talks, we frequently are approached by audience members who, having just learned about the traits and characteristics of psychopathy, conclude that their boss, peer, or subordinate must be a psychopath. Although it is neither appropriate nor even possible for us to offer an opinion, we are admittedly struck by the audacious behaviors attributed to their coworkers by these individuals—and the similarities they exhibit to psychopathic behavior. Over the years, additional individuals have reported similar concerns to us after having read about psychopaths in *Without*

Conscience or in newspapers and business magazines. Some of the personal stories we hear most likely are descriptions of true psychopaths, but, of course, many are not. What is clear is that a large number of people believe that they do work for a boss, or with a coworker, from hell.

We estimate that about 1 percent of the population has a dose of psychopathic features heavy enough to warrant a designation of psychopathy. Perhaps another 10 percent or so fall into the gray zone, with sufficient psychopathic features to be of concern to others (see page 27). Most people have very few or no psychopathic characteristics. But what about the business world? There can be no simple answer to this question, for the philosophy and practices of organizations range from ethical and altruistic to callous and grasping, perhaps even "psychopathic." Presumably, the former would have fewer resident psychopaths than would the latter, although no doubt there are exceptions. For example, a religious or charitable organization—by its nature trusting and lacking in street smarts— might provide a comfortable niche for a smooth-talking, charismatic psychopath.

Unfortunately, there is no scientific evidence concerning the number of psychopaths in business, for several reasons. First, few organizations will provide the sort of access to their staff and files required to do proper assessments with a standardized instrument, such as the PCL: SV. Second, psychopaths have a talent for hiding their true selves, so one could expect many to go unnoticed and uncounted, leading to an underreporting of psychopathy in business. In the case of particularly successful psychopaths, it may be only the patsies (former pawns) who see behind the masks. Third, psychopathic-like traits and behaviors are also exhibited by some individuals who are not truly psychopathic, which could lead to overreporting, that is, viewing someone as a psychopath when he or she is not. Nonetheless, based on many anecdotal reports and on our own observations, it is likely that psychopathic individuals make up much more than 1 percent of business managers and executives.

Disordered Personalities at Work

In the journal *Psychology, Crime, and Law*, researchers Board and Fritzon administered a self-report personality inventory to a sample of British senior business managers and executives. They concluded that the prevalence of histrionic, narcissistic, and compulsive personality disorders was relatively high, and that *many* of the traits exhibited were consistent with psychopathy: superficial charm, insincerity, egocentricity, manipulativeness, grandiosity, lack of empathy, exploitativeness, independence, rigidity, stubbornness, and dictatorial tendencies.

Many people demonstrate what might appear to be psychopathic characteristics at some point in our lives; readers need only review themselves against the definitions and descriptions of psychopaths (see page 27) to see how this might be possible. But we should be careful not to confuse the presence of a few psychopathic-like traits with the disorder itself. How many times have you been abusive at work, but are quite the opposite with your family or life partner? Or you may be charming and manipulative with business associates, but forthright with friends. Or you may not feel guilt or remorse while "cheating" on your taxes, but feel terribly guilty if you hurt your child in any way. Or you may have had to defend a difficult business decision that hurt coworkers but feel bad inside nonetheless. Judging oneself or others on the basis of one or two traits or behaviors that appear to resemble those of psychopaths (but typically are much less severe) is dangerous. Only a relatively few individuals demonstrate *most* of the expected traits and characteristics in a *consistent* manner across *all* aspects of their personal, professional, and social lives. Even so, it is often difficult to see behind their chameleon-like façade. Psychopaths demonstrate the expected traits and characteristics in a *consistent* manner across *all* aspects of their lives, but they may hide them well.

"Boss from Hell"?

Your boss is cold, hard-driving, and ruthless. Before concluding that he is a psychopath, you should carefully consider the possibilities that your judgment is at fault and that his behavior is more a reflection of a personal leadership style than of a psychopathic personality. Because management style is rooted in training, personality, and experience, there are as many styles of management as there are managers. It is not surprising, then, that the match between employee expectations of how a boss *should* act and the supervisory style actually *exhibited* by the boss is not often perfect, leading to disappointment, conflict, and misinterpretation.

How employees view management or leadership style and its impact on performance and effectiveness has long been the subject of study by organizational psychologists. One of the earliest investigations into the styles of supervisors was conducted from 1946 to 1956, but the findings still have relevance today. Employees were asked to describe their leaders' behaviors on the job, and leaders in turn were asked to describe their own behaviors and attitudes. A large-scale mathematical analysis of the hundreds of descriptions was then conducted in an attempt to categorize the responses into the smallest number of critical items. The results of these Ohio State studies showed that there are two large groups of behaviors, or "factors," that go into our evaluation of our boss's style. These factors are labeled consideration and initiating structure.

Consideration refers to those behaviors and attitudes that deal with the interpersonal interactions between employee and boss. Highly considerate bosses treat people with respect, consider the egos and self-esteem of others in their decisions, and build working relationships on mutual trust. Bosses low on consideration are, as might be guessed, perceived to be uncaring and inconsiderate of the feelings of employees; they are seen as distant and cold. It is easy to see that reports of bosses berating employees in front of others, ignoring them when common courtesy demands otherwise, and failing to build relationships based on mutual trust and respect might actually reflect a boss low on consideration, rather than a true psychopath.

Initiating structure, the second supervisory factor, means that a leader is expected to decide on the work goals and tasks to be completed, flesh out the roles of the team members, and delineate the standards of performance or key success measures—in essence, to "lead." Bosses high in this factor take an active part in determining what needs to be done and how to do it. Traditional boss roles, such as planning, organizing, communicating, setting expectations, and defining the "big picture" fit in the high end of this factor. Bosses low in initiating structure tend not to be involved in the work at hand. A boss who dominates or who issues orders every step of the way may just be too high on initiating structure and not a true psychopath. Conversely, if the boss is rarely involved or even interested in the work you do, he or she may be very low in this factor—a "laissez faire leader"—or may not be a leader at all. Low structuring is not necessarily an indication of psychopathy either, although you may feel personally slighted and possibly angry.

Most people want a boss who is considerate and trusting and who builds rapport. Whether we also want our bosses to be high or low on initiating structure depends on whether we want someone to tell us what our job is and how to do it (most appropriate for new jobs or untrained employees), or we prefer to do our job with little interference from the boss (most preferred by seasoned workers). Both are equally valid styles as long as there is a match between employees' needs and the boss's approach to management.

While this two-factor model of leader behavior is well founded and makes intuitive sense when describing observed supervisory behavior, subsequent research on leadership has shown that these two variables alone (that is, how much consideration and structuring make up the boss's style) are not enough to predict who will be an *effective* leader. Whether a boss is high or low in these factors is not related to how effective a supervisor will be; the boss-employee relationship is much more complex than this and involves other things, not the least of which is the work situation itself. Yet we all tend to refer to these factors (sometimes by other names) when asked to rate how "good" or "bad" our leaders are.

"Coworkers from Hell"?

"Bad" bosses are not the only people we hear about. We have also heard a lot about coworkers and colleagues with negative attitudes, antisocial tendencies, manipulation, irresponsibility, poor performance, and a tendency to disrupt others who are trying to work. Clearly, these individuals are particularly difficult to work with and to manage, but there may be plausible explanations other than psychopathy for their behavior. To understand this we need to consider the factors people commonly use when evaluating colleagues and coworkers. Again, organizational researchers have discovered an important factor: it is called *conscientiousness* by the industrial psychologists who study it.

Individuals who are highly conscientious tend to focus on doing a good job; they like being accurate, timely, and thorough. They take pride in completing the jobs they start, are very responsible and detail oriented, and like to be seen by others as competent. Low-conscientiousness coworkers can get sloppy about meeting deadlines, achieving goals, or finishing what they start. They can come across as irresponsible, unfocused, disruptive, and poor performers. Sometimes they rely on others to help them get their work done—or others may feel the need to "cover" for them so as not to hurt the team's or department's overall performance. Clearly, most of us prefer to work next to individuals who are conscientious in their work. It seems fairer to us for others to carry their own weight on the job, especially if they are drawing a salary similar to the one we receive.

A lot of research has shown that conscientiousness is a primary dimension of personality, rather than just a style or personal preference.

People vary on this trait as much as they do on other personality traits—we all have various degrees of conscientiousness in our makeup. However, being at the extremely low end or extremely high end of the scale, while disconcerting to some of our coworkers, is not necessarily a bad thing. Your effectiveness at work depends, once again, on the match between your degree of conscientiousness and the specific job you do. Examples of jobs requiring moderate levels of conscientiousness typically include artists, creative research scientists, or visionary leaders, because of the need to step out of the box or take risks when creating new works of art, pursuing new knowledge, or leading in uncertain times. Conversely, jobs like design engineer and nuclear power plant operator require high degrees of conscientiousness; managing many important details is critical to their success.

While the "fit" between levels in conscientiousness and job requirements may not be perfect in real-life situations, there is no reason to suspect that coworkers low (or high) in conscientiousness are psychopaths.

Psychopath or Difficult Person?

Individual differences in consideration, structuring, and conscientiousness are normal parts of human behavior in any organization. However, there are some clusters of psychopathic traits that *do* come across as low consideration, extreme structuring, and low conscientiousness. If demonstrated together, they could raise the suspicion that one is dealing with a psychopath.

What would a psychopath look like according to these common business models? Many psychopaths would clearly be rated *very low* on consideration (rude, arrogant, and self-centered, among other things), at the *extreme* when it comes to structuring jobs (either uncaring or overbearing), and *very low* on conscientiousness (irresponsible, impulsive, arrogant, self-centered, and seemingly unwilling to accept responsibility). As we stated before, these factors alone do not indicate psychopathy, but they certainly are warning flags. But what else does one need to look for?

Psychopaths, although capable of hiding some of their attitudes and traits from others, are in fact amazingly consistent in their psychological makeup. Years of study have uncovered their unique personality structure, reflected in the four components or dimensions of psychopathy (see page 27): interpersonal, affective, lifestyle, and antisocial. All psychopaths score very high on the affective dimension, but there are variations in their scores on the other three dimensions, giving rise to a number of psychopathic "styles."

What we know is that virtually all exhibit some form of asocial, antisocial, or aggressive behavior, whether overt or covert. They are all egotistical, having a sense of entitlement and the assertiveness to demand it, which often makes them appear selfish in relationships. They all have a grandiose sense of who they are and *insist* that others give them the respect due them. They are not as goal oriented as the rest of us when it comes to actual diligence and hard work, although they will frequently tell others how ambitious they are and weave a (phony) hard-luck story about how they overcame immense odds growing up poor or underprivileged or from an abusive home. Yet they are all irresponsible when it comes to attending to appropriate behaviors (for example, not doing the job they were assigned or making promises they do not keep), both on and off the job. And they rarely, if ever, experience guilt or remorse for any of their transgressions, even the most outrageous and hurtful.

A Fundamental Mistake

One of the biggest and most painful mistakes we make is to assume that everyone has much the same capacity as we do for emotional experiences. Because we have little difficulty in putting ourselves in the emotional shoes of another person, we are surprised at the callous indifference some people appear to show to the pain and suffering of others. What we often fail to realize is that there are some individuals, including psychopaths, whose own emotional life is so shallow that they cannot construct an accurate emotional facsimile of those around them.

Recent brain imaging research indicates that the experiences and events that most people find emotional are associated with activation of several brain areas, including the limbic system, which is sometimes referred to as the "emotional brain." But these same experiences and events *fail to activate components of the limbic system in psychopaths.* Indeed, psychopaths respond to what should be an emotionally arousing event (such as an emotional word or a gruesome picture) as if it were *not* emotional at all. Curiously, in psychopaths, the parts of the brain that *are* activated by such events tend to be associated with language processing. Their response seems to be more cognitive or linguistic than emotional. Their callous indifference to the plight and inner pain of others is more akin to that of a predator to its prey. But we often fail to realize this—a fundamental mistake—preferring instead to believe that everyone shares the same inner turmoil and pain.

Individuals who interact with psychopaths frequently, though, also note some clear differences. Some psychopaths come across as more impulsive or erratic than others do. The more impulsive psychopaths require immediate gratification and use short-term predatory strategies to get what they want. The less impulsive types tend to appear less predatory in their pursuit of gratification, instead relying on opportunities coming to them. This difference is possibly due to different physiological factors, but the exact mechanism is unclear at this time. Some psychopaths (arguably the less intelligent ones) are driven to satisfy the most basic instinctual needs, such as food and sex, while others seek higher-level satisfaction in power, control, or fame. Some are more subtle or clever in their manipulations of others, using charm and linguistic skills to get others to obey and conform. Others are more blunt, attempting to con in clumsy ways, and then resorting to abusive demands when their "charm" does not work. This latter type acts out their aggressions in violent, vindictive, ruthless ways, while the former are less reactive—perhaps more in control of their inner drives—relying on suggestions, intimidation, and "passive aggression" to get their way.

Manipulators and Bullies—Different Styles?

Forensic research on psychopaths has recently revealed that there are, in fact, several psychopathic *subtypes* within the global syndrome of psychopathy. These subtypes—the classic, the macho, and the manipulative—are described in the sidebar below. It is an open question at this time whether these subtypes are a reflection of the individual's brain physiology or a result of personal growth and development. Yet all seem to represent primary themes or styles that dominate their particular psychopathic approach to life and relationships. Would these types show themselves on the job?

Variations on a Theme

A high score on the PCL: SV can result from many different combinations of features. For example, statistical analyses of the scores of large numbers of offenders and patients have revealed three main "psychopathic styles." All three share the affective features of the disorder (that is, shallow emotions; lack of empathy, guilt, or remorse), but differ somewhat on the other dimensions.

The *classic style* consists of those with a *high* score on each of the psychopathy dimensions: interpersonal, affective, lifestyle, and antisocial. They exhibit virtually *all* the features that define psychopathy.

The *manipulative style* consists of those with a *high* score on the interpersonal and affective dimensions, and somewhat *lower* scores on the lifestyle and antisocial dimensions. They manipulate, deceive, and charm but are less impulsive and antisocial than are the other types. They are talkers more than doers.

The *macho style* consists of those with a *high* score on the affective, lifestyle, and antisocial dimensions, and a *low* score on the interpersonal dimension. They are aggressive, bullying, and abrasive individuals, less charming and manipulative than the other types. They are doers more than talkers.

When we analyzed the anecdotes and stories from readers and program participants as well as others we have worked with, and then added in our own research, we discovered two distinctive styles of corporate psychopath that seem to fit well with what we know of two of these psychopathic subtypes.

Some psychopaths, the *corporate manipulators or cons*—like the manipulative type—are adept at using others in pursuit of fame, fortune, power, and control. They are deceitful, egotistical, superficial, manipulating, and prone to lying. They do not care about the consequences of their own behavior, rarely thinking about what the future might hold. They never take responsibility, despite promises to deliver on goals, objectives, and personal favors. When confronted, they will blame others for the problem at hand, not accepting responsibility for their actions. They are rude and callous to individuals who have nothing to offer them, feeling superior and entitled. They never think about the harm they inflict on people or institutions, often coming across in interactions as totally devoid of human emotions, especially empathy. To apologize for something they did is foreign to them, as they do not experience remorse or guilt.

They Just Don't Get It

In 2005, John Rigas, eighty-year-old founder of Adelphia Communications, and his forty-eight-year-old son, Timothy Rigas, were convicted of securities fraud and conspiracy and for bilking investors in what the judge described as one of the largest frauds in corporate history. John Rigas was sentenced to fifteen years in prison, and his son to twenty years. Referring to the former, the judge said, "Long ago he set Adelphia on a track of lying, of cheating, of defrauding."

The responses of the Rigases were revealing. "I may be convicted and sentenced," said the elder Rigas, "but in my heart and conscience I'll go to the grave believing truly that I did nothing but try to improve conditions" for the company and his family. His son, Timothy Rigas, told the judge that, "Our intentions were good. The results were not."

Yet, despite all this, the manipulators can be surprisingly successful in dealing with others, relying primarily on their excellent ability to charm and weave a believable story to influence others. They are adept at reading situations and people, and then modifying their approach to best influence those around them. They can turn on the charm when it suits them, and turn it off when they want. Because of their chameleon-like ability to hide their dark side, they can quickly and easily build trusting relationships with others, and then take advantage of them or betray them in some way. Manipulators seem to experience a gamelike fascination in fooling people, getting into other people's heads and getting them to do things for them. This ability to win psychological games with people seems to give them a sense of personal satisfaction.

While they may come across as ambitious—a trait they will play up—they actually have few long-range goals of any consequence, relying more on their innate ability to seize an opportunity that interests them at any given moment and then weave it into the story they tell others. Should something else more exciting come along—a new job or a new love interest—they will move quickly toward the new opportunity, a tendency that can make them look somewhat impulsive and irresponsible to observers. While they may blow up at coworkers, flying into a rage and then calming down just as quickly (as if nothing has happened), they can also control their anger if it is in their best interest to do so—saving their vindictiveness for a later time.

Another group of psychopaths is much more aggressive. This group, the *corporate bullies,* seems to reflect many of the traits of the macho psychopath: they are primarily abusive rather than charming. Bullies are not as sophisticated or as smooth as the manipulative type, as they rely on coercion, abuse, humiliation, harassment, aggression, and fear to get their way. They are callous to almost everyone, intentionally finding reasons to engage in conflict, to blame others for things that go wrong, to attack others unfairly (in private and in public) and to be generally antagonistic. They routinely disregard the rights and feelings of others and frequently violate traditional norms of appropriate social behavior. If they do not get their way, they become vindictive, maintaining a grudge for a considerable amount of time, and take every opportunity to "get even." They frequently select and relentlessly attack targets who are relatively powerless.

Targeting the Vulnerable

Among the most attractive targets for a psychopathic con man are women who are insecure, lonely, or isolated from friends and family in a foreign country. In Canada recently, a man posed as a former Hong Kong police officer and claimed he now was working with the local police. He scammed wealthy women from Asian "satellite families," in which the husband worked in Hong

Kong and the family lived in Canada. He was able to insinuate himself into their lives, and in several cases was able to convince a woman that she should divorce her husband. In each case, he demanded money to invest in his business schemes, and if a woman resisted, he threatened or assaulted her and said that his criminal contacts in Hong Kong would harm her husband.

The man was ultimately convicted of extortion and defrauding one of the women and was sentenced to prison. The judge referred to him as a "snake who slithered into her life and ruined her life."

This particular type of crime is played out in communities around the world. In most cases, the victims are afraid and embarrassed to come forward. Not all the victims are wealthy, but all are targeted by snakes.

Bullies react aggressively in response to provocation or perceived insults or slights. It is unclear whether their acts of bullying give them pleasure or are just the most effective way they have learned to get what they want from others. Similar to the manipulators, however, psychopathic bullies do not feel remorse, guilt, or empathy. They lack any insight into their own behavior, and seem unwilling or unable to moderate it, even when it is to their own advantage. Not being able to understand the harm they do to themselves (let alone their victims), psychopathic bullies are particularly dangerous.

Of course, not all bullies are psychopathic, though this may be of little concern to the victims. Bullies come in many psychological and physical sizes and shapes. In many cases, "garden variety" bullies have deep-seated psychological problems, including feelings of inferiority or inadequacy and difficulty in relating to others. Some may simply have learned at an early age that their size, strength, or verbal talent was the only effective tool they had for social behavior. Some of these individuals may be context-specific bullies, behaving badly at work but more or less normally in other contexts. But the psychopathic bully is what he is: a callous, vindictive, controlling individual with little empathy or concern for the rights and feelings of the victim, no matter what the context.

In addition to these two specific types—the manipulator and the bully—we have seen a handful of cases that are even worse. *Corporate puppetmasters*, as we labeled them, seem to combine the features of each in a sophisticated way. They are adept at manipulating people—pulling the strings—from a distance, in order to *get those directly under their control* to abuse or bully those lower down in the organization. In essence, they use both strategies—manipulation and bullying—much like historical figures such as Stalin and Hitler, individuals who surrounded themselves with obedient followers, and through them controlled much of their countries' populations. Any sign of disobedience (often accentuated by a paranoid stance) led them to attack their direct supporters as well. To the puppetmaster, both the intermediary (the "puppet") and the ultimate victim are expendable since neither is viewed as a real, individual person. We believe that corporate puppetmasters are examples of the much more dangerous classic psychopath.

Origins of Aggression

Developmental research indicates that early childhood is a time of considerable physical aggression, peaking between the ages of two and four. After a gradual decline with age, aggressive (and antisocial) behavior again peaks in late adolescence and then, in most cases, decreases in early adulthood; this pattern is described as *adolescent-limited*. However, the antisocial and aggressive behavior of some individuals is *lifetime-persistent*, meaning it can extend well into adulthood. Some of the features of the lifetime-persistent pattern (such as impulsivity, narcissism, callousness), but not others (such as verbal deficits, neurological problems, high anxiety), are similar to those found with psychopathy.

Is it possible to identify aggressive and other traits in children that are potential precursors of those found in adult psychopaths? Recent research in behavioral genetics indicates that it is indeed possible to do so (see page 47). Of particular importance is what has been referred to as a pattern of *callous-unemotional* (CU) traits, similar to the interpersonal/affective features of psychopathy listed on page 27. These traits can be measured in preschool children and are predictive of later aggressive and other behavioral problems.

Researcher Paul Frick and his colleagues have suggested that these CU traits arise out of low levels of fear-induced inhibitions (that is, they are not deterred by the threat of punishment), resulting in impairments in the development of moral socialization and conscience. Donald Lynam and his colleagues have provided evidence that the combination of attention deficit/hyperactivity disorder (ADHD; per the *Diagnostic and Statistical Manual of Mental Disorders*, 4th edition [DSM-IV]) and conduct disorder (CD; per DSM-IV) represents the "fledgling psychopath." This combination of adolescent disorders is thought to reflect problems in inhibiting behavior that is potentially unacceptable or harmful to self or others. These problems in self-control, along with CD traits, appear to be important in the development of psychopathy.

Corporate Psychopaths We Have Known

Hervey Cleckley and many current researchers have suggested that the manipulative psychopaths would do well in business, politics, and other professions because of their ability to con others into believing they are honest and ethical and have talent, experience, and a flair for leadership. While the bullying psychopaths might seem ill-suited for work in these areas, our research suggests otherwise. In management positions, their reputations keep rivals and subordinates at a distance, allowing them to use their power to get what they want. Furthermore, members of top management, not close to the day-to-day action, may hear rumors of such bullying behavior, but discount them as exaggerations due to envy and rivalry, or even accept the behavior as part of the person's strong management style. To the degree that bullying psychopaths have bolstered their reputations as major contributors to the successful running of the business, they are immune to criticism or might receive a token "slap on the wrist" occasionally. The puppetmasters are much more immune to organizational discipline because they themselves are in control of a greater number of employees, as well as systems, processes, and procedures designed to protect the organization and its members.

Doing the Crime but Not the Time

A Canadian ad executive, Paul Coffin, pleaded guilty to fifteen counts of defrauding the federal government of $1.5 million. For five years, he and his wife had lived the good life by double billing for his services and submitting bogus invoices for fictitious employees. During the investigation, he had been uncooperative and experienced many memory "lapses" about his criminal activities.

He received a conditional sentence (no jail time). The judge accepted the man's suggestion that *instead* of prison he should deliver a series of lectures on *ethics* to university students. The proposed topics of these heartfelt lectures are: "Never compromise your integrity, no matter what the perceived benefit." "The only person who can rob you of your reputation, credibility, and good name is yourself."

Consider, also, the case of the former president of Hollinger International, David Radler, who pleaded guilty in the United States to a $32 million mail fraud, and agreed to testify against other company executives. In exchange, he received a sentence of twenty-nine months and a $250,000 fine. However, being Canadian, Radler probably will serve his time in a Canadian prison. Because his crime was not a violent one, he almost certainly will receive day parole (free by day, locked up at night) *after five months* and full parole after ten months.

No doubt, the convicted executives of Enron, Tyco, and World Com *wish* they had committed their crimes in Canada, or at least were Canadian citizens.

In our original research working with almost 200 high-potential executives, we found about 3.5 percent who fit the profile of the psychopath as measured on the PCL: SV (pages 26–28). While this may not seem like a large percentage, it is considerably higher than that found in the general population (1 percent), and perhaps more than most businesses would want to have on their payrolls, especially as these individuals were on the road to becoming leaders in their organizations. Of these individuals, we found that all had the traits of the manipulative psychopath: superficial, grandiose, deceitful, impulsive, irresponsible, not taking responsibility for their own actions, and lacking goals, remorse, and empathy. Of these individuals, two exhibited bullying, as well. From the cases we have reviewed from others in the field, as well as from readers, this level of incidence seems correct.

The average PCL: SV score for the corporate psychopaths was 19 (out of a top score of 24), which is well within the research range for psychopathy. In evaluating these findings, it is important to note that scores at this level indicate the presence of enough psychopathic features to be problematic for the organization.

Mistaking Psychopathic Traits for Good Leadership

Early research by psychologists and psychiatrists suggested that the behaviors of most psychopaths were too dysfunctional to make long-term survival in organizations possible and that they might be better suited to work on their own or in some other career. But based on our

own research and that of others, we now know that some organizations actively seek out and recruit individuals with at least a moderate
dose of psychopathic features. Some executives have said to us,
"Many of the traits you describe to us seem to be valued by our company. Why shouldn't companies hire psychopaths to fill some jobs?"
A proper, scientific answer is that more research is needed to determine the impact of various doses of psychopathic characteristics on
the performance of different types of jobs. The "optimal" number
and severity of such characteristics presumably is higher for some
jobs (such as stock promoter, politician, law enforcement, used-car
salespeople, mercenaries, and lawyers) than for others (such as social
workers, teachers, nurses, and ministers). Until such research is done,
we can safely say that those who believe that "psychopathy is good"
clearly have not had much exposure to the real thing.

Anyone working with or for a psychopath will be painfully aware
of his or her destructiveness. For an organization, one psychopath,
unchecked, can do considerable harm to staff morale, productivity,
and teamwork. The problem is that you cannot choose which psychopathic traits you want and ignore the others; psychopathy is a
syndrome, that is, a package of related traits and behaviors that form
the total personality of the individual. Unfortunately for business,
the "good" traits often conceal the existence of the "bad" when it
comes to a psychopath.

An important reason for mistaking a true psychopath for a leader
is that a talented psychopath can easily feign leadership and management traits sought after by executives when making hiring, promotion, and succession planning decisions. A charming demeanor and
grandiose talk can easily be mistaken for *charismatic leadership* and
self-confidence. Furthermore, because of its critical importance to effective leadership, charisma, when it *is* found in a candidate, can lead
to a "halo" effect—that is, a tendency for interviewers and decision
makers to generalize from a single trait to the entire personality. The
halo effect acts to "fill in the blanks" in the absence of other information about the person and can overshadow more critical judg-

ments. As mentioned earlier, even seasoned researchers—who *know* they are dealing with a psychopath—are often fooled into accepting things at face value.

The Dark Side of Charisma

Psychologist and researcher Robert T. Hogan and his associates have pointed out that *charisma* can hide a multitude of problems. "There are certain people who have good social skills, who rise readily in organizations, and who ultimately derail . . . because their apparent qualities hide a dark side."

He notes that more executives are fired for personality problems than for incompetence. Most problematic are "narcissistic, psychopathic managers who exploit subordinates while currying favor with superiors. . . . Before they fail they cost their organizations large sums of money by causing poor morale, excessive turnover, and reduced productivity."

The ability to *influence* events and decisions and *persuade* peers and subordinates to support your point of view are critical executive management skills. Not everyone has these skills at the level required by general management jobs. Organizations constantly seek people with these skills and invest significant sums of money in training, coaching, and development of staff to improve them. To find someone who seems to have a natural talent for influence and persuasion is rare. When found, it is hard for decision makers to look past it. We know that psychopaths are masters of conning and manipulation—especially if covered over by a deceitful veneer of charm—leading to the perception that they have strong persuasion and leadership skills.

Visionary thinking, the ability to conceptualize the future of the organization, is a complex skill requiring a broad perspective, the ability to integrate multiple points of view, and a talent for looking into the future—that is, to *think strategically*. Psychopaths are not good at establishing and working toward long-term, strategic objectives; they are much more opportunistic. Yet they can weave compelling stories about situations and events of which they know very little into surprisingly believable visions of the future. Because visioning is so difficult for the average person to understand, it is little wonder that the vague but convincing, illogical but believable, rambling but captivating, and compelling but lie-filled discourses of the psychopath (see sidebar below) can look like brilliant insight into what the organization should do. This is especially true in times of crisis, when few can make these lofty predictions and many are looking for leadership to fill the vacuum.

Style Trumps Substance

In many cases what is actually said is the least important part of a social interaction. The content of the message often is obscured by the manner in which it is delivered and by the visual impression the speaker makes on us. We all understand this; impression management and manipulation are normal social mechanisms used by everyone.

Politicians, advertisers, and salesmen are not the only ones who understand that "looking and sounding good" often blinds people to what should be obvious to them: distortions of the truth, empty clichés, hyperbole, and fatuous nonsense. "I don't know what he said. But he's so good-looking. What's not to believe?"

In the last and most decisive battle for Gaul, the enemy was mercilessly overpowering Julius Caesar's army. His troops were significantly outnumbered and they were surrounded; the end seemed near for Caesar and his long campaign to take Gaul. But seeing that all would be lost, he put on his armor and his bright crimson cloak—so he would be easily seen by the enemy—and led his reserve troops into the middle of the battle. Still outnumbered, his troops rallied, and the enemy soldiers, realizing that they were being charged by *Caesar himself*, faltered. History records Caesar's victory, his valor, and his fighting acumen. We know that he was charismatic, a strong orator, influential, and persuasive, and a visionary leader whose strategies are still taught in military schools to this day. Was Caesar a great leader, or was his success the result of psychopathic impulsivity and extreme risk taking by himself and his soldiers?

It is important to note that psychopaths—like great leaders—*are* risk takers, often putting themselves and others (in Caesar's case, his own life and that of his army; in the case of business, the entire company) in harm's way. Risk taking, often difficult to quantify or differentiate from foolhardiness, is a trait that closely lines up with what we expect of leaders in times of crisis. But how much risk is appropriate? How much risk will be effective in saving the day or, in more mundane business settings, achieving objectives? Another trait, *impulsivity*, accentuates risk-taking behavior, leading to acting without sufficient planning and forethought. And *thrill seeking* often involves taking dangerous risks just to see what will happen. Elements of extreme impulsivity and thrill seeking can also be mistaken for *high energy, action orientation, courage*, and the ability to *multitask*, all important management traits.

Despite the risks to his own life, Caesar's risk-taking behavior in this last battle for Gaul was far from psychopathic. He was a *prudent* risk taker, sizing up the realities he faced, the resources he (and the enemy) had, the probabilities that would influence the outcome, and the risk to his legion posed by *not* taking a risk. He was also not a thrill seeker, at least not to the degree exhibited by psychopaths. He and the Roman legion he commanded were a disciplined machine, hardly the image of a rampant leader and his band of psychopaths fighting for the thrill of it.

Cowboys *Not* Wanted

Are psychopaths particularly well suited for dangerous professions? David Cox, a psychology professor at Simon Fraser
University, doesn't think so. He studied British bomb-disposal
operations in Northern Ireland, beginning his research with the
expectation that because psychopaths are "cool under fire"
and have a strong "need for excitement" they would excel at
the job. But he found that the soldiers who performed the ex-
acting and dangerous task of defusing or dismantling IRA
bombs referred to psychopaths as "cowboys"—unreliable and
impulsive individuals who lacked the perfectionism and attention to detail needed to stay alive on the job. Most were filtered out during training, and those who slipped through *didn't
last long.*

It is just as unlikely that psychopaths make good spies, terror-
ists, or mobsters, simply because their impulsiveness, concern
only for the moment, and lack of allegiance to people or causes
make them unpredictable, careless, and undependable—likely to
be "loose cannons."

Psychopaths' emotional poverty—that is, their inability to feel
normal human emotions and their lack of conscience—can be mistaken for three other executive skills, specifically the ability to *make
hard decisions*, to *keep their emotions in check*, and to *remain cool under
fire*. Making hard decisions is one of those management tasks that
executives have to do on almost a daily basis. Whether it is to choose
one marketing plan over another, litigate or settle a lawsuit, or close a
manufacturing plant, all major decisions have emotional components
that must be dealt with. Nonpsychopathic executives are often required to suspend their own emotional reaction to events in order to
be effective. They have feelings, but the constraints of their jobs often preclude them from sharing them with others, except family
members or close confidants. Of particular importance, as dictated
by some business realities, is appearing cool and calm in the midst of

turmoil. One can imagine Caesar calmly putting on his red robe as he contemplated the possibility of his own death.

Certainly, New York City mayor Rudolph Giuliani did so for extended periods in the aftermath of the World Trade Center attacks, and he has been credited with keeping the city under control as the problem was analyzed and dealt with.

When the Hippocratic Oath Is Hypocritical

There are scores of cases in which medical doctors have violated the Hippocratic Oath (or a modern version), which describes their responsibilities to their patients. Many have committed murder and have been appropriately dealt with. In many cases, however, the penalties for misconduct are mild, much like those typically meted out to corporate miscreants.

Several years ago a medical doctor was found guilty of unprofessional and unethical conduct for having financial dealings with two of his patients, a seventy-three-year-old woman and her forty-eight-year-old hearing-impaired son, both of whom were incapacitated by a steady stream of narcotics that he supplied. He took over their life savings, home, and car. He also billed government medical plans for services he did not perform. His dealings made him a great deal of money.

The penalty for such "infamous conduct"? A ban from practicing medicine for six months and a fine of $45,000. No jail time. He moved to another locale and has done extremely well ever since.

In summary, we suggest that it is easy for someone—anyone—to confuse behavior that is psychopathically motivated with expressions of genuine leadership talent. This is especially true when the prospective new hire has an arsenal of skills and traits that can be effectively packaged as leadership talent, when the *persona* is so tightly bound up in business expectations, and when the psychopathic fiction "I am the ideal leader" is so effectively staged.

ACT IV
DOUBTS DANCE AWAY

Frank waved to the security guard as he parked his car near the building. He grabbed his briefcase and went directly through the entrance to the cafeteria for his coffee. It was Tuesday, gourmet coffee day, so he went straight for the good stuff. He always liked getting in early after a business trip so he could get a head start on the work he knew had piled up on this desk during his absence. Waving to a few staff members as he left, he went to his office, turned on the light, stopped, and stared. His office looked the same as it did when he left Friday night, except for the wastebasket that he had put near the door and that Marissa, the cleaning supervisor, had emptied and returned to its spot behind his desk.

"Hmmmm," he muttered as he walked over to the credenza, placed his briefcase down, and opened it. He turned, and as he placed his coffee on the coaster on his desk, he saw a computer disk in a bright yellow case on the pile of papers he had left.

"I hear the meeting went very well," said Dave from the doorway.

"Yes, it did. They liked the material," said Frank, picking up the disk.

"That was a close one, wasn't it," said Dave, laughingly.

"Dave, come in. Let's talk," said Frank, deciding to take a firm approach with Dave; he wanted to get to the bottom of what had happened over the weekend. Dave took a seat across the desk and crossed his legs. Frank continued, holding the disk in his hand and waving it. "Dave, what happened on Sunday? I tried to reach you after I looked at the material you left for me. I was—"

"I was away that morning," interrupted Dave. "When I got your message, I realized that something terrible had happened. I rushed to the office, hoping that this was just a simple mistake—that maybe you had dropped the disk on your way out—and found it here," Dave turned slightly and indicated the center of the carpet, "so I immediately realized what had happened. I knew you were already on the plane, so I decided to e-mail it to you and John just in case you didn't have your computer with you."

Dave paused and Frank turned the yellow disk over in his hand, asking, "This is what you left me for the meeting?"

"Yes, Frank, why?" Dave looked puzzled. "Didn't I do the right thing getting the file over to the meeting?"

Frank turned to his briefcase and pulled out the blue disk he had found in the package from Dave on Friday. "Then what is this?" he asked.

"That's my draft material. Blue is for drafts, yellow for final product," said Dave matter-of-factly.

"Dave, there was nothing in the folder to indicate that there was a final product file, yellow or otherwise. Why did you give me the draft disk, when I . . ."

"Frank," said Dave, getting serious, "I gave you both disks—it's not my fault you dropped one on the way out. I did what I could to help you. It was a mistake, I understand, but I didn't tell John about you leaving the file. I covered it up and things worked out, didn't they?"

"Dave . . ." started Frank.

"Frank, I don't know what you are implying here, but I gave you the draft material as well because I know you are a stickler for details and like to check everyone's work. I figured you might want to see the background material, too."

"Your draft came from a magazine!" said Frank, raising his voice slightly, and toughening up his tone.

"I know that," dismissed Dave. "Don't you remember pointing that article out to me as an example of an excellent presentation? I scanned it in and used it as a template for your presentation to the committee. I thought it was what you would want. Wasn't it as good as the article you admired?"

Frank was perplexed. Dave's story made sense. Yes, he had praised the story about the competitor and showed it to Dave.

"And the numbers and charts?"

"They were just placeholders until I got the data I was collecting. The final is the same format, but with our numbers, graphics, and pictures." Dave paused, a serious expression crossing his face. "I wasn't doing anything devious here, Frank, and I'm a bit disappointed that you're suggesting I did."

"I'm not suggesting that, Dave; I'm just trying to understand what happened."

"Well, you said it yourself, you dropped the file on the way out. A simple mistake; nothing to make a federal case over. I was hoping to get a pat on the back for both a great presentation and saving the day. But . . ."

"The presentation was terrific, Dave. You did a great job, thanks. I really mean it. Everyone was impressed," said Frank.

"I appreciate it, Frank, thanks. Do we have the go-ahead?"

"Yes, full steam ahead," said Frank smiling. "Put together your recommendations for the team, and let's meet tomorrow to discuss timing."

"Yes, boss!" said Dave, giving a mock salute, but smiling broadly. Frank rose and extended his hand to Dave; they shook firmly and Dave left the office.

Frank worked all day and into the evening. At about 7:30 P.M. Frank called his wife to say he was on his way home. He sometimes felt that he had to make up the time he spent out of the office, but his wife knew that he just missed the excitement and enjoyed working late.

As he hung up, Pete, the cleaning person, entered the doorway. "Excuse me, Mr. Frank," he said backing out into the hall.

"Oh, that's okay, Pete, I'm just leaving. You can come in." Frank packed his briefcase, grabbed his jacket from the back of the office door, and waved to Pete. He paused, thought a moment, and asked, "Is Marissa around tonight?"

"Yes," said Pete. "She's down the hall to the left."

"Thanks, have a good evening," said Frank as he headed down the hallway.

9

Enemy at the Gates

Carla hurried down the corridor, coffee in hand and file folders under her arm. She hated to be late for these meetings, but she had just received some new information that might help with the decision making today.

10:02, glared the large clock at the head of the room.

"Sorry I'm late," said Carla, putting down her folders onto the conference table at her place. Pulling her wallet from her purse, she retrieved two dollars and placed them in the center of the table. Despite all the changes the company had undergone during the past year, this one ceremony—a dollar a minute for lateness—was maintained. Some time-management consultants had recommended it years ago to the executive committee as a means of disciplining themselves, and it stuck. They just loved it; now every meeting involving directors and above is run by this rule. The pot, when the fine was a quarter a minute, used to come up to enough after a year to buy pizza for the entire company staff. Now, with inflation, the fine was up to a buck, but the resulting improvements in timeliness led to fewer pizzas overall.

"Glad we're all here. Thank you," said Johnson, the CEO. "You all interviewed Morgan and Tom for the new director of communications job, and this meeting is to share our impressions, review what information we got from references, et cetera, and make a decision. Are we all on board with that?" he asked, looking around the room at the members of the selection team assembled in the conference room.

Heads nodded around the table.

Carla handed out two candidate packets to each member of the team. These contained the results of their interviews, reference checks, background checks, and assessments from the executive recruitment firm. "The cover sheet gives the summary of all that we have. I'll give you a minute to read through it," she said, as they perused the page while she took out some other notes from her pile.

"It's pretty obvious that they're in a dead heat according to the competency list. They both got high marks from their references on understanding the business, building external relationships, oral communication style, written communication, and business acumen. Morgan did a bit better in problem solving and decision making overall, but one reference said he tended to take on too much of the detail work himself and didn't delegate enough. Tom got the opposite review; he tended to delegate too much, sometimes handing off details his last boss thought he should have handled himself."

"I got the same impression during my interviews," said Nate, the hiring manager. "Tom told me he liked to develop his people, and delegation was a means to that end. Morgan didn't seem to think doing it all himself was a problem; actually, he was quite proud of the fact. But then he didn't have the same staff level as Tom."

The conversation continued with a detailed review of the remaining competency areas. At the end of this topic, the two candidates were about even in their attractiveness to the group.

"Any developmental areas mentioned?" asked Johnson, paging through the reports.

"Yes, on the next page you'll see them listed. Tom hasn't had much exposure to the rest of the business side; he's primarily been in communications. Morgan, on the other hand, came to communications from a marketing background," answered Carla, "so he's had more exposure."

"I like that about Morgan," added Nate. "While Tom did have an appreciation for the business based on his MBA, Morgan could really talk to the day-to-day issues. I'd have to score him higher on that one."

"How about Morgan; did he have any developmental areas?" asked Johnson.

"Yes, he had very little supervisory experience in his career. He started as a market analyst and then moved up into a senior-level position, still as an individual contributor. He made a lateral switch to communications because they had an opening and he had always liked journalism," responded Nate. "Morgan moved up twice in three years, but it was only in his last job that he got to supervise people."

"So delegation would be one of his developmental areas," added Carla, making a note on her file. "I did get some feedback on Tom's style from one source, who suggested Tom was pretty tough on his people. No real information about Morgan's management style from his references."

"I spoke with Morgan at length about his supervisory style, and although he doesn't have much hands-on experience, he said all the right things," added Nate.

"I got the same impression," said Carla. "Morgan came across with a lot of management theory, but he really didn't have the experience."

"Well, I think we can take care of that with some training," added Nate.

The group continued to discuss the strengths and weaknesses of each candidate, sharing their personal impressions as well as the data from the references.

"How about their abilities to handle the media issues we're facing. What are your thoughts?" he asked, looking toward Nate.

"Regarding Tom," Nate started, "I liked the fact that he had quite a bit of media exposure and personally represented his company during one of their product crises. Morgan has had almost no face time with the media. He did, though, create a sophisticated communications plan, which I circulated to you about a week ago."

"What did the tests show?" asked Johnson, referring to the battery of psychological tests that every top-level candidate takes as part of the hiring process.

"Tom was more outgoing and assertive, almost too much so," reported Carla, "and Morgan came out reserved, maybe not assertive enough. However, overall, the results were interesting."

"Interesting?" asked Johnson, smiling. "That's a new one. What do you mean by 'interesting'?"

"Both came out well on conscientiousness, openness to ideas, intelligence, and socialization," continued Carla, "but, surprisingly, Tom's scores were the highest the consultant has ever seen in a businessperson."

"Say more about that," said Nate, moving forward in his seat.

"There are certain ranges we look for, specific to each open position. Morgan did well, high enough on all scales to be a good fit. But Tom got *perfect* scores on all the scales. I'm not really sure what that means, but I do wonder how he could have done so well."

"Maybe he's a perfect fit for us?" asked Nate.

Johnson looked at his watch and told the group that he had another appointment to prepare for. Getting up from his seat, he suggested they continue the meeting without him and asked them to let him know of their decision by the end of the day.

This chapter will focus on how the company can forestall the hiring and promotion of corporate psychopaths. While no procedure is a guarantee against manipulation, vigilance based on greater understanding can improve one's defenses.

We start by briefly summarizing the typical personnel procedures used by businesses to hire, promote, and manage employees. As we explain the process, we invite the reader to look for potential weak spots, cracks, or loopholes in these processes, where a psychopath might be able to slip through or operate unnoticed. We will also offer suggestions for closing some of these entry points.

Managing the human assets of an organization is one of the most challenging functions of the executive, and we suggest that doing it well is most critical when it comes to identifying and handling potentially problematic individuals. The human resources department of any company is responsible for many functions, including finding and hiring new employees, administering compensation and benefits issues, managing employee and (where applicable) union relationships, developing and providing employee orientation and training programs, administering the performance appraisal process, and management development. Some larger HR departments also provide advice and guidance to executives on change management issues, executive development and coaching, and succession or replacement planning.

Among the most critical functions, relating to both the handling of psychopaths and the long-term viability of the business, are *hiring practices* and *succession planning systems*.

Hiring and Selection: The First Line of Defense

The most value-adding HR management function centers on finding, attracting, and retaining the best performers. The purpose of any hiring process is to assess the qualifications of candidates and determine who can best do the work available. Stated another way, the goal is to find the best match between the abilities of the candidate and the needs of the business.

The *hiring manager* with a vacancy to fill, and coworkers who are filling the gap in the interim, sometimes wonder why it seems to take a long time to fill a job. The answer lies in the diligence required to make the right choice. During this screening process, the company is trying to determine if the candidate is the best one for the job, and the candidate is also deciding if he or she really wants to work for the hiring company. The hiring process is actually a series of *screens* or *hurdles* through which the candidate must pass before being offered a job.

In general, once someone has vacated a position, the hiring manager reviews the work to be done and possibly redefines some of the requirements contained in the job description. Job descriptions are almost never meant to cover all of a person's duties, but they do include the most important. While formats vary considerably from company to company, the basic elements include a *title*; statement of *role* played in the organization; a list of duties or *responsibilities*; a list of the basic *knowledge, skills, abilities,* and *attitudes* (called *KSAs*) required for good performance; and sometimes a list of *goals* and related *measurement standards*. Writing a job description can be a tedious process, but it is critical to making a good hire and to weeding out those who are unqualified. Based on the job description, the hiring manager typically prepares a *requisition* that is a formal request to hire. At this point, many other people get involved, including compensation professionals, who decide the starting salary range; finance staff, who review the budget and head-count constraints; and, finally, members of upper management, who review and approve the hire.

The next step is to advertise the open position on a company job-posting board, or, more frequently, through ads in the newspaper, in professional magazines, or on the Internet. If the job is at a sufficient level, such as a senior manager, or requires very specific expertise, such as a high-level chemist, a professional recruitment firm may be retained to prescreen candidates.

Before the advent of the Internet, advertisements would lead to perhaps ten résumés being received. Today, Internet advertisements can lead to stacks of résumés or letters of interest from candidates. The purpose of any résumé, from the candidate's perspective, is to get the company's attention and an invitation for an interview. From the company's perspective, the résumé is an initial screen. Someone—usually an HR staff member—has to read all the résumés and whittle down the stack to those few that appear to be from viable candidates. Résumés are grouped into qualified, marginally qualified, not qualified, and, sometimes, overqualified. Ideally, a small number of viable résumés will be presented to the hiring manager, and then only a handful of candidates will be selected for further consideration.

SCREENING RÉSUMÉS

The major weakness in using a résumé as a screening device is, of course, the tendency for applicants to *overstate or falsify their qualifications*. It is common knowledge among executive recruiters that many of all executive résumés contain some form of distortion or outright lies—and these are the norm. Most of the exaggerations are in the areas of background experience and education. Some applicants claim more responsibility, greater financial accountability, enhanced job titles, and higher-level reporting relationships than they really had. Some pad their résumé with fake years of service, slurring dates to cover gaps that they cannot explain or jobs they wish to forget.

Fictional Résumés

"You can't argue with the written word," noted Pogo, an animal character in Walt Kelly's comic strip, popular with college students several decades ago. The same folk wisdom was evident in a humorous radio dialogue of the same era, which used as proof of various assertions, "It's in the book!" Unfortunately, the belief that if it is in writing it must be true is alive and well when it comes to evaluating an impressive-looking résumé. Surveys by those in the recruitment business indicate that about one third of résumés for managerial positions contained lies, that 15 percent of top executives lied about their education (degrees, dates), that friends often were passed off as former "bosses," and that education, responsibilities, and compensation were exaggerated. No surprises here, but a few simple checks and verifications would have caught most of these fabrications.

In some cases, it is only the hiring company that suffers from fraudulent applicants. But in other cases, the applicant is a psychopath who, once hired, puts lives at risk. There are scores of such examples—think of the many movies that "star" an impostor as medical doctor. Or consider the ease with which Seymour Schlager managed to become a top executive scientist at the largest medical device company in the United States. His résumé was impressive, listing his degrees and experience as a doctor, lawyer, Ph.D.-level microbiologist, and AIDS researcher. What he didn't indicate, though, was that he had been convicted of the attempted murder of his wife and that his medical license had been lifted. Much of his work experience was made up to cover over his time in prison. On at least one résumé sent to prospective employers, he listed as his return address the prison in which he was housed. Even the most cursory check would have disclosed this and other damaging information about who he really was. But such a check was not made.

Many applicants will tailor their résumés for a specific company to better reflect a match between their own knowledge, skills, and abilities and those described in the company's advertisement. This is actually a reasonable approach to take, as it highlights what is important to the hiring company and makes one's résumé stand out among the many others. However, doing this assumes that one *truly* has the qualifications and experience cited. Psychopaths, notorious liars, often will cross the line between good marketing and outright lying. In our work with psychopaths, we have seen résumés that contain jobs the applicant never held, companies that never existed, promotions that never happened, professional memberships that do not exist, awards and commendations never received, letters of recommendation written by applicants themselves, even fake education, degrees, and professional credentials (for example, a license to practice medicine), among others.

To uncover possible psychopathic deceit, it is essential that *every* piece of information contained on the résumé be verified. This is time intensive but worth the effort. However, résumé verification is usually done *after* the interviewing phase, when the choice is down to two or three candidates, and always after the candidates give permission to do so. This puts the hiring manager at a disadvantage during the interview, because he or she has only the résumé data to go on, and the psychopath is so good at lying.

At the very least, education and professional credentials should be checked before the initial interview. Education can be verified through the registrar's office at the university cited on the résumé, and should include type of degree (such as a BS/BA or MS), year, and area (finance, business, engineering, and so on). Sometimes applicants misrepresent their actual degree by substituting something that sounds more impressive (for example, engineering is a more difficult field of study than engineering technology). These details should be carefully checked.

Professional credentials and licenses, especially those granted by the government to protect the public from abuse (such as in the fields of medicine, psychology, engineering, and others) can be checked through the appropriate authorities. Many governments and professional societies have online databases that can be searched quite easily. Internet search engines such as Google can be very helpful in obtaining information about candidates, some of whom will have their own web page.

Faking It

A medical doctor was sentenced to prison for fraud. But this was not a simple case of bilking people of their money. Instead, he received millions of dollars from pharmaceutical firms to conduct scores of research projects involving human subjects. Unfortunately for the sponsoring firms, many of the research protocols he generated for them were made up, fudged, or otherwise fake. For example, he bought urine from his employees and passed it off as having come from patients in his "research" projects. Investigators described what he had done as "one of the most corrupt research enterprises ever discovered by law enforcement."

Following his conviction, the doctor offered to cooperate with investigators to expose other doctors involved in phony medical research. He also expressed concern at being "visualized as nothing more than a common crook." But there is nothing at all common about callous greed that puts the health of others at risk.

Also, because advanced degrees often require the writing of theses or dissertations, and seasoned technical professionals sometimes write articles and scientific papers, cautious companies may find it worthwhile to get a copy of these documents and let their technical staff read and assess them. Google Scholar is a good resource for this purpose.

The weak point in screening résumés, at least for the company wishing to avoid hiring a psychopath, is, of course, the résumé itself. Unfortunately, other than uncovering the most outrageous lies, little can be done to assure the accuracy of this initial screen. In general, one should not be too blinded by an impressive résumé. The job of the résumé is to get the applicant in the door—the first hurdle—but deeper digging is necessary to assure that what has impressed you is accurate.

SCREENING INTERVIEW 1

Individuals whose résumés seem to be a good fit for the open position are invited for an interview or series of interviews. Sometimes the first contact is by phone, an approach that saves the company considerable time and expense and allows a larger pool of candidates to be seriously considered. Telephone interviews benefit the applicants as well, because many more of them get a serious shot at the job than can be afforded by face-to-face interviewing alone.

The telephone interview is designed to get to know the candidate on a more personal level and to collect more details about his or her work experience. Typically, a candidate's motivations and personal interest in the job can be explored by asking questions like, "Tell me more about . . ." and "What got you interested in applying for this job?" A savvy candidate can catch glimmers of what the company is looking for and strategically offer examples of work experience that respond to their often unspoken concerns; those with good communication skills can, thereby, advance their candidacy. Psychopaths, of course, are quite astute at noticing what others need to hear and will begin their verbal manipulation during this interview; it is nearly impossible to differentiate them from legitimate applicants at this time.

To get the most out of telephone interviews, a company may wish to record them, with the applicant's permission, of course, and allow the hiring manager or other HR staff to review them. The staff can then prepare preliminary lists of follow-up questions to be asked during subsequent, face-to-face interviews. Seasoned psychopathy researchers are often impressed with the conversational skills of psychopaths when in their presence, only to find during subsequent listening to the tapes that their banter is filled with *flowery phrases, inconsistencies, lies, distortions,* and *bad logic.* At least these researchers have the advantage of other collateral information (such as criminal records) about the psychopaths, which the company—at least at this point in the process—does not have.

As a company interviewer, though, one must be careful not to place too much credence on subtle discrepancies gleaned during telephone interviews. Despite the ubiquity of telephones, many people are not at all skilled in speaking over them, especially when stress takes over good judgment and smooth conversation, as is the case during a job interview. At the very least, detailed notes about any inconsistencies should be taken by the interviewer and used to address concerns in follow-up interviews.

SCREENING INTERVIEW 2

Candidates who pass the initial phone screen are invited in for face-to-face interviews with key staff. The interviewers often include HR staff, the hiring manager, and, in many cases, a technical person from the department with the vacancy. The perspective of each is different, but they share the common goal of finding out as much about the candidate as they can in a limited amount of time in order to make an informed hiring decision.

With their experience and expertise in assessing people, the HR staff is often thought by others to possess the best chance of determining the people skills and fit of the applicant. HR alone, of course, cannot determine these things; it is up to the entire screening team, a concept we will discuss in detail below. Some hiring managers also expect the HR staff to determine the mental health (a generic term, often misused) of the applicant. This is clearly an unreasonable expectation, and totally out of the realm of HR work. Short of a psychological assessment, formal evaluations of mental health are not possible by untrained interviewers—and perhaps not relevant to a given job. The reader should keep in mind that psychopathy is *not* mental illness; it is a personality disorder, and psychopaths are well known for coming across as particularly "sane" to others. They display few, if any, of the idiosyncrasies, foibles, and neuroses that make the rest of us unique.

The hiring manager takes on the bulk of the interviewing task, while the others on the selection team play supporting roles. The hiring manager must find out many things before making a decision. Some of the questions and concerns on the mind of the hiring manager include:

- Does this person have the skills I need to get the job done?
- Will he or she fit in with the department or team?
- Can I manage this person?
- Does this person demonstrate honesty, integrity, and a good work ethic?
- What motivates this person?
- Do I like this person, and will he or she get along with others?
- Will he or she focus on tasks and stick to the job until it is done?
- Will this person perform up to the level the company requires for success?

The interview is the primary source of answers to questions such as these and makes it, therefore, a critical event in the selection process. Good candidates have a clear agenda: they want the job, they want to advance their careers, they want to work for a particular company on particular types of projects, and so on. These are all quite legitimate. Psychopathic candidates may also have a *hidden* agenda: they want to play "head games," and they want money and power because they feel entitled to it—not in exchange for real work. They want to talk the interviewer into giving them the job, and they ultimately want to take advantage of the company. The employment interview is the ideal setting for the psychopathic candidate to shine.

Surprisingly, though, many managers make two critical mistakes when approaching the employment interview: *not preparing* for the interview and *not being trained* in interviewing techniques. Both of these mistakes play directly into the hands of a psychopathic candidate by giving him or her too much control of the interviewing process.

Many managers we have known simply do not prepare the right questions for the task; some do not prepare any at all. To the candidate, the interview is the chance to impress the company with his or her ability to do the job and the motivation to do it well. Good management candidates will have mentally rehearsed their presentation and potential scenarios prior to the interview. They will have read books on interviewing techniques and have ready answers for the most common questions, including the challenging ones, such as "Tell me your greatest weakness"; "How would you handle it if . . . ," and; "If you could do something differently in your career, what would it be?" It is well worth the time and effort for the hiring manager to carefully prepare questions designed to elicit the *specific* information needed to make the right choice among a slate of candidates, and to force the candidate to go beyond pat or rehearsed responses.

The second mistake some managers make is not receiving training in interviewing techniques. Some interviewers prefer a free-flowing, unstructured approach to the interview, a style that goes against most of what we know about good interviewing techniques. Without formal training, the interviewer is forced to rely on "gut feel" or personal impressions. While this approach may work for seasoned interviewers with good candidates, it leaves the average interviewer open to manipulation by a psychopathic applicant.

Basic training on how to conduct and manage an employment interview is the least one should do to defend against psychopathic manipulation during employment interviews. While many training programs on interviewing techniques are available, most share a similar format: an *opening, initial exploration, detailed questions, providing information about the job and the company, follow-up on concerns,* and *close.*

The purpose of the *opening* is fairly obvious and dictated by the culture of the country where the interview is taking place. Handshakes, offer of a beverage, inquiry about travel to the interview site, and talk of the weather are common. These icebreakers pave the way for the real work.

During the *initial exploration*, the interviewer asks general questions about the candidate's background, experience, expertise, and education. The typical start of this line of questioning is to solicit an explanation of the candidate's career moves, sometimes in chronological order and sometimes in reverse order.

Once this introductory material is reviewed, the interviewer proceeds to ask *detailed questions* on specific aspects of the applicant's background that seem to be relevant to the open position. As with any good line of questioning, there are three levels of responses that the trained interviewer is listening for: the *overt answer* to the question, the *impression* the candidate is making on the interviewer, and the *underlying* competencies, motivations, and values the overt answers reflect.

Overt answers address concerns about facts like:

- What did the candidate really do in this job?
- What role did he or she play, supportive or leading?
- How much influence did the candidate exert on the outcomes of projects?
- How did the candidate handle problems that came up?

Impressions include:

- How does this candidate come across?
- How serious is the candidate about his or her career and this job?
- Is he or she likable?
- Is he or she bright?
- Did the candidate prepare for this interview?
- Is the candidate being forthright with information?

Underlying competency information gleaned by a good interviewer includes answers to concerns such as:

- Does this person communicate well in a somewhat stressful face-to-face conversation? Does the candidate stay focused on the question asked or ramble along?

- Did the candidate exhibit good judgment in the career moves he or she made?
- Did the candidate grow in his or her job and take on more responsibilities over time or merely do the same thing repeatedly?
- Did the candidate demonstrate leadership, integrity, effective communications, teamwork, and persuasion skills (among others)?

One common mistake interviewers make is to concentrate only on the overt answers and their own impressions and to *not* delve into the underlying competencies, motivations, and work values of the candidate. The reason for this is understandable: it takes a tremendous amount of work to craft questions designed to elicit competency-based responses, and a lot of experience conducting interviews to be able to interpret them correctly. In large companies, where structured interviews are the norm, the HR staff typically prepares a list of questions based on the information contained in the job description about responsibilities, competencies, standards, and so forth. A good job description leads to useful questions, while a hastily prepared job description leads to vague or poor questions. These questions are then distributed among the interviewers (assuming multiple interviews). Interviewers are then taught how to pose the questions in order to elicit the most useful information. Good listening skills and note taking by the interviewer are critical, as multiple candidates and the passing of time tend to cloud recollection of specific responses, and may lead to reliance on recalled impressions or gut feelings, which may be faulty

The next phase involves *providing information about the job and company* to the candidate. Research has shown that the more candidates know about the day-to-day ins and outs of a job, the better able they are to decide for themselves whether there will be a good match between their aspirations and expectations and what the job has to offer. A candidate who opts out of a job because of information learned during an interview saves both parties time and energy that could be better spent in other pursuits. A common mistake made by interviewers, though, is to get so caught up in their description of the job and their department that interview time flies by and subsequent questioning does not take place. Some interviewers, unfortunately, like to hear themselves speak, and candidates are naturally reluctant to interrupt. Therefore, it is prudent to put this discussion toward the end of the interview, and definitely avoid starting with it. The interviewer's goal should always be to get answers to every question that may come up about the candidate once he leaves. This may be a tall order, but it is a worthy objective of any interview.

During the course of an interview, there may be some bits of information revealed or comments made that just do not sit right with the interviewer. There may be areas of performance and experience that were not sufficiently addressed because the interviewer did not ask or did not explore more carefully, or because they were glossed over by the candidate. For example, when a candidate states: "My team won the company award for bringing the project in under budget and ahead of schedule," the interviewer may wonder:

- Was the candidate the leader of the team, or did he or she fill in when the boss was away?
- Was the candidate an active (nonleader) participant or merely the recorder of the meeting minutes?
- Did the candidate use this team experience to demonstrate leadership, despite not having the actual title?
- Did the company recognize the candidate's performance by assigning another project with more responsibility?

Details like these may not have been addressed during the initial line of questioning, or may come to mind based on subsequent information provided by the candidate. The *follow-up on concerns* phase is the time to pursue details that do not jive or that conflict. Inconsistencies may be the result of hasty answering or the result of distortion, exaggeration, or possibly invention. During this phase, the interviewer drills down even further into the details of the candidate's past in search of the critical information needed to understand what the candidate's experience really entailed. It is also a time to clarify inconsistencies, to get a read on his or her true motivations, and to answer the question: What did the candidate *really* do on the job, and is it important for the position we need to fill?

A typical question asked during this phase of the interview might be, "I'd like to go back to your description of the project team you were on. What was the *specific* role you were assigned?" [The candidate answers.] "What was your relationship like with . . ." and so forth. This line of questioning is sometimes difficult for less experienced interviewers because they lack the verbal skills or tact to ask specific questions without offending the candidate, or they do not like to confront others in general. Yet pointed questions may be the only way to satisfy the concerns of the interviewer, and perfectly clear answers should be the only way for the candidate to maintain his or her candidacy. Again, answers can be analyzed on many levels, providing more information about competencies, motivations, and values.

We might note here that a formal clinical assessment of psychopathy such as with the PCL: SV cannot be conducted without access to corroborating information *before* the interview. This allows the interviewer to question and resolve inconsistencies that occur within the interview and between the interview and other "hard" sources of information. This may mean simply pointing out the inconsistency and asking the candidate to "help me out here." Or, it may require systematic probes and judicious challenges. In any case, the interviewer must recognize that everyone engages in some form of impression management, but psychopaths are masters at it.

Finally, a positive *close* to the interview is important in order to maintain good rapport with the candidate. Candidates will often ask what the next steps in the hiring process are, and the interviewer should have an answer that is appropriate to the situation.

RETAIN CONTROL OF THE INTERVIEW

One of the problems that researchers who interview psychopaths face is losing control of the interview. Psychopaths avoid answering direct questions, but rather introduce topics into the conversation that are interesting to the interviewer. Before you know it, you are the one being interviewed and your plan is derailed. You lose sight of what the interview was about in the first place.

Psychopaths often perform exceedingly well during an interview. They experience little social anxiety and discomfort during interpersonal encounters that most would find daunting. This allows them to weave convincing tales of professional experience, integrity, and competence, and to use an array of technical terms and jargon with such confidence and panache that even the experts are fooled. The astute interviewer might be able to determine whether or not these tales reflect more than a superficial knowledge of the topic. Even so, the task will not be an easy one. When a psychopath is challenged on any detail during an interview, he or she will simply shift gears, subtly change the topic, and generally weave an altered tale so believable that even an interviewer who *knows* the individual is lying might have doubts. The psychopath's goal is to convince HR interviewers and the hiring manager that he has the ideal background, experience, and motivation to fill the job, and that he is bright and very likable. The candidate can be so convincing that the psychopathic fiction, "I am the ideal employee," may be readily accepted by the interviewer.

Once the hiring manager is convinced, he or she will champion the applicant's candidacy, and there may be little that can be done to prevent it. An obvious solution to the misleading résumé problem is to verify its contents, but this step is often delayed until *after* the interview. Psychopaths and other candidates who distort their résumés capitalize on this fact.

When dealing with any job candidate the interviewer must keep in mind who is in control of the interview. The goal of any interview is to gather facts, verify them, and make an informed choice. The following suggestions or guidelines are based on interviewing *best practices*, and are useful when interviewing all types of candidates.

STICK TO THE PLAN

Armed with questions designed to get a reasonably accurate picture of the candidate's knowledge, skills, abilities, and attitudes, the interviewer should make sure that *all* the questions are answered to his or her satisfaction. The more information gleaned from the interview, the better the final decision making. Psychopaths as well as other clever interviewees will attempt to shift the interview to a friendly conversation about themselves and, if the interviewer is predisposed, a discussion of the interviewer. While this may leave the *impression* that the candidate is a good conversationalist and generally open and friendly, it misses the point of the hiring interview, which is to get the facts. Better to stick to the plan and get as much information about the candidate as possible in the time allotted.

ASK FOR WORK SAMPLES

It is customary in the arts and entertainment field for job candidates to show up with examples of their work in the form of a portfolio, which may include photos for models, movies for visual media professionals, and articles for journalists. This allows the hiring manager to see the actual product of each candidate's efforts and judge its quality, style, and appropriateness to the open position. In the case of business job candidates, the hiring manager should ask to see examples of actual reports written, presentations made, and projects completed. These, of course, should have any identifying or confidential information blanked out, but the great bulk of the work can be read and judged. If a candidate cannot provide copies, ask that they be brought to any subsequent meeting for review on site, should there be a follow-up meeting.

While we would not be surprised if an enterprising psychopath created a phony report or found one on the Internet just to satisfy a

potential hiring company, the effort may be more than most psychopaths are willing to invest. Should you suspect that the portfolio
is falsified or not the work product of the candidate, the only way to
uncover this may be to drill into details behind the actual report as
you question the candidate. But this approach assumes that the hiring manager has the technical expertise to do so, and, if not, may
best be left to a technical interviewer on staff.

FOCUS ON ACTION AND BEHAVIOR

Most interviewees speak vaguely about their past without providing
sufficient detail about what they really *did*. Others exaggerate their
contributions, giving themselves the appearance of being more important to the outcome than they actually were. A full answer should
include a statement of some goal to be achieved or problem that had
to be solved, followed by a review of the actual things the candidates
did, whether directly or tangentially, to address the goal, and, finally,
the outcome of their efforts, including what impact their efforts had
on the results.

CLARIFY DETAILS

When faced with responses that do not provide sufficient details, the
interviewer must go back during follow-up questioning to flesh out
the complete picture. The interview should redirect candidates to
specific areas of interest as much as possible, especially about broad
concepts like leadership. "Who, what, when, where, and why" types
of follow-up questions can help get to the truth behind the experience being described.

Supporting roles are quite important, and the job being filled may
require this sort of background and experience, but supporting roles
are different from supervisory and management roles (which often
involve the command and control of events, actions, and outcomes).
The interviewer should be clear on the level of authority the candidate claimed to have had, and then pursue a line of questioning
aimed at finding out just how much influence, decision making, and

freedom to act the candidate actually exerted on his or her past jobs. There can be many reasons for the candidate to continue to provide vague answers, including nervousness, forgetfulness, or the fact that he or she is exaggerating. The interviewer should keep this in mind while pressing for details.

LOOK FOR APPROPRIATE FEELINGS

One of the hallmarks of a psychopath is the inability to express a full range of normal emotions. For example, when telling a story that would normally elicit visible emotional reactions in most people, psychopaths often come across as cold and shallow, or as B-grade actors. Psychopaths do not understand what others mean by their "feelings," yet they will attempt to mimic them on demand. This often leads to superficial expressions or even exaggerations of emotion inappropriate to the event being described. There are many cases of psychopathic criminals describing the most heinous crimes in a matter-of-fact conversation, to the consternation of interviewers—but they may also claim to feel remorse or experience religious enlightenment to the parole board considering their early release. The most stunning examples of the "emotional disconnect" between feelings and actions are when serial killers describe their crimes. (See sidebar, page 228)

They Just Don't Get It: 2

Paul Bernardo and Karla Homolka videotaped their torture and rape of several young women, whom they later killed. As part of a "battered wife syndrome" plea bargain, Homolka testified against Bernardo and received a twelve-year sentence. He received a sentence of twenty-five years before eligibility for parole. When Bernardo was asked at his trial why he had kept the tapes, he replied, "I couldn't bring myself to throw (them) out because this was the last memory of these girls."

A police video showed Homolka walking through the house in which two murders had been committed. She matter-of-factly asked a detective if she could have the rug on which one of the young girls had been dismembered. "My sister wants it," she explained. In another room she casually asked the detective if "the furniture had been damaged as a result of their investigation."

Bernardo and Homolka also videotaped the drugging and rape of *Homolka's younger sister*, Tammy, who died as a direct result of their actions. At her funeral, Bernardo placed a gold ring on a chain around Tammy's neck, and Homolka slipped a wedding invitation into the casket.

Later, in a letter to a friend, Homolka complained that her parents were more concerned about Tammy's death than about her forthcoming wedding to Bernardo. "Fuck my parents. . . . My father doesn't even want us to have a wedding anymore. Screw that. We're having a good time. If my father wants to sit at home and be miserable, he's welcome to. He's wallowing in his own misery and fucking me."

Homolka is now out of prison, still portraying *herself* as the victim—but now of the criminal justice system.

Exaggerated or inappropriate displays of emotion commonly expressed by psychopaths during an interview might include indignation or rage. Exhibiting these emotions during an employment interview, of course, would raise questions about the candidate's emotional control and judgment regardless of the reason—psychological or otherwise. Some display of emotion is normal and to be expected during these expositions, as, for example, when describing passion for one's work, disappointment over a failed project, or termination of a close coworker. Sometimes the absence of an emotional component to an answer may raise questions. The key is to look for emotions appropriate to the story being told, and to be sensitive to how realistic (as opposed to superficial) these emotional expressions appear. This is the one time when "gut feel" and the interviewer's "emotional antenna" have a valuable place in the interviewing process.

The Emotional Disconnect

We have described the "emotional disconnect" in psycho-paths as an inability to experience or express normal feelings concerning the effects their actions have had on other people (p. 226). Some of the most dramatic examples come from those who have killed others.

Six weeks after receiving parole for robbery and murder, Jack Abbott (see p. 54) killed a waiter who was a part-time actor. Ab-bott wondered what all the fuss was about: "There was no pain, it was a clean wound. He had no future as an actor—chances are he would have gone into another line of work."

The Green River killer, Gary Ridgeway, pleaded guilty to the sexual murders of forty-eight women. In one of the interviews with law enforcement, he enters the room, sits down, looks up, and points out that the camera is not directly on him. The camera is moved and he proceeds to describe what he had for breakfast and how he had slept the previous night. Later, he talks about his horrific crimes in the same emotionally flat manner he had used when describing his breakfast.

TAKE NOTES

It is easier to recall impressions and feelings about the candidate than specific facts, so it is a good idea to make detailed notes during the interview and write them on the résumé itself or on the list of questions provided by human resources. These notes should be clear enough that others reading the document can decipher them. It is also useful to review these notes *during* the interview to help formulate follow-up questions. Simply telling the candidate that you need a moment to review your notes is a reasonable request and is often welcomed by a candidate, as it allows him or her to take a break.

DO NOT DECIDE ALONE

A well-structured hiring process will include a meeting of interviewers—a selection committee—to discuss the qualifications and relative merits of the candidates. This is good practice because different interviewers see different strengths and weaknesses in any single candidate, and these should be compared and discussed. It is invaluable in the case of screening out a potential psychopath. Recall that psychopaths attempt to build private one-on-one relationships with those who have utility to them. By definition, this would include all interviewers and decision makers involved in the hiring process.

As informal students of human psychology, psychopaths may easily ascertain the specific psychological needs and wants of each interviewer and then customize their approach to best advantage. On the surface, each interviewer will come away with a positive impression, and, to the degree that decision making relies on this good feeling, they will all agree that the psychopath is the ideal candidate, almost too good to be true.

By increasing the number and varying the *types* of interviewers beyond the human resource professional and hiring manager, the chances of finding discrepancies that lie behind the "ideal employee" façade increase. Expanding the interview schedule with a technical expert, a future peer or subordinate, the current job holder (if still on staff), a member of upper management, and even the department staff assistant can provide different perspectives that might uncover important information. We also know that psychopaths treat individuals differently depending on their perceived *status*. Psychopathic responses to perceived "lower-status" interviewers may include condescension, flirting, disparaging side comments, and displays of entitlement, among other things. "High-status" interviewers may provoke discussion of overly ambitious career aspirations and expectations, bravado and deceitful boasting, and even the disparagement of another "lower-status" interviewer. By getting all of the interviewers in a room together for a discussion of the candidates, the *selection committee* can flush out these discrepancies. By reviewing the candidate's interview results together, critical inconsistencies, and possibly deceitful claims, can be uncovered. A good meeting facilitator will get each person to test his or her impressions, feelings, and facts about each candidate. Lists of positive and negative aspects of the slate of candidates can then be used to make the final selection.

Adding interviewers to the schedule is time consuming and expensive and is not often done when the open position is a lower-level one. As a result, these candidates will get less thorough treatment by fewer people, including, perhaps, lower-level interviewers who may not have sufficient training and experience. This situation also arises when candidates just out of college are interviewed with little experience to validate, save their academic performance, course work, and college extracurricular experiences. Such individuals, if they are psychopaths, could cause a lot of problems down the road if they slip past the company's defenses because they were not evaluated sufficiently.

B-Scan

We analyzed the succession plans of a few hundred North American executives and noted that the similarities between the developmental issues for some managers identified as "high potentials" and psychopathic-like features were startling. Our list of questionable characteristics—dysfunctional behaviors, attitudes, and judgments—was refined to form the B-Scan, a research instrument for use by companies as part of their evaluation for succession planning.

We obtained clear differences between a group of successful, high-performing executives and a group of *convicted* white-collar or economic criminals (that is, individuals who defrauded their companies and other innocent victims). In a follow-up investigation, we also found predictable differences between the successful high performers and corporate psychopaths.

Research on the B-Scan continues.

KNOW THYSELF

As we learned in earlier chapters, psychopaths' objectives are to ingratiate themselves with their targets, establish trust, talk their way through any inconsistencies, build strong relationships with those in power, and then take parasitic advantage of everyone. During employment interviews, psychopaths (and others skilled at impression management) will quickly assess the interviewer's value system, personal needs, and psychological makeup, and then tailor their speech and behaviors to make a good impression. A worst case would be for the interviewer to be so taken in that he or she does not challenge the data contained on candidates' résumés, or does not push back very hard on vague reports of their performance on the job. A savvy interviewer will push past subtle influence attempts and stick to the interview agenda.

Only by having a clear understanding of his or her *own* strengths, weaknesses, biases, and idiosyncrasies can the interviewer hope to maintain the course of the interview and not fall prey to ingratiation. This is not an easy task, as it requires personal insight into one's *private self* and *public self* (see page 69). The more you know about your own weaknesses, biases, and hot buttons, the better prepared you will be to fend off attempts by psychopaths and others to influence you.

LYING IS HARD TO DETECT

Many individuals believe that they are good at telling if someone is lying or not. Few of us can really tell. Even those who are trained to detect lying and deception are not particularly good at it. Criminal justice personnel are often asked to determine whether someone is lying or not, but recent research shows that their results are no better than that of the average untrained person. It is best not to guess whether an interviewee is lying, but rather to rely on corroborating evidence to get at the facts and ultimately the truth.

Look Me in the Eye

A series of advertisements that offered to pay investors an absurdly high rate of return contained this statement, "Look us in the eye before you invest."

Hare called the company and asked to make an appointment to "look someone in the eye." The secretary asked why he would want to do that, to which Hare replied, "Because the ad asked me to do so. I think they want me to see how honest they are." The secretary laughed and said, "You've got to be kidding." Hare assured her that he was serious. She hung up.

The ad, of course, was a cynical ploy to tap into the common but mistaken belief that intense scrutiny of the eyes will reveal deceptive intent. This belief is a powerful tool for con men, as are solemn "up-front" declarations of honesty and integrity. Consider, for example, this quote from Enron's 1998 annual report: "We do not tolerate abusive or disrespectful treatment. Ruthlessness, callousness, and arrogance don't belong here."

Of course they don't. Besides, who can argue with the written word? Or with honest eyes?

VERIFYING THE FACTS

The best places to start the search for corroborating evidence are the prior employers listed by candidates on their applications, provided that they have granted permission to the hiring company to contact references. It is customary *not* to contact current employers. Applicants often do not tell their current employers that they are considering a new job, and their request not to call them should be respected.

Verifying employment has a specific meaning in the business world. Verification is a highly structured process in which the hiring company contacts previous employers, reports to them the candidate's name, title, salary or wages, and start and termination dates as noted on the résumé and application form. The prior employer is asked to say "yes" or "no" to each statement. There is no real exchange of *new* information, with the possible exception of whether or not the prior company would rehire the candidate. The response to this question can be deceiving, since many companies have policies prohibiting the rehire of previous employees. Even the word *termination* does not mean that the person was fired; only that he or she left the company. The actual reasons or circumstances for leaving are rarely given or are limited to carefully constructed statements. The purpose of this caution is to protect the prior employer from litigation or claims by the candidate that he or she did not get a job because of something defamatory the prior employer said. Some employees terminated for *cause* (this technical term refers to stealing, policy violations, taking illegal drugs, or abusing coworkers, among other things) leave with signed agreements from their previous employer assuring them that a negative reference will not be given; only a neutral one. This leaves the hiring company at quite a disadvantage, especially as *performance ratings*—the most important information about candidates—are almost never given. This is the information the hiring manager wants and desperately needs in order to make an informed choice among candidates.

Another difficulty is what to make of the information if discrepancies are noted. Some discrepancies are clearer than others. For example, "assistant director" is a different, higher-level job than "assistant to the director," and candidates are expected to know the difference. Discrepancies in reported salaries are always problematic, although some candidates will show reduced salary on their résumés because they do not want to have their candidacy discounted based on that fact alone. Other discrepancies are harder to assess. For example, candidates will sometimes increase their actual salaries to a round number, a practice that does not suggest deceit; employment dates may be vague or unclear simply because candidates do not remember them or because they wish to cover over legitimate gaps in their employment history. Contrary to common belief, being out of work between jobs is not necessarily a negative. In today's economy, it can take months to get a new position as individuals search for the right career move. It is also not problematic for individuals to accept lower-level interim jobs—and include them on their résumé—as they search for a higher-level one, especially during times of economic downturn when senior level jobs are scarce. This may even indicate that the applicant is responsible and takes supporting his or her family seriously. Certainly, it is best for job applicants to be forthright, and interviewers should understand that career digressions are sometimes necessary, and take an open-minded approach.

Without much new information coming from the formal verification process, some hiring managers may try to circumvent the human resources department and call previous supervisors directly. This sometimes works, but many companies train their supervisors well in this regard, telling them to direct all employment inquiries to human resources, and explaining to them the dangers of answering these "off-the-record" questions. Not every company follows this strict procedure, however, so hiring companies often use this route to find out how the candidate performed on his or her previous jobs.

REFERENCE CHECKING

Reference checking is an important step in the hiring process and should not be downplayed, despite the time it might take to do well. On résumés and applications, most candidates list references who will provide favorable information. This is to be expected but should not dissuade the hiring manager or the HR staff from making contact and learning more about the candidate. Psychopaths, though, can be expected to pad their résumés with false references—for example, friends posing as past employers—or to provide names of individuals who do not exist at all.

Many candidates also provide the names of personal and professional references who will vouch for them. These individuals are a good resource if they are questioned carefully. Unfortunately, some references may verify résumé information that is false, such as job titles, scope of responsibilities, salary level, and performance. This situation is very hard to get around unless you know the reference personally—perhaps through a professional organization.

For each reference it is important to have a list of key questions that focus on verifying known information and soliciting new information, but keep in mind that the data collected are often only impressions or hearsay. Recall, also, that psychopaths leave behind *pawns*, *patrons*, and *patsies* in their wake, each with his or her personal perspective of the candidate. Patrons will be expected to give glowing reviews, while patsies and some pawns will provide a decidedly negative picture of the same person. Dramatic differences in their reports may provide a clue to potential problems.

Former bosses can provide valuable firsthand knowledge about the person's qualifications, work ethic, diligence, accuracy, ability to get along with others, approach to problem solving and decision making, and other hard-to-define characteristics. A good approach is to ask the reference how the candidate handled work situations that the candidate related during the interview. Because these situations were also discussed in detail during the interview, the hiring manager now has two points of view to compare. One cannot expect them to be a perfect match, but any distortions or exaggerations should be readily apparent. Other typical questions include:

- What is the applicant's record of accomplishment when it comes to project management and completion of assignments?

- What are the applicant's strengths, both technical and personal?
- What are his or her weaknesses or development needs?
- Which management approach worked best with this applicant?

The last question is particularly important, as it can begin to get at the real management issues of interest to the hiring manager and should be asked once rapport is established. Also, it allows the previous supervisor a chance to deepen the conversation into any concerns that may be lurking under the surface. The purpose is to get a clear, detailed, and accurate picture of the candidate from someone who actually *knows* the candidate, and then use this information to validate one's impressions from the interview.

In addition to questions about the applicant's technical expertise, background, and experience, it is important to learn about the applicant's *impact* on others.

- Is the applicant a team player?
- How did the applicant treat peers and, especially, subordinates?
- Do people feel comfortable with and trust the applicant?
- Were there any peers, subordinates, or other members of management who had issues with the applicant? How did the applicant handle them?

Another area of questioning should focus on any *changes* in perception, such as surprises or disappointments that occurred over the course of the applicant's employment; reports of any strange or erratic behavior would come under this line of questioning.

- Did the applicant ever surprise or disappoint?
- Were there any trust issues?
- Would the reference rehire the applicant?

There are other sources of information about performance and scope of responsibility that hiring managers can pursue. The most common include the interviewer's professional acquaintances who also work for the candidate's previous employer. In some industries, key individuals know each other and may be willing to offer their opinions. These individuals may not know the candidate, so this is a hit-or-miss approach, and the information provided may be biased. However, it is worth trying if the information gleaned is interpreted with caution.

CHECKING BACKGROUNDS

Another source of information about candidates involves *background checking*. This has been made much easier in recent years with the advent of the Internet. There are also companies that will provide professional background-checking services for a fee. These typically include criminal record, credit reports, education, licenses and credentials verification, and even driving records. While the amount and quality of information is not guaranteed, it can be used to verify what is already known and possibly to uncover issues of concern. Having a criminal record is not in and of itself a rejection factor. Many individuals who have broken the law in years past make good, solid employees. But in some industries, such as banking and securities, a history of fraud is an automatic red flag. Used wisely, background information can help the company make a more informed choice.

"Please God, Help Me Plunder"

Joyti De-Laurey, a thirty-year-old former personal assistant at a British investment bank, was sentenced to a seven-year prison term for stealing more than $7 million from her employers. She used the money for a lifestyle that would be considered extravagant even by the rich and famous. She obtained the money by forging her bosses' signatures on checks and transfers, and then moved money from their brokerage accounts to her checking accounts. The scam was so simple and obvious that her lawyer *blamed her bosses* for the crime because they were too busy making money to monitor her behavior.

One of her bosses stated that he had noticed that his account was "light" by two or three million dollars but assumed it was his mistake. He also thought she was "a talented woman" and considered promoting her because "she knows exactly how to work for me." Her lawyer argued that she was guilty of nothing more than "honest greed."

Perhaps, but De-Laurey also had a grotesque sense of ethics and entitlement, and a convenient belief that God was on her side. The latter was evident in her "Bibles of Daily Thoughts," notebooks containing her letters to God. "Dear God. Please help me. I need one more helping of what's mine and then I must cut down and cease in time all the plundering," she wrote. "Please ensure my job is safe and my integrity is unquestioned."

PUTTING IT ALL TOGETHER

The purpose of this multistep selection process is to gather as much information about potential hires from as many sources as possible so that a company can make a good decision. By combining information from multiple raters (that is, interviewers, references, and recommendations), the company creates a more thorough picture of each applicant, improving its chances of picking the right person for the open job.

A thorough hiring process is very similar to the approach used by psychologists and criminal justice professionals in assessing criminal behavior, although obviously the criteria being rated are quite different. A prison record is a de facto "résumé" of an offender's "accomplishments" and includes "references" and "performance reviews" from social workers, psychologists, and criminal justice officials. When evaluating psychopathy, researchers combine their interview notes with what others have observed and documented in the record. Having access to collateral information is as important to screening for psychopathy as it is to making the right hiring decision. While the company has a different objective in mind and rarely probes into the deep psychological motives of an applicant, a solid selection process has the potential for capturing enough information about the applicant's behavior at least to raise some red flags.

Executive Hiring and Promotion

When trying to fill technical positions, having clear job requirements eases the hiring process. There are certain things that chemists, engineers, computer programmers, and financial analysts, among others, are expected to know, and specific experiences that they are expected to have had at various points in their careers, making the screening of candidates somewhat straightforward. The selection of a senior manager is significantly more difficult. One reason for the difficulty in selecting the right executive is that the nature of the executive's job is so amorphous or so tailored to the individual that it is difficult to ascertain exactly what knowledge, skills, abilities, and attitudes are required. It should be obvious to the reader by now that a good job description is critical to understanding the qualifications to be sought in new hires and promotional candidates. Unfortunately, many executives we have met just do not have an adequate job description with which to work.

Also, there is some overlap between things psychopaths do and good executives do, at least on the surface. A complete understanding of the differences is important because one can be mistaken for the other, and the amount of damage a high-level bad hire can do to the organization can be significant.

INTERNAL VERSUS EXTERNAL CANDIDATES

Choosing between an internal promotional candidate and an external hire is sometimes like comparing apples to oranges. Internal candidates for promotions, of course, are better known to the company than outsiders, but this often works against them, because the external candidate usually seems much better qualified than the internal one. Because more is known about the internal person's personal weaknesses and idiosyncrasies, it is more likely that decision makers will have formed negative opinions that work against his or her candidacy. Conversely, organizations usually discover much *less* about the external candidates, making them appear more qualified. This kind of uneven comparison makes it much easier for a psychopathic candidate to join an organization, beating out an internal candidate who is otherwise qualified. Would you choose the "devil you know or the devil you don't know"?

The matter is made more complicated if you *already* have a corporate psychopath on staff (without your knowledge) who has established an influence network and already has a *patron* on his or her side. In this case the (possibly) better-qualified external candidate is at a disadvantage. Recall that the psychopath spends considerable time and energy building relationships with key decision makers in the organization, in case he or she needs their support later on. The psychopathic fiction, "I am the ideal employee," created in the minds of his or her supporters can be easily transformed into a very believable "I am the ideal *leader*." In this case, the internal psychopath will look *much* better than any but the most outstanding external candidate.

Furthermore, the psychopath also has a clear advantage should the company compare him or her with internal candidates. Recall that corporate psychopaths spread considerable *disinformation* about their rivals (unbeknownst to the company or the rival), which leads to doubts and concerns, thus effectively knocking other candidates out of contention.

This is a real problem for the company trying to fill a top-level job. The best defense for this type of systematic manipulation is to add more hurdles or screens, in the form of executive recruiters and formal succession planning.

EXECUTIVE RECRUITERS

Executive recruiters specialize in the identification of talent and then recommend candidates with the appropriate background and credentials.

Psychopaths Wanted

University researchers have used a variety of techniques to study psychopathy in the general population. The challenge is to get them to come into the laboratory and to agree to provide enough information about themselves for a proper assessment to be conducted. A common procedure is to put an ad in the newspaper, such as the following:

Are you charming, intelligent, adventurous, aggressive, impulsive? Do you get bored easily and like to live life on the edge? If you would like to make some easy money by participating in a confidential interview, please call to set up an appointment.

But who would volunteer for such a study? Real psychopaths, psychopathic wannabes, crooks, would-be mercenaries, or those who just need the money? All of these, it appears. Indeed, a recent study found that the average score on the PCL: SV of those who answered such an ad was very high, with half the scores approaching those of incarcerated criminals. Among the latter, some had been arrested for a variety of crimes, while others had managed to engage in a range of unethical behaviors without ever being charged.

The use of professional executive recruiters adds a layer of security in this type of selection, as they have often placed the executives they recommend in more than one company over the course of their careers. They therefore have access to an extensive performance database (both track record and personal chemistry) from their previous dealings with these executives. Much of this information comes from hiring managers at other companies who have used their services to fill vacancies. Also, in some industries, key applicants tend to circulate through the same companies and can provide information about each other to the recruiter. Although information from peers might be biased, it often is uncensored and may reveal questionable behaviors of the sort covered in this book. Using their vast databases, astute recruiters should be able to find a good match between the company requirements and the profiles of their candidates, and to screen for any hint of previous indications of psychopathic behavior. While a corporate psychopath may be able to fool a recruiting firm *some* of the time, the more the recruiter knows the candidate's history, the less likely it is to occur again.

SUCCESSION PLANNING

The alternative to external recruiting is internal promotion. Succession plans provide orderly continuity of leadership for the company, and they are the most effective means of identifying and grooming leadership talent for promotion. If well designed, they can minimize the chance of a corporate psychopath's slipping through. Formal succession planning can be cumbersome, but when compared to the alternatives, it can reap benefits.

Many companies start the process by identifying key management *positions* in their organization and then clarifying the criteria for success. Like the hiring process, formal succession planning is composed of several screens or hurdles through which potential future leaders must pass. In many companies, the person in charge of succession planning solicits recommendations from key managers about subordinates who have the potential for higher levels of responsibility, or more generally, the "right stuff." The initial evaluations are based on information gleaned from their performance appraisals, record of accomplishments, and personal interactions with the manager making the preliminary recommendation.

Subsequently, formal assessments are done, often including *psychological evaluations*, a *"360-degree"* rating, and *assessment center* performance. Psychological assessments usually involve in-depth interviews with a psychologist as well as the administration of psychological tests. A report is then given to the candidate during a follow-up meeting with the psychologist, and the company often receives a summary as well. A 360-degree rating involves the completion of confidential surveys about the candidate by peers, current and former bosses, and subordinates. These typically include questions about the candidate's performance, attitudes, and competencies considered important by the company. Assessment centers are well-structured training events designed to evaluate many candidates simultaneously during a simulated work setting. Participants are asked to "run a company" or solve some business issue while they are observed and rated by company personnel and business experts. At the conclusion of the exercise, feedback on how well the participants did and suggestions for improvement are then given to each candidate, and a summary is given the company as well.

All of this assessment information is reviewed by a management committee charged with running the succession plan. It is used to determine each candidate's *potential*: specifically, how far along a management career path or how high up in the management ranks the candidate is reasonably expected to progress. *Readiness level*—how long before a candidate can be considered ready to assume greater responsibility and authority—is also evaluated at this time.

Those with sufficient potential and acceptable readiness levels are assigned a personal *mentor* who is responsible for overseeing the company's investment in this person. Together, they create an *individual development plan* that outlines the growth and improvement needs of the candidates, based on ratings of competencies, knowledge, skills, abilities, and attitudes, as well as personal information, such as aspirations, and any career constraints, including geographic preferences and family commitments. Recommendations for improvement often include training programs, rotational assignments, special projects, and regular meetings with a professional *coach*.

For those with high-level potential, job rotations through a variety of departments, such as finance, sales, marketing, research, human resources, and manufacturing, are often assigned to provide a broader understanding of the business. Many companies also require the completion of international assignments, which will give the candidates exposure to different cultures, languages, and sets of business problems.

As the reader can appreciate, formal succession planning provides multiple assessments from a variety of sources across a lengthy period of time, thus assuring that almost every aspect of the future leader's behavior has been reviewed and cross-checked. If the reader feels that the process is quite bureaucratic, this is in fact the case, for succession planning systems were originally developed during the period when bureaucracy was the organization model in vogue. Succession planning was an attempt to improve the chances of making the right promotional choices while removing cronyism, nepotism, and other "old boy network" influences from the process. Formal succession planning is one of the few bureaucratic processes that *transitional* companies can benefit from and should retain.

Yet we would argue that there are still some risks involved, and holes in the process can be taken advantage of by manipulative employees. One problem is that the psychopathic employee has had a significant amount of time to establish a cadre of supporters, some of them patrons who, shielded from any negative information, advocate for the psychopath's candidacy. The second problem is the disinformation spread by the psychopath, with the express purpose of disparaging rivals and enhancing themselves.

There are several approaches to counter these problems. First, the management committee should keep close tabs on all candidates, take every opportunity to interact with them personally, and solicit information from those who are in the best position to provide candid data. These sources include supervisors, especially those handling special projects and international assignments, and subordinates who have experienced the high-potential candidate firsthand. It is always possible that some misinformation will be included in even the most well-prepared plans, but by increasing the number of sources and balancing their perceptions, any perceived discrepancies should raise a red flag and prompt further review and validation.

Second, companies should avoid identifying for grooming only one person per position. This approach, called "crown prince/ princess" by experts, almost guarantees that once chosen, a candidate, psychopathic or not, will be given the higher-level job in time, without the added security of internal comparison. To avoid this, *several* candidates are identified for *each* important position (referred to as a *talent pool*), and no one person is guaranteed the promotion.

A third approach would be additional psychological assessments, including interviews and written tests designed to measure personality traits. Because of the special knowledge required to do this, companies often outsource it. It is important that the psychological assessment be considered just one source of data in the list of criteria used by the company to make its decision. In the end, it is the performance and observed behavior of the candidates that should be the deciding factors.

Guess What? Some People Lie

Personnel managers and psychologists rely heavily on self-report psychological tests or instruments in which the individual responds to a set of questions or items about his or her personality, attitudes, and habits: "I am a truthful person," "I like to take chances," "I care about the welfare of others." Although most of

these tests contain scales designed to detect faking and dissimulation, it is not difficult for anyone with even a modicum of smarts
to beat them. A personnel manager who takes the results of such
tests at face value or who relies heavily on them for making personnel decisions runs the risk of being conned by someone more
test wise than the test administrator.

Even relatively uneducated prison inmates are able to slant
the results of most psychological tests, appearing psychologically healthy or mentally disturbed, depending on the context.
Some inmates even run their own testing service, providing
advice to other inmates on how to respond to the items in a
given test.

One psychopathic inmate studied by Hare ripped off some
other inmates and, thinking his life was in danger, was able to
produce a psychological test profile that indicated he was so disturbed that the psychologist recommended he be transferred to
the psychiatric wing of the prison. After being in the psychiatric
wing for a few months, and believing that things in the prison had
cooled down, he took another psychological test, and this time
appeared normal. He was sent back to the prison, where he soon
got into trouble again. He took another test in order to get back
into the psychiatric wing, but this time the psychologist had figured out what was going on, and the inmate's ploy to be transferred again out of the prison was unsuccessful.

EXECUTIVE COMPETENCIES

It is critical that all human resources data be reviewed carefully and
challenged repeatedly to ascertain their validity: Were the goals actually achieved? Were projects completed on time and within budget?
Did sales, revenues, or production quotas actually increase? Are the
numbers correct? Following this, the human cost needs to be evaluated: did the candidate leave a trail of bodies in his or her wake, or
inspire others to take on a challenge and come through with success?

When considering management and executive candidates, performance in important competency areas often commands attention. Some examples are:

- *Business acumen:* Does the candidate understand the business issues facing the organization? Does he or she understand regulatory, social, environmental, political, industry, scientific, and technical trends?
- *Perspective:* Does this person have a "big picture" view? Can he or she see the forest (as well as the trees)?
- *Thinking:* Can the candidate think strategically, plan strategically, and implement a strategy?
- *Communication:* What is the candidate's communication style? Does he or she communicate effectively?
- *Presentations:* How well does the candidate make presentations? Can he or she sell ideas effectively?
- *Media relations:* How does the candidate represent him- or herself and the company to the media?
- *Relationship building:* How effective is the candidate at building relationships with internal people (such as peers, supervisors, and subordinates) and external people (such as customers, members of the public, local government, and professional contacts)?
- *Judgment:* How effective is the candidate at problem solving and related decision making?
- *Interpersonal style:* What is the candidate's interpersonal style? How does this person interact with others?
- *Values:* What are this person's core values, personal motives, and drives? How do his or her values influence his or her decisions and behaviors?
- *Career goals:* What are the candidate's career aspirations? Are they realistic?
- *Development:* What are the candidate's limitations or developmental needs?

But these are only the basic requirements for an executive's job. There are some other very important competency areas relevant to the topic of this book that should be considered during every hiring program or succession planning assessments.

Handling Challenges to Organizational Responsibility and Effectiveness

Executives are presented with challenges every day as a routine part of their job. Their ability to meet these challenges goes beyond whether they are good at specific technical competencies such as communication and interpersonal skills and decision making (among others). Broadly speaking, executives are expected to make organizationally responsible choices, and they are judged by how effective these choices are in advancing the aims of the corporation. Over time, a pattern of responses to the expectations of organizational responsibility and effectiveness emerges, which can be used to define the "true" person. While individual lapses in judgment may garner attention in many cases, the ability of psychopaths to cover or explain away their individual decisions makes evidence of these lapses difficult to obtain. Rather, it is the long-term impact of their behaviors in a variety of situations and their dealings with a variety of people that can shed more light on who they really are. In this sense, it is the *choices made in response to organizational challenges* that provide a clear picture of the person as an executive.

SOME "RED FLAGS" TO CONSIDER

The following list is presented to give the reader a sense of some of the long-term consequences of psychopathic features that might be observed in a business setting. While no single consequence is necessarily indicative of psychopathy, all of them are problematic if not addressed in training and coaching sessions. At the very least, evidence of these outcomes should send up the "red flag" and warrant further investigation and evaluation.

INABILITY TO FORM A TEAM

The most debilitating characteristic of even the most well-behaved psychopath is an inability to form a workable team. Noted in narcissistic and Machiavellian businesspeople as well as psychopaths, the inability to form a team is a critical factor in career derailment. Psychopaths' failure as leaders and managers is based on their unwillingness and inability to collaborate with others, especially those whom they see as adversaries. Being highly competitive, and in the name of the "good fight," they withhold or distort information to the detriment of the team and ultimately the company. When placed on a team they will exhibit disruptive tactics and behaviors designed to either take over the team themselves or disturb the working of others.

Often, they will attempt to derail a team before the first meeting by challenging the need for the team itself, and will use typical organizational rationale (for example, "meetings are a waste of time") to buttress their disruption, but crafted to sound as if they have the company's best interest at heart. Or they may participate in a half-hearted manner, often showing up late and making a scene when entering, or leaving in the middle of the meeting to do tasks that are "more important." They disrupt the team's progress by distracting it from its purpose, criticizing the team, its objectives, and individual teammates, including "bad-mouthing" to others when it suits their purpose. Being highly competitive and unwilling to listen to the directives of anyone whom they cannot value (i.e., those who do not have high utility for their career), they will attack the team, berate the members, and sabotage the leader. Recall that psychopaths believe they possess or are entitled to higher status than others and will treat coworkers like pawns in their drama. Predictably, they attack others who attempt to manage or evaluate them.

When teamwork is in their *own* interest or is useful to them (as a means of manipulating others), they will attempt to take over the team. In doing so, they often come across as domineering or bully-ing. Not surprisingly, psychopaths describe themselves as team play-ers, lacing their descriptions with examples of how the team was so poorly led that they were forced to take over and save the project. The psychopath is a real team player; but there really is only one member of his team.

Teamwork is critical to the success of modern organizations. The ability to form or participate on a team is critical, and those who can-not do so are seldom successful. The best sources of information about these disruptions are the other team members. Problematic ex-ecutives will always justify their behaviors toward the team, but the decreases in morale, productivity, and cohesion will be evident to those who are experiencing them firsthand. Routine solicitation of feedback from team members about the team and each participant's actions is a way to capture this important information.

INABILITY TO SHARE

Living peacefully in any civilized society requires the citizenry to share a variety of life-sustaining things. Likewise, corporate citizens need to share resources in the interest of the greater good, reflected in higher profits, job security, or a stress-free workplace. Because they do not see others as equals or as having any legitimate claim to re-sources, psychopaths (as well as some narcissists and Machiavellians) see no need to share resources. In fact, their parasitic, competitive na-ture drives them to actively siphon off resources from others. Psy-chopaths do not readily share credit for a job well done, important information required by the task at hand, money needed to imple-ment a project, workspace, time, and personal effort, among other things.

Not sharing information is a common offense, and is often justi-fied, upon confrontation, by a "need to know" rationale. While cer-tain governmental agencies charged with national security can operate in this mode, keeping secrets from one's boss or a subordi-nate in most organizations is not justified. "The right hand not knowing what the left hand is doing" is a common embarrassment in organizations under the best of circumstances; to purposefully create such dilemmas is contrary to organizational success.

However, it is easy to understand why psychopaths hoard information. The failure of others makes it easier for them to appear successful. Knowledge really is power in an organization. Psychopaths who keep others "out of the loop" use the power this gives them to their own personal advantage, which they see as more important than the interests of the organization. When a psychopath does share information, it is with an ulterior motive. Keeping others in the dark can make others look stupid, and this is a form of neutralization used by psychopaths against their detractors. For example, "They wouldn't understand" was the condescending rationale used by one psychopath we met to justify not sharing information with his coworkers. Another claimed to be protecting the department from the disruptions of a coworker, stating, "She would only get upset and then we'd have a bigger problem"; a statement designed to bolster the psychopath's superiority and plant the seeds of distrust of the "emotional" coworker. Clearly, comments that discount the value of coworkers or teammates, especially their ability to think and reason as equals, are consistent with the elevated (grandiose) self-perceptions psychopaths have of themselves. They are too self-centered to see the danger of this approach, let alone its unfairness or unethical nature.

An extension of the inability to share information is the inability to share credit with others (unless there is some benefit to the psychopath). Credit sharing can be difficult to measure, as upper management does not have easy access to the truth about the relative contributions of employees. Complaints from coworkers who feel that they are not getting the information and other resources they need to do a good job, or who feel they are contributing to the outcome but not getting proper credit, may be the only hint that something is amiss. Supervisors and human resources staff should pay attention to complaints of this kind, some of which may turn out to be groundless. Others may uncover serious managerial and morale problems.

DISPARATE TREATMENT OF STAFF

Because psychopaths see people playing different roles in their *psychopathic drama* (that is, pawns, patrons, patsies, and police), they will treat some better than others. This disparate, and often subtle, treatment of others may never really be known except to the individuals themselves. And, for reasons explained in chapter 10, they may never come forward to report their feelings. As a result, it may take a very long time for coworkers and management to figure out what is really going on, if they see it at all.

Unfortunately, it is usually only the most gross or egregious treatment of others that gets attention and prompts action. But even this treatment is readily explained away and justified by the corporate psychopath. For example, one psychopathic manager promoted a junior staff member as a reward for her good work, even though another person in the department had more experience and was more deserving of the promotion. The person who was passed over was considered a rival by the psychopath because he had received some positive attention from others in the company. The promotion was designed to block the potential rival's career and to guarantee continued support from an obedient, indebted junior person.

In another case, an individual who had been in a supervisory position for only three years was nominated as a high potential, with an eye toward taking a position as vice president within the next two years. Although there were clearly more qualified people in the organization, the psychopathic nominator was able to persuade the succession committee of his choice. In this case, considerable money, from a limited fund, was spent on developmental activities over the objections of others on the committee. At the end of two years, the "high-potential" candidate was no more ready to assume the responsibilities of a vice president's job than at the time he had been nominated. When he was not promoted he left in disgust, having been promised a great career by his psychopathic boss.

In a third case, a truly high-potential secretary worked for a boss who was well connected politically, but completely incompetent. Realizing the talent of his secretary, he promoted her into an assistant position and began giving her increasingly larger projects to complete. On the surface, this looked like good management practice. The employee was highly motivated, worked toward an MBA at night at a well-respected school, and completed each assignment perfectly. Over time, it became clear to the assistant that her boss really did not know what he was doing and was giving her work that he should be doing. She persevered, however, thinking that her efforts would eventually be recognized by either her boss or those around her. But with the increase in responsibility came increased badgering, abuse, and, ultimately, bullying. Wanting to do a good job, and still learning to be more confident in her own abilities, the assistant took the abuse, convincing herself that she had to pay her dues. Yet in every case, her work was garnering praise for her boss. After five years of abuse, she began sending her résumé to recruiters and discovered the true value of her background, education, and experience. Wanting to stay at the company, however, she went to human resources. She learned that her boss had been complaining about her so much and so often—blaming her for failures on projects to which she was not even assigned—that she could never be considered for promotion. In fact, she had come close to *termination* on more than one occasion. Both she and the human resources staff member were surprised that she had no knowledge of her "poor performance record." All she had ever heard was that there was more for her to learn; all HR had ever heard was that she was an incompetent secretary. Taking her aside, the HR member offered her a transfer to a lower level in a different part of the company, but privately suggested she move on to another company where her talents would be rewarded; her boss was just too well connected.

Vigilance and skepticism on the part of individuals in authority may be the only way to see through this type of scenario.

INABILITY TO TELL THE TRUTH

Most of us were taught, as children, not to lie, and we grew up to be reasonably honest people. Young psychopaths learn how to lie very well. Interviews of criminal psychopaths reveal the most grossly distorted stories and blatant lies, presented in an entertaining, somewhat self-serving, but altogether matter-of-fact style. Even in the face of contrary evidence, the psychopath can lie so well that listeners doubt themselves first, rather than question the psychopath.

Honesty is one of the most important traits in an organization. We have almost never seen an executive's file in which he or she was rated less than perfect on honest and ethical behavior. The problem is twofold. First, it is unpleasant and not socially acceptable to claim that someone is dishonest or unethical. And second, just how do you measure honesty? Is offering a customer a less-than-quality product dishonest business or good materials management? Is avoiding questions about layoffs and downsizing until final decisions are made dishonest or good employee relations? These are difficult calls to make—they are challenges to organizational responsibility and effectiveness—but the psychopath can easily slip through the fog, by appearing honest and ethical on the surface, yet doing things that many would agree are dishonest and unethical.

Pathological lying is a hallmark of psychopaths. They cross back and forth easily between lying and honesty during conversations because they do not have the guilty feelings the rest of us have when we try to tell a lie. Their lies are always woven with a thread of truth, which, if questioned, they indignantly point out in their own defense. Questioning a well-positioned corporate psychopath's honesty can bring its own punishment in the form of retribution against the challenger: "Can you believe what Harry said to me? He called me a liar when I shared with him the information about . . ." one of our psychopaths told an executive about a coworker he wanted to derail.

Organizations can forgive mistakes if the intention was honest and motivated by the best interest of the company. Psychopaths often use these excuses to get themselves out of a jam if caught in a lie, making it difficult to separate the honest employee from the dishonest.

INABILITY TO BE MODEST

Not everyone is modest, yet it is an admirable trait where it exists. Modest people do not brag about their accomplishments but typically enjoy doing a good job for its own sake or accepting only an occasional pat on the back as reward. Many who are modest shun the spotlight, preferring to let the record speak for itself. Modesty may be valued by most employees, but *immodesty* can be equally accepted, if it is justified. Occasionally letting others brag about their successes helps to build relationships. But there is a thin line between justifiable pride and arrogance that is not lost on coworkers.

Both narcissists and Machiavellians tend to be *immodest*, but it is the psychopath's *arrogance* that stands out so clearly to coworkers. Unfortunately, when dealing with higher-ups, the ability of psychopaths to manage and promote their arrogant self-perceptions, and to package them as self-confidence and strong leadership, effectively hides their true nature. Genuine modesty among psychopaths is so rare as to be nonexistent. Its absence, while not an indication of psychopathy directly, can help to corroborate other suspicions.

INABILITY TO ACCEPT BLAME

Taking responsibility for one's own mistakes and not blaming others is highly valued in corporations, as well as in society. Psychopaths rarely, if ever, take responsibility for their actions, even if they clearly made mistakes or their actions and decisions led to failures. But they go a few steps farther; they will not only *blame* others but also create "evidence" that others are to blame. This takes effort, but psychopaths easily integrate it into their game, seizing on opportunities to bring harm to others' careers or professional standing. Clearly, this is a form of lying and quite different from the shifting of blame or pointing fingers that most of us sometimes engage in. This is active, instrumental aggression. Because covert blaming is hard to uncover, it often takes a series of failures of projects under the functional control of the psychopath to produce any significant results.

Fast-paced companies are particularly vulnerable to this problem, as they tend to move people too quickly into new jobs without sufficient evaluation of their current performances. For example, after a year and a half on the job, a manager with psychopathic tendencies was promoted to a higher-level job in a different division. He came with a reputation of decisiveness, good communication skills, and charismatic leadership. His success at initiating innovative new products earned him a reputation as a genius among others in the field. Six months after he left his old position, things started to go wrong. Sales were down, rework was up, and profit margins sagged. The products he had championed were simply not meeting the expectations of either the customers or the company. Despite the fact that his decisions regarding the product were faulty, and implemented contrary to the data collected by the marketing research and manufacturing departments, he easily and effectively blamed those left behind for not picking up the ball. He blamed manufacturing for not being able to build the product to the tight specification of his design; he blamed marketing research for selecting the wrong demographics, and he blamed his replacement for not giving the project the attention and care he had given when he was in charge.

INABILITY TO ACT PREDICTABLY

We are all more comfortable with people who are somewhat predictable, even those who are different from us. Businesses need to know that those working for them will show up at work, perform their jobs according to accepted safety and quality standards, get along with others, and not disrupt the work of others. Even creative types, who may surprise us with their genius, are considered predictable once their day-to-day work habits are understood. What a business cannot afford is what is commonly referred to among management as a loose cannon. These individuals wreak havoc on the normal flow of business as well as on the day-to-day social intercourse of other employees. They disrupt meetings, come up with irrational ideas, embarrass others and the company, and surprise even the most seasoned. Few executives like surprises, and they pride themselves on being aware of the goings on of their business. Because you never know when it will go off, a loose cannon can be the executives' worst nightmare.

Unless one truly understands the machinations of corporate psychopaths, it is almost impossible to predict what they will do. Rarely are others privy to the inner workings of their mind, making them dangerous employees to have on staff.

Astute psychopaths control their behavior while in the presence of those in higher authority, especially if they have identified them as potential pawns or patrons. In most cases, the best sources of information about their erratic behavior are coworkers or supervisors close to them.

INABILITY TO REACT CALMLY

The ability to remain calm during a crisis is the hallmark of good leadership. Psychopaths are quite adept at maintaining their cool when in situations being observed by those in power, especially if this trait is valued by the organization. Yet when out of view, they can overreact in socially inappropriate ways. Many who observe this phenomenon will report them as being dramatic. Occasional outbursts by supervisors, such as when responding to a dangerous safety violation, are acceptable and even expected. But psychopaths tend to overreact in response to perceived personal insults or insufficient demonstration of respect for their authority. This harms the work group, and ultimately the company, because it puts everyone on notice that the psychopath must be treated with kid gloves. Psychopaths become unapproachable, which defeats the purpose of good supervision, open and honest corporate cultures, and free flow of information. Groups subjected to dramatic bosses often lose their cohesion and team spirit, falling back on an "every man for himself" mentality.

Because psychopaths are able to moderate this behavior while in the presence of authority they respect, it can go unnoticed for considerable amounts of time—until they move on and the stories start to emerge. Unfortunately, the only evidence available before a psychopath's departure is rumors and tension in the department. Insightful HR organizations can learn more about what is really going on if they follow up on such information.

INABILITY TO ACT WITHOUT AGGRESSION

Bullying and intimidation have no place in business; they disrupt work, hurt people, and are unfair to those who cannot defend themselves, which often includes most of the company staff. In business settings, overt aggression comes across as *bullying*, while its covert form is *coercion* and *intimidation*. Few executives would argue that these can harm the company. Learning about this type of behavior is often difficult, though, as most bullying is done in private.

Because of the legal ramifications of such behavior, many companies institute no-bullying policies and create confidential mechanisms for affected employees to report this behavior. Codes of conduct often have provisions concerning bullying and intimidation. In some European countries, it is also against the law. To be effective, the policy must be clear and communicated to all. Supervisors and managers must receive training on how to recognize bullying and to deal effectively with it. Employees may also receive training on how to confidentially report abuses in their workplaces.

Psychopaths, despite their charming and engaging personas, are masters of manipulation, intimidation, and coercion. Overt bullying often is a tool of their trade. The problem is that these behaviors, as well as threats of litigation, may also be directed toward those who investigate the complaints.

ACT V, Scene I

CIRCLE THE WAGONS

"Do you have a minute?" asked Frank, peering into John's office.

"Yes, sure, what's up?" asked John, the vice president, putting down his pen.

"I need to talk to you about Dave," started Frank, entering the office, closing the door and taking a seat. "I've been hearing a lot of bad reports about him the past couple of months, and one of my best analysts just asked to be transferred off Dave's project team."

"Transfer? That's not good. You think Dave's the issue?"

"Well, I know he is," said Frank, exasperatedly. "One of my guys came to me two nights back, after hours, to tell me what has been going on." John leaned forward, interested in what Frank had to report. "He said that since the project started, over six months ago, things have been getting steadily worse. Dave has been disrupting and dominating the team to the point that many don't want to work with him anymore. He apparently doesn't come prepared, often comes to the meeting late, leaving a whole room full of people idle, yells at folks, cuts people off while they're making their status reports, and embarrasses them if they make a suggestion. People are afraid to speak up, and they're losing interest in the project because they feel they can't do anything right by Dave."

"That's really odd, Frank. Dave has always come across as a good leader, and I thought he was well liked. Have you spoken to him about this?"

"Yes, the first time was about three months ago, when I read his interim report. It was a mess: a hodgepodge of material he seemed to cobble together because I asked. There was no organization, no synthesis, and no accurate timeline. He couldn't—or wouldn't—even answer some basic questions about the details and figures. I told him I expected more of a status report, complete with his personal analysis and recommendations, and more details about dates, costs, and so forth."

"How did he respond?" asked Frank.

"Well, at first he went ballistic on me, ranting about how we have too many meetings at this company, I should trust him, and on and on. I had to close the door because he was disrupting the floor. After he calmed down, we spoke and I outlined my expectations. He seemed to understand and said he would improve."

"Did he?" asked John.

"Yes, actually he did—dramatically, I'd say. His next two reports were outstanding. I didn't agree completely with the timeline, and some of the material was overly self-serving, but most of it was what you would expect. So I was surprised when I heard things had gotten worse on the people side of the equation; I was under the impression that the team was working well together. Plus, some other things have come up."

"Could it just be a personality clash between Dave and your guy on the team?" interrupted John. "Maybe Dave's style is getting in the way."

"No, I don't think so. This was the second transfer request this week, and my secretary has heard other rumblings through the department. He tried to give one of the temps something to type last week and she told him that he had to get it approved first. Well, he made a big scene and got her crying before she finally agreed. Plus—"

"Frank," started John, slowly, "I have to tell you that Dave came to me about three or so months ago. He complained that you were getting on his case."

"He went to you about me?" said Frank, at first surprised, and then getting annoyed.

"Yes, well, we're on the softball team, you know, so over a beer I asked him how things were going, you know, the usual chitchat, and he started in on you. He seems to have a very short fuse."

"What did he say?" asked Frank.

"Basically, it boiled down to your being too demanding, too detail oriented, stuff like that. I told him that's why you make the big bucks." They both laughed half-heartedly. "I also told him that getting things done on time and in budget is what makes success here, and that he should focus more on pleasing you."

"So maybe it was your pep talk that got to him, not mine," suggested Frank.

"Neither here nor there, Frank. If he's hurting the team and disrupting others, then that's a problem. You should meet with him again," started John. "Did you say you saw him yesterday?"

"No," Frank said. "I wanted to touch base with you first, put together a strategy."

"I think you can meet with him, tell him you've heard things, and see where it takes you," offered John.

"There's more, John," said Frank seriously.

"Oh," John paused. "What?"

Frank continued, "I've heard that Dave hasn't been writing the reports himself or meeting with the other departments to coordinate the different phases. Even some of the other department heads are wondering why Dave is not meeting with them himself. Some say he's not doing any of the work he's supposed to. Apparently, Dorothy is doing most of the heavy work for him."

"There's nothing wrong with delegation, Frank. Maybe he's developing her, or she just wants to be helpful." John paused and thought. "Dorothy? She's not one of yours, is she?" he asked.

"No, she's from Jerry's area. Dave insisted we put her on the team because she's very motivated and can help with the artwork. I really had no problem with it and neither did Jerry," added Frank.

"Hmmm, that's odd. Dave was complaining about some female on the team—I don't think he gave me her name—who wasn't carrying her own weight. He was blaming her for some of the delays; he had to spend all his time tutoring her and fixing her mistakes. I suggested he move her off the team, but he said you wouldn't allow it; you had made a deal with Jerry to give one of his hotshots some exposure to the product development process and couldn't back down."

"Well, no. Putting Dorothy on the team was Dave's idea, and, interestingly enough, Dave never complained to me about her. Jerry does think highly of her, yes, but she needs more experience. I never heard that she wasn't doing well at all; in fact, Dave praises her all the time. He thinks that *Jerry* is holding her back." Frank and John looked at each other.

After a pause, Frank continued, "We've—I've—got a problem, John. There are too many contradictions here. I need to deal with it."

"You're right, we need to find out what is really going on. Look, I have a meeting in a few minutes. Why don't you come back late this afternoon? Bring Dave's file and whatever else you can dig up. Let's review everything first, and then decide what to do."

"Okay," said Frank, getting up and heading toward the door. "I hope this is just a big misunderstanding," he sighed.

"Doubtful, Frank," said John.

10

Hot Buttons and Weak Spots
PERSONAL SELF-DEFENSE

Nancy loved being a traveling nurse. Like many travelers, Nancy had put in her time at a major city hospital, got the experience she needed, and then, at age thirty-two, decided to make a career change. Travelers, she found, get more money, and a bit more respect from the medical staff than the regulars do.

As a young nurse, Nancy was appalled by the egocentricity of the surgeons she worked with; she had been surprised, actually, that they were entirely different than she had fantasized about in school. She used to wonder why some of them weren't sent for psychotherapy, or at least an anger management course. A wise old nursing instructor explained to her, following a public dressing down she received from a doctor, that they act this way—rude, crude, and lewd—because of the intense pressure they face every time they cut into a human body.

"They really do feel for their patients deep down inside," assured the instructor, "but years of making life-and-death decisions hardens them, and their only outlet is to act out in the OR." Nancy accepted this explanation for a while, and it helped her deal with her frustration, but then she learned about traveling nurses and saw an opportunity to work at her craft knowing that she would be on the road in a few months. She knew she couldn't change who the doctors were, and it appealed to her that she could change the working relationship between her and them, so she made the switch.

Then one day she met Marshall. They happened to sit next to each other on a plane as Nancy was moving to a new job in the Midwest, and they struck up a conversation. As often happens when we find ourselves locked into a seat next to a stranger for a few hours, Nancy started to talk about herself to Marshall. Normally not very talkative, Nancy found herself captivated by this handsome man in a dark gray suit who seemed to take an interest in her. When she found out that he was a physician, she got nervous. *Oh, jeez, not a doctor,* she thought, but his calm demeanor and friendly smile eased her concerns.

"My career choice came late in life," he admitted. "It was difficult juggling my schedule to attend classes, particularly the labs, but my boss at the time understood, probably because he was a veteran, too."

"You were in the war?" asked Nancy, beginning to wonder whether Marshall was much older than she had surmised.

"Well, for a short while, but then I got shot down."

"Oh, my God," she said, gasping.

"Yes, well, that's the nature of war—it truly is hell. I couldn't just leave my guys there; I had to save them," he added casually.

"My dad got a Purple Heart in Vietnam; did you get one?" Nancy interrupted excitedly.

Marshall turned toward her, smiled briefly, and then stared coldly. "Medal of Honor," he said so seriously that Nancy feared that she might have offended him.

"Oh, that's really impressive," she said meekly, worrying even more that she had blown the opportunity to finally meet a decent man. "Tell me what happened," she added quickly, hoping to repair the conversation; then, just as quickly, she remembered that her father would never talk about his combat experience. It was just too painful for him. Nancy felt that the conversation was heading into a death spiral, and she didn't know how to save herself.

Marshall, leaning back, closed his eyes briefly and then proceeded to tell her about his war experiences. Nancy listened intently. She couldn't help but be impressed by the valor Marshall showed that day and she felt pride for him and, in a moment of reverie, her late father.

"After I got out I got a job as a private pilot and made good money, but I then decided I wanted to help sick people more than ferry rich ones to and from exotic vacation spots," he said, rolling his eyes. "I guess having the medics sew me back together," Marshall paused, looked away and then back, "I guess I was grateful, and it was then that I decided that I should help others."

Nancy was touched, and toward the end of the flight, when Marshall asked for her phone number, she eagerly obliged.

Marshall and Nancy dated for about four months. While her crazy schedule kept her close to home, Marshall, who lived and worked eighty miles away, made the trek whenever he could steal enough time to stay with her. He always arrived at her place with flowers, candy, a small piece of jewelry, expensive champagne, and sometimes a naughty negligee. Nancy loved all the attention. They dined at fancy restaurants, and being proud of her ability to support herself as a traveling nurse, she often offered to pay.

Their conversations were different than any she had ever had with a man—serious, humorous, lighthearted, and deep. She was always surprised by how much Marshall knew about the world, about people, and about medicine.

At times, she would fantasize about their spending their lives together, but she would catch herself before she got too carried away. Her girlfriends—most of them nurses, as well—repeatedly warned her about *doctors,* but she knew they were envious of her catch and would have fallen for Marshall if they had met him. She never told him about her dreams, for fear of scaring him off. Yet day by day she felt her commitment to him increasing, and judging by his words, she felt he was growing more attached to her as well.

When he told her he was going to borrow some money to start his own private practice—he was tired of the long hours his hospital job required—she got excited and then very nervous. While his current job was hectic, at least he could get time off occasionally. She knew that once he started his own business he would be consumed by it. Entrepreneurs often worked very long hours trying to build their new businesses, and she feared that their visits would diminish.

Maybe I could work in his office as his nurse, she fantasized. *Maybe I could be his business partner!* She had loaned him some cash once to pay a medical school bill, but she could not afford to help him with his new business. *No, I would have to be the office nurse,* she mused before shaking herself from her reverie.

With her four-month assignment ending soon, Nancy hit on the right idea. She decided to apply for an OR position at Marshall's hospital. He would be leaving anyway, so there wouldn't be any conflict or potential for embarrassment, but at least she would be in the same city. And maybe, after a few months, they could move in together. She decided not to mention this to him, fearful that he might misunderstand. *Men get so crazy when they think you're trying to get them to commit,* she reminded herself. She wanted to have the job and her own apartment ready before surprising him one evening with the good news.

Nancy took her cafeteria tray filled with a salad, soup, and tea, and headed toward the group of nurses congregated at one of the tables. Her morning interviews with the medical staff at Marshall's hospital went well, and she now wanted to meet some of her potential coworkers. As a traveling nurse, Nancy enjoyed the chance to meet new people, work in new environments, and then move on before the insanity got to her. "Hi," she said approaching the group. "Is this seat taken?"

"It's yours," responded Rhonda, the most senior person at the table, and the one with the most outgoing personality.

"Thanks," said Nancy, sitting down. "I'm Nancy R, an OR nurse interviewing for an assignment in—"

"We know," interrupted Sally. "We get the scoop from HR on all the new travelers," she said, pointing to one of the women at the end of the table, who nodded. "Welcome."

As Sally made the introductions of those at the table, Nancy carefully noted their names, having learned early on that remembering coworkers' names was a critical first step to success at any location. Some staff nurses resented a traveler. Nancy was not sure why, but she always made it a policy to start on the best terms with everyone she met at her new assignments.

"Have you met the crazies yet?" asked Susie, referring to the OR medical staff.

"Well, I was interviewed by Dr. S, who seemed real decent, and then Dr. H."

"Oh, those are the *normals*," interrupted Susie. "Wait until you meet the second shift!" The others at the table rolled their eyes.

"Does Dr. M work on the second shift?" she asked, her curiosity about Marshall getting the better of her.

"Haven't heard about that one," said Rhonda, puzzling. "Are you sure he works here?"

"Oh, well, I heard his name mentioned earlier today, and I was just wondering," said Nancy, hoping she had not said too much.

"We did have an M, Marshall M, on the third shift. He was a transporter, but he doesn't work here anymore," chimed in Sandra, the union rep for the nurses. A few of the women at the table visibly stirred at the mention of Marshall, but Sandra continued. "Got into a bit of trouble with one of the residents. Don't know any *doctor* by that name, though. You, Sally?"

"No, not since I've been here, which is going on twelve years," said a quiet, older nurse at the end of the table.

"Well, Marshall was a looker all right, did an okay job, but always fantasized about being a doctor someday. I think he moved to County General, not sure," added Rhonda.

"Oh, I must be mistaken," said Nancy, beginning to get nervous. She hurriedly finished her lunch and got up to make her exit. "I've got to see about my new apartment. Sorry, I have to run."

"So we'll see you in two weeks?" asked Rhonda.

"Yes, yes, I'll be here!" chimed Nancy with a big smile.

As she got into her car, she picked up her cell phone. She decided to call Marshall to find out what was going on. His cell rang and rang. She realized that she did not have his address. As her anxiety grew, she decided to drive over to County General Hospital.

Nancy parked her car in County General's visitor's lot and walked to the main entrance. When her turn came, she said to the guard at the desk, "Hi. I'm here to see Dr. Marshall M. He's a surgeon."

The guard flipped the pages of his hospital phone directory and searched. "He's a doctor here?" he asked, puzzling over the list on his desk.

"Yes. He just started here, I heard."

"Oh," said the guard without looking up. He turned to the computer screen and typed. "Hmm. Are you sure about the name, miss?"

"Yes. Maybe he—"

"Well, we have someone by that name; looks like the night shift, but he's not your surgeon." The guard looked up, adding, "Sorry. You might want to call his office to get the location. We have quite a few buildings here."

"Thanks," said Nancy, a tight smile across her face. "I'll do that." She headed for the door and then stopped. Glancing at her watch, she thought for a moment. Turning, she walked over to the coffee shop at the end of the lobby and bought a large cup of tea and a doughnut. Taking a seat with a view of the entrance, she decided to wait.

What to Do?

Having a psychopath in your life can be an emotionally draining, psychologically debilitating, and sometimes physically harmful experience. We have received numerous letters and e-mails from individuals who believe a psychopath has victimized them. Their often detailed and pleading communications have given us a glimpse into the impact that psychopathic manipulation and abuse has had on their lives. In some cases, we have suggested that individuals call the local police or civil authorities. In many cases, we referred them to qualified psychologists, psychiatrists, counselors, members of the clergy, or other professionals in their area who are best suited to provide the help they need.

Look into His Heart—and Look Again

"He is such a caring man. So intelligent. He can always find the right words to reach your heart. You must love him."

—Woman who befriended a rapist/murderer on death row

"I've lied all my life, but I'm not lying now."

—Defendant in a fraud trial

Over the years we noticed a pattern in the reports from letter writers and those we interviewed. Much like psychopaths, who operate through a parasitic assessment-manipulation-abandonment process, the targets themselves seemed to unwittingly share a parallel response pattern. In this chapter, we will attempt to outline the development of the psychopath-victim relationship in such a way as to enlighten the reader to traps and pitfalls along the path. We believe the best defense against the dark art of psychopathic manipulation is to fully understand how psychopaths operate and to take every opportunity to avoid them.

1. Learn All You Can About Psychopathy

In chapter 3, we described psychopathic traits and characteristics in some detail. We believe that the best defense against psychopathic manipulation is to learn all you can about psychopaths and their nature. While even experts are sometimes fooled, improving your ability to see past their "mask of normalcy" is crucial to your ability to *resist* their machinations. And knowing how to recognize and interpret their true motives may help you make the decision to distance yourself from them.

2. Avoid Labeling Someone a Psychopath

You should resist the temptation to label someone a psychopath, especially if you are not formally trained and qualified to conduct psychological assessments. The term itself has many negative connotations—some of which may not apply to the individual in question—and once used has a tendency to stick. Careless or inappropriate application of the label would be unfair and might lead to litigation and other forms of retaliation. For most practical purposes, it is sufficient to be aware that a given individual appears to have many of the traits and behaviors that define psychopathy. Trying to "psychoanalyze," redeem, or change one of these individuals is a "mug's game" you cannot hope to win.

A Few Trees Do Not a Forest Make

Don't make the mistake of turning one or two characteristics or symptoms into a general personality assessment or diagnosis. "He's impulsive, short-tempered, and just plain nasty. I think he's a psychopath." The careless use of the term is particularly common in personal disputes. If we don't like someone, or if the person is seen as an adversary, a competitor, a threat, or as not meeting our needs, we may tend to use any piece of "revealing" information, relevant or not, to conclude that he or she *must* be a psychopath. Keep in mind that a qualified professional would use the term only with strong evidence of a very heavy dose of the defining features, and even then, judiciously.

3. Learn All You Can About Yourself

"Know thyself" is perhaps one of the wisest bits of advice ever spoken. Self-knowledge will strengthen your immunity against psychopaths' games; it is crucial for your psychological, emotional, and, possibly, physical survival. Psychopaths feed on what they see as naïveté and innocence.

We are all somewhat reluctant to hear about our faults and weaknesses. Some people avoid going to the doctor because they don't want to know whether their aches and pains reflect something serious. Some avoid talking to psychologists because they fear they will learn something uncomfortable about themselves. Psychopaths are well aware of these concerns and capitalize on them. In effect, a perceptive psychopath may know you better than you know yourself.

The more you know who you are, the better able you will be to defend against psychopathic influence.

4. Understand Your Own Utility to Psychopaths

The most common types of *utility* attractive to psychopaths relate to money, power, fame, and sex, but in organizational life, this list grows to include access to information, communication, influence, authority, and so forth. Psychopaths target not only executives and celebrities, but others with more subtle value (such as informal power and influence), as well.

It can be difficult to appreciate what your worth might be to a psychopath, in part because society often requires us to play down our assets. A realistic assessment, however, supported by information and feedback from friends, family, and professional colleagues, can help you clarify your strengths and value to others.

Psychopaths use impression management to get you to share your assets with them. They may prey on your generosity, trusting nature, or sense of charity. They may cause you to take pity on them, if that feeling gets you to help them in some way or gets you to use your influence with others who could help them fulfill their needs. The difficulty lies in separating those in real need, whom you should help, from those who rely on psychopathic manipulation to get you to do so.

A good defense is to routinely apply some *critical thinking* and common sense to social interactions, particularly those that involve people you do not know well. We all like to be complimented, but there is a difference between harmless social stroking and oily flattery designed to ingratiate and manipulate. The problem is that we don't always notice the difference, particularly if we do not have a realistic picture of who we are, and if we are dealing with a psychopath skilled in painting the sort of picture we would like to see. Excessive or incongruous compliments and flattery should be a signal for you to pay critical attention to what is coming next. Ask yourself, "What does this person *really* want of me?"

5. Understand Your Hot Buttons and Weak Spots

We all have *hot buttons* and *weak spots*. Hot buttons are those things that provoke an automatic—often emotional—reaction from you, get you excited, or set you off. For example, you may react with envy and depression when your colleague gets promoted, and with sudden frustration or anger when someone cuts you off in traffic, gets credit for your work, or is critical of the way you dress. You may react with pleasure when complimented on your looks, with anticipation and joy when your candidate is ahead in the polls or when a player on your team hits a home run. Hobbies are often hot-button topics and tend to provoke positive reactions out of most people. Likewise, passion for one's work can provoke intense energy and excitement, especially when someone takes an interest in what you do for a living.

When someone presses one of our hot buttons, our attention may be diverted from more important things in our social environment, and our evaluation of a person or situation may be colored by the feelings and reactions triggered by the hot button. This reflex-like tendency—to let hot buttons get the better of us—is not lost on the psychopath or any manipulative person. They will identify your hot buttons and will push them to test their utility. They will use this information to establish in you a mood that is conducive to their current interests and schemes.

It is difficult, except in the most blatant situations, to tell whether someone has purposely pushed your hot button or has inadvertently done so without any particular intent to manipulate or use you. In fact, many legitimate friendships are started when someone has pushed a hot button in an effort to genuinely befriend you. A psychopath's attempt to use your hot buttons against you—for example, to make you lose control in front of someone of importance—will quickly be labeled a mistake by him or her, if challenged. You may even receive a public apology. However, if the psychopath's motive is to embarrass or humiliate you in front of others, then the damage is already done to your *reputation*, as described in chapter 11.

Often, the psychopath will press your buttons privately, convincing you that he or she understands and shares similar feelings—a ploy to build rapport. For example, you may complain about being irritated or hurt by some inconvenience, slight, or perceived insult by another employee. The psychopath need only say, "Oh, my God. She didn't!" and you will begin to feel that the psychopath understands and possibly even shares your feelings about the offending event or person. The astute psychopath will then listen to you spill your guts about things, events, and people, thereby ingratiating himself with you and providing information that can potentially be used to manipulate you later on in the relationship.

Learning all you can about your hot buttons is a first defense against having them pushed unscrupulously. Unfortunately, it is far easier to become *aware* of one's hot buttons than to learn to *control* them. Feedback from others, including family members, close friends, or professional colleagues (through 360-degree assessments), is the best source of information about your hot buttons, especially those of which you are not aware. Practice, with the assistance of a trusted friend or professional coach, can help you learn to control or at least moderate your reactions. Eventually, you will improve in your ability to quickly recognize a hot-button reaction as it starts, allowing you time to put on the brakes and to regain control of your reactions.

Like all predators, psychopaths are attuned to the *weak spots* of those with whom they interact. There are many types of human weakness, and the astute psychopath knows most of them. For simplicity, we will focus on three common categories: flaws, lacks, and fears.

What is wrong with you—too heavy, too thin, or too shy? We often see *flaws* in ourselves that others do not see. Some are real, but many of these exist only in our imaginations. Psychopaths are adept at identifying those things that *you* like least about *yourself*, and at using them as *currency* in their dealings with you.

The psychopath will try to convince you that he or she accepts you as you are, despite any flaws you think you have. This is a very powerful and reassuring message for someone to hear and is the foundation for the psychopathic bond. Eventually, the psychopath may reveal that he or she shares the same flaws with you, deepening your sense of connectedness and anticipation that a strong personal relationship can be built.

Having a realistic picture of your flaws is important for your defense against psychopathic manipulation. This usually involves paring down the list in your mind to those that *really* matter, and then challenging those that remain on your list. You may decide to improve some and accept others. Once you make these assessments and decisions about your flaws, it becomes more difficult for others to manipulate you through them.

What is missing in your life—self-esteem, love, understanding, excitement, or enough chocolate? Believing we have less than we should of something influences our thoughts, feelings, and behaviors. We sometimes resent those who have more than we do. We begin to doubt our own abilities to provide and achieve. We may decide we are failures. We feel the need to fill the void, sometimes at any cost.

Craving the things we *lack* leads to a vulnerable state, psychologically, emotionally, and sometimes physically. In this state, people are consumed with thoughts and dreams of fulfilling their desires, making them easy targets for psychopaths who are all too ready to help. For example, promising to give you what you crave—but with no intention of delivering—is a common technique used in pyramid scams and street games, such as three-card monte. In these economic schemes, often perpetrated by *manipulative* psychopaths, you are led to believe that you can make a lot of money, but you usually lose everything before realizing you have been taken. In another example, a psychopathic puppetmaster may entice you to join him in a criminal act to help him pay a debt or to get even with someone. The crime may involve stealing money, supplies, or trade secrets from

your company; damaging property belonging to others; or even hurting your own family members. This is especially appealing if the psychopath convinces you that you will *never* get caught and that the
victims will only get what they deserve. Perhaps, but you now are indebted to the psychopath. This will come back to haunt you.

Giving Them What They Deserve

Grifters are well described in the movies. Typically, they are
portrayed as highly intelligent and creative individuals who target only greedy "marks" who deserve what happens to them.
Their elaborate schemes make for good entertainment, almost a
morality tale in which the grifter feels justified in using the mark's
larcenous nature as a lever for the swindle. The grifter may be a
rogue, but a charming one who otherwise is ethical and unlikely
to swindle decent people.

The reality, of course, is not so benign. Many of the grifter's
victims are simply gullible, trusting, or naïve, and hardly deserve
to lose their life savings to a charming rogue simply because they
present weaknesses or vulnerabilities that can be exploited. Paul
Newman's character in *The Sting* may be likable but has few
counterparts in the real world.

What are you afraid of—intimacy, loneliness, or speaking in
front of a group? All of us have fearful moments, times when we are
plagued by questions and doubts. Unless these thoughts are debilitating or intrude in our day-to-day lives, they are within the range of
normal. Yet our fears, once identified by the psychopath, provide
clues as to how we will react in certain situations and events, and thus
become potent tools for manipulation. Defense against this use of
our fears is difficult, for they are the product of both nature and nurture, and therefore not easy to modify. A certified counselor or mental health professional may help us to appreciate how vulnerable we
become in the face of what we fear and to adopt protective strategies.

6. Understand How Psychopaths Manipulate Others

The more that you understand about how psychopaths operate, their *modus operandi*, the better prepared you will be to avoid being manipulated by them. In chapter 3, we reviewed the phases that make up the parasitic lifestyle adopted by many psychopaths: (1) *assessment* of the individual's potential utility, weaknesses, and defenses; (2) the use of impression management and manipulation to ingratiate themselves with the individual and then to siphon off resources; and (3) *abandonment*, the phase in which the individual is no longer of use to the psychopath.

Nonetheless, even the most experienced psychologists can be taken in by the blandishments of a charming psychopath, so there is never a guarantee that you will be safe. However, this should not dissuade the reader from learning more about how psychopaths manipulate others.

Powerful Allies

Crime is the result of a complex mix of socioeconomic and psychological factors, many of which are beyond the control of the individual. However, loopholes in the law, inconsistent judicial responses, fascination with the dark side of human nature, thinly disguised fascination with those who bend the rules or do it their way, and a curious tendency to rationalize even the most egregious misbehavior also are important reasons for the prevalence and tolerance of criminal behavior in our society.

As a society, we tend to attribute the causes of an antisocial or criminal act more to outside forces than to choices an individual makes. Indeed, this diffusion of responsibility is big business; witness the large number of psychologists, psychiatrists, social workers, and counselors ready and eager to explain or exculpate criminal behaviors. This is good for criminals in general and for psychopaths in particular. The latter make effective use of the belief that everyone is good at heart, only needs a chance, and is capable of genuine reform. Perhaps this is why so many of those in the helping professions find themselves in big trouble by trying to help a psychopath. As one psychopath put it, "I love do-gooders because they do me such good."

Many victims are unwitting participants in psychopathic manipulation. We have found repeatedly, in the cases reported to us in e-mails, letters, and interviews with victims, that *many did not know that they were dealing with a psychopath until it was too late*. While the specific details of each case may differ, the feelings, attitudes, behaviors, and outcomes the victims described seemed to form a pattern or process. What follows is our understanding of these stages, roughly in the order they seem to appear: temptation (your curiosity goes up, your guard comes down), bonding (you believe you have found the perfect relationship), collusion (wanting to please them, you give in to their expectations and demands), self-doubt and denial (you blame yourself for their unhappiness; you are blind to the truth), abuse (you take what they dish out), realization (you see that you have been played the fool), shame (you feel too embarrassed to tell others or seek help), anger and vindication (you want to get even; you repair the damage done).

7. Avoid Temptation (Good Luck!)

First impressions can be deceiving. Unfortunately, the first impressions most of us have of psychopaths are positive. Their manifest charm, attractive appearance, verbal fluency, and adroit use of flattery and ego stroking can be very effective. But these impressions are like the promise offered by the jacket of a bad book. The unfortunate difference is that we seldom buy a book without first flipping through the pages or at least reading some reviews, whereas we often accept the psychopathic façade at face value. With psychopaths, what you see is not what you get, but it may take a lot of pain before you realize this. Because not all psychopaths are alike in their presentation, you may experience the pain more than once. Perhaps we all would be better off if we were to exert at least a modicum of cautious—even suspicious—evaluation in new social encounters, particularly those that potentially can have some impact on our lives. At the very least, we should reevaluate our first impressions as more information about the individuals becomes available. Note that not everyone feels comfortable during an encounter with a psychopath, for reasons that are not entirely clear.

"But He Just Needs a Good Woman"

The ability of psychopaths to get others to take enormous risks for them is stunning to outside observers. In many cases, it is professional women who do the dirty work and, in the process, destroy their own careers.

In *Without Conscience*, Hare described at length the exploits of John Grambling, a well-educated, well-connected, and sophisticated scamster whose ability to steal or obtain money fraudulently from family, friends, and banks was so remarkable that one banker suggested that he "should be compelled to wear a bell around his neck." He was caught, convicted, and sent to prison.

Coincident with his release after seven years, a psychiatrist at his prison attended one of Hare's workshops. The psychiatrist had read *Without Conscience* and informed Hare that, while in prison, Grambling had an affair with the prison psychologist and that they planned to marry following his release. This same psychologist did psychological evaluations for the parole board and previously had attempted to gain Grambling's early release. The psychiatrist stated that the interesting thing about the affair was that he had showed a copy of *Without Conscience* to the psychologist, but that it apparently had no effect on her "love" for Grambling.

The psychologist's actions were in violation of state and professional guidelines. She lost her job and her reputation. We don't know the psychologist's motives for her actions, but we do know that what she did is not at all uncommon in prisons.

---

8. Avoid the Psychopathic Bond

Subtle charm, impression management, and manipulation techniques may convince you that a psychopath likes who you are. You may feel excited at this time, believing that the psychopath genuinely likes and respects you. You also may "know" that the relationship, whether personal or professional, will grow.

Over the course of a long conversation or a series of meetings, a psychopath will try to convince you that he shares many of your likes, dislikes, traits, and attitudes. This need not be stated openly; in fact, psychopathic manipulation can be so subtle that you might be guided to this conclusion just by hearing the psychopath's life story. Of course, psychopathic stories are carefully crafted to mesh with an individual's hot buttons and weak spots. In all of the cases we have reviewed, the thought of finding someone who shared their values, beliefs, and life experiences was very seductive.

At this point, the psychopath tries to convince you that his integrity is without question, and that the relationship is based on honesty and trust. At this stage most individuals report having shared a goodly amount of personal information with the psychopath, believing that the things they had learned about the psychopath's life were true and deeply personal. They did not suspect that they were being lied to or that much of what they had heard was fabrication.

Psychopaths eventually guide you into believing that the two of you are unique, very special, and destined to be together. They portray themselves as the perfect friends, employees, or business partners. This may take considerable time and effort on their part, and the grooming will be subtle. The sad truth is that the psychopathic bond is a sham; it does not exist except in your mind. You now are potentially open to psychopathic use and abuse.

Sensitivity to the bonding process is good preventive medicine. Be wary of falling for someone's story too quickly. Solid relationships take time to develop and grow; apply critical thinking and careful assessment along the way. If you feel that this person is *too* good to be true, try to prove yourself wrong.

9. Do Not Collude in the Psychopath's Game

Once the psychopathic bond is firmly established you will find that your hot buttons and weak spots are used to gain your compliance and to reaffirm the relationship. Surprisingly, the resultant back and forth may strengthen rather than weaken the relationship. Criticism ("You're too fat; nobody else will love you!"), threats ("I'm not putting up with this anymore, I'm leaving!") or intimidation ("Don't make me hurt you!") are effective manipulation and coercive techniques. This is especially true in relationships in which you find yourself doing what the psychopath asks (even if it is not in your own best interest) in order to maintain the intense bond. Healthy relationships tend to be balanced, with each person giving and taking. Psychopathic relationships are one-sided; you give and the psychopath takes (money, a place to live, sex, power, control).

Fighting Satan

Derry Mainwaring Knight was sentenced to six years in prison in England for defrauding a number of wealthy and influential Christians who believed they were helping him to fight devil worshippers in a satanic cult. He had ingratiated himself into a church community and convinced the members that the devil had taken hold of him and that the only way to break away was for him to become head of his own organization, the Sons of Lucifer. In this way, he said, he could destroy the satanic cult from within. But to do so, he needed to buy a great deal of expensive satanic regalia and black magic artifacts.

The rector of the church was hooked, and enlisted the support and financial aid of many prominent politicians and businessmen. One even provided a Rolls-Royce automobile so that Knight could impress other members of the cult. The money he received was spent on a lavish lifestyle. He was charged with nineteen counts of fraud.

In his defense, he stated that he had no need to defraud anyone because he made up to $25,000 a week from his prostitution ring! Following his conviction, his mother stated that he had bilked her of $92,000. She also said, "He often told me that you can always take Christians for a ride because they won't take you to the law. Jail is probably the best thing that could happen to him."

In many cases, friends, family, and coworkers see what is going on and may try to warn you. Well-meaning comments such as, "He's no good for you," "Get out of that relationship," and "You can't trust him or her" often go unheeded or may lead to your estrangement from family and friends. The psychopath reinforces the isolation, and sometimes, as in the case of psychopathic cult leaders, demands it.

They Don't Get It: 3

Sebastian Burns and Atif Rafay were given three life terms for savagely murdering Rafay's mother, father, and sister in Washington state for $500,000 in insurance money. Rafay and Burns apparently believed that most people were stupid, that intelligent people were above the law, and that the only crime is to get caught. But it is Burns who stands out as the more calculating, callous, arrogant, and grandiose.

Following their conviction, Burns addressed the court in a two-hour rambling, self-serving oratory described by the judge as "chilling" and by the prosecutor as something he had never seen before: "But then, I've never seen anyone like Sebastian Burns before. He's a psychopath," he said.

Reporters described Burns as being tremendously articulate, more like a high-school debater than a convicted criminal, and as holding some audience members spellbound. The judge commented, "Mr. Burns, you are not immoral, you are amoral. You have no moral rudder whatsoever. You are an arrogant, convicted killer. You will be responsible for your premeditated, naked, vicious massacre of this family." Burns portrayed himself as a victim and said the police got him to brag about the murders so that he would impress important criminals who were trying to recruit him.

Hare's view is that the court performance by Burns was bombastic, disjointed, contradictory, confusing, and confused. The fact that some members of the audience found it compelling is a tribute to the ability of some psychopaths to put on a good show without saying anything of substance.

While he was in custody, the twenty-six-year-old Burns was caught having sexual relations with his forty-three-year-old married public defender. The Bar Association recommended that she be suspended for one year, but the state supreme court increased her suspension to two years and ordered that she undergo a psychological evaluation before being reinstated.

If you find yourself being dominated by a boss or coworker or on an emotional roller coaster, seek outside confirmation. If you find that the interactions are damaging, it is time to end it. Often, family, friends, and coworkers can assist you or provide you emotional support as you transition out. In abusive situations, you may need to get the advice and assistance of the authorities or other trained professionals.

10. Try to Deal with Self-Doubt and Denial

The opportunistic, deceptive, and manipulative behaviors of psychopaths can be as bewildering to the victims as they are devastating. Many victims become racked with self-doubt, blaming themselves for whatever has happened. Others deny that there is any problem at all. In each case, doubts and concerns about the psychopaths in their lives are converted into *doubts about themselves.* The problem is greatly exacerbated when a victim cannot convince others, including family and friends, that someone else is the cause of the problem. "Everyone thought that *I* was the problem" is a common refrain of those who have dealt with a psychopath.

If you are lucky, others may see things for what they are. In an organizational setting, these can be coworkers with no utility to the psychopath, former victims, or the organizational police (see chapter 6) who are sensitized to the possibility of manipulation and deceit. In one's personal life, these can be family members and friends.

Unfortunately, it is very difficult to convince someone in the grips of a psychopathic bond that they have missed something or do not have a complete picture of what is going on. Even when data are presented to these victims (perhaps a suspicious motel receipt or a mysterious charge on a personal credit card), they exhibit denial. Like the psychopath, they may blame others for falsifying the information, they may slough it off as a misunderstanding, or they may even conclude that it is nobody else's business because of the degree of trust they put in the psychopath.

It is very difficult to help someone consumed with self-doubt and denial. The best that family, friends, and coworkers can do is to help the victims get the assistance they need either through referrals to an employee assistance program or other trained mental health professionals. At the same time, concerned observers should be alert to the possibility of continued or escalating abuse at the hands of the psychopath.

11. If Abused, Seek Help Immediately

Should victims raise questions to the psychopath about his or her behavior or decide to ask the psychopath about inconsistencies they have noticed, they risk retribution. At first, the psychopath may vehemently deny any improprieties, and turn the game into an attack on the complainant. At this stage, most victims will feel ashamed that they doubted the psychopath, and will come to doubt themselves even more. Should they persist in expressing doubt or concern, they will certainly suffer escalating abuse at the hands of the irritated psychopath.

Abuse can take many forms but usually affects us in three ways: psychologically, emotionally, and physically.

Physical abuse, the most obvious, can be manifested in blackened eyes, bruises, cuts, and so on. Often, as in the case of abused spouses, physical aggression goes unreported. Family members, astute friends, and coworkers who notice it may try to intervene, but are often forced to stand by helplessly because the victim refuses their assistance. *Any* type of physical abuse is dangerous, as psychopaths—along with other abusers—tend to escalate their attacks over time.

Emotional and psychological abuse is much harder to evaluate by outsiders, although it can be devastating to those in a psychopathic relationship. Emotional abuse often leads to anxiety, distress, depression, inability to sleep, and generalized fear. Psychological abuse can lead to lowered self-esteem, feelings of unworthiness, self-doubt, and psychological pain. Individuals abused by psychopaths feel they are not themselves or something is wrong with *them*. They often blame themselves for the abuse, wondering, "What did I do wrong?" Because our thoughts and feelings affect how we behave, victims may begin to do poorly on their jobs and get easily distracted, agitated, reticent, or overly emotional. Psychopaths use emotional and psychological abuse to control their victims.

If a victim of abuse, you should seek advice and counsel from those around you—friends, family members, or trusted colleagues—or, depending on the type of abuse, the authorities or human services providers dealing with these types of issues.

Is Your Partner a Psychopath?

Recent research indicates that about 20 to 25 percent of the men who persistently abuse and batter their wives or partners are psychopaths. In many jurisdictions spousal assault results in jail time, but some courts give the abuser a choice of going to jail or taking part in a court-mandated treatment program, particularly if he is well educated, articulate, and without a previous criminal record. This may be the only time a psychopath will voluntarily seek treatment. The problem is that he will *appear* to make good progress, receive a document attesting to this progress, and will return to his partner a "much-improved man."

The reality is that there is *no evidence* that psychopaths derive any benefit from treatment or management programs. The consequences of this exercise in futility are borne by the partner. Psychopathic batterers should not be given the option of avoiding jail by undertaking treatment.

12. What to Do When You Realize You Have Been a Pawn

Eventually, the unexplained lies, inconsistencies, negative feelings, and feedback from friends and family reach a point when the victim begins to realize that he or she has been a pawn in a psychopath's game. It may take a lot of validation, and a lot of time, for the realization to sink in.

Love Fraud

Donna Andersen is a freelance writer in Atlantic City, New Jersey, who was conned and bilked of her savings by a psychopathic bigamist, James Alwyn Montgomery. In trying to make sense of what had happened to her, she read Hare's book *Without Conscience*. "His book described Montgomery precisely," she wrote on her website (www.lovefraud.com), to which the reader is referred for extensive personal accounts of her own experiences and those of others who have been burned by psychopaths (whom she refers to as *sociopaths*). She wrote, "Montgomery told me two kinds of lies:

- **Lies mixed with truth**. His story would be plausible, but I'd notice inconsistencies. When I questioned the discrepancies, he would either explain them away or accuse me of being paranoid.

- **Totally brazen lies**. A normal person, even one prone to exaggeration, would never think of making the extraordinary claims that Montgomery made. For example, Montgomery said he was awarded the Victorian Cross, Australia's highest military honor, for his heroism in the Vietnam War. Well, he never won the medal. He never served in Vietnam. And even though he walked my dog every morning wearing a Special Forces beret, he never served in the military."

Once you understand what has happened, you may feel like a patsy or a fool. Many former victims report saying to themselves, "How could I have fallen for these lies?" or "I'm such a fool." This is a normal feeling, but it is not without its costs. People who feel like fools wish to hide their foolishness. Rather than seek out confirmation or validation of their new view of the psychopath, they tend to avoid others. They sometimes believe that others have not seen what is going on, and while this may be the case, it is far better to confide

in trusted friends and family than to allow the perception of foolishness to fester. Talking about your experiences and writing in a journal are good ways to dissipate your foolish feelings. You may also
want to begin documenting what had transpired since you met the
psychopath. Clearly, you should check your finances, personal documents, and other valuables that might have been taken or misused by
the psychopath. It is important that you distance yourself and take
action to protect yourself from further contact and retribution.

13. Work Through Your Feelings of Shame

Shame is a natural response to abuse. Because of this, many abusive
situations go unreported. It is imperative that any feelings of shame
be discussed with family, friends, or a trained professional. The first
reason is that you do not deserve to feel shame, just as you did not
deserve to be abused. It was not your fault; the psychopath is a predator and you were a target and victim. The second reason to seek help
is that shame itself leaves you vulnerable to continued psychopathic
manipulation. Consider some abused wives who, despite beatings
and verbal assaults, beg their abusive husbands to take them back or
go on to new abusive partners. It is just as easy for a psychopath to
use your own shame against you as it was to use your flaws, lacks, and
fears in the first place. Do not let shame for being conned prevent
you from seeking help and guidance; do not let the psychopath use it
as a weapon against you.

14. Anger and Vindication

By the time victims contact us, they are in the stage where they feel
intense anger toward the person who manipulated and abused them,
and they want to get even. We believe that this may be a healthier
stage to be in, *as long as the victim does not act on these feelings.*

Anger and the need for vindication are normal emotional and psychological responses, part of the repair and regrowth process. The anger often comes from the residual feelings victims have had all along but could not express because of fear and submission. It is critical that former victims work on their angry feeling with a trained mental health professional.

The need for vindication seems to be satisfied, at least for some people, by confirmation that the person who victimized them was truly a psychopath. Many victims have reported that the more they learned and understood about the psychopathic process the better they felt.

Some individuals want to uncover the psychopath for what he or she is. This is best left to the authorities if a crime has been committed. However, warning friends about the behaviors to watch out for can be useful and possibly save someone else from falling into a psychopath's web of deceit.

ACT V, Scene II

UNRAVELING THE PUZZLE

Frank arrived at John's office a little after 3 P.M., his arms loaded with files.

"Want some coffee?" asked John, standing at the credenza with a coffeepot in his hands.

"Yes, that would be great. I think we might be here a while," answered Frank, putting his files on the coffee table and walking over to John. "What did you find out?" asked John.

"A lot, and it's not good. Apparently, the team problem is just the tip of the iceberg. I pulled Dave's personnel jacket, spoke at length with some of the folks on the team, and got an earful from some of the other department heads, including Tim in purchasing and Matthew in security."

"Security? Oh, boy, this is going to be good. Why don't you start at the top?"

"Well," began Frank, "while checking Dave's personnel file I noticed some discrepancy between his original letter, his résumé, and his application blank."

"Yes, what kind of discrepancy?" asked John, leaning forward.

"Apparently, he listed three different, although very similar, college degrees on these documents. I wasn't sure if this was intentional or just a clerical mistake, so I asked Melanie to check his education. Turns out that the university on his résumé was actually one of those online diploma mills. It's bogus."

"Why hadn't Melanie brought this to our attention before?" asked John with concern.

"Well, she hadn't checked his background because we offered the job to him on the spot, remember? She said that normally she follows up on these things once—"

"I remember, yes, we jumped the gun," said John, shaking his head. "What else did she find out?"

"He doesn't have a criminal record."

"That's nice to know," interrupted John.

"But he does have quite a few speeding tickets. Not really an issue, but since we're taking a closer look, I asked her to get everything she could." Frank sipped his coffee and continued, "I also found a note in his file from Tim asking Dave to—" Frank pulled out the note and read, " 'stop ordering supplies and equipment directly from suppliers.' " Frank looked up to find John staring at him. "Yes, apparently he's been using his signature authority to buy a new computer, some peripherals, and a few small things without going through channels. Eventually, one of the internal auditors questioned Tim and he followed up with a note to Dave."

"What did Dave say to Tim?" asked John.

"He said he was sorry, was new to the company, wouldn't do it again, et cetera."

"And nobody ever mentioned this to you?"

"No, Tim bought Dave's story and decided to put a copy of the note in his personnel file should anything ever come up about it," answered Frank. "Melanie also suggested I talk to Matt in security, and he told me that Dave had caused a scene one day when a guard wouldn't let him park up front."

"Well, Matt's group can sometimes blow things out of proportion," said Frank.

"It wasn't the only incident. Dave tried to enter the building after hours when he was new and didn't have card access. He apparently went ballistic on the young lady at the desk, threatened to have her fired, and so on. So she wrote it up. Eventually, he asked me for access, and now, according to Matt, Dave and this guard are 'best buddies.' "

"Please, let's not start any rumors about that kind of thing."

"I've got some more from Melanie."

"Okay," said John, pouring a second cup of coffee.

"She tried to check some of Dave's references and found that out of the four he listed, one no longer worked at the company, two would only give neutral comments, and one said he was a 'great guy.' However, Melanie said that when the phone was answered on the last one, it sounded more like a fraternity house than a company." John frowned, and Frank continued, "so she did some digging around and came up with two contacts at Dave's last two companies who agreed that he was trouble." Frank picked up his notes and read, "Quote 'He's a loose cannon, always chewing people out, lies a lot, a back-stabbing ass-kisser,' unquote."

"Pretty much what your guys are telling you," stated John.

"Yes, the picture fits. And the new product project—"

"Yes?" said John, hesitantly.

"The whole idea, from concept to action plan, even the executive committee proposal presentation, was Dorothy's work. Dave just tapped into her and took her ideas as his own."

"You got that from Jerry?" asked John.

"Yeah, he never suspected, but Dorothy found a copy of the presentation on Dave's desk and saw that her name wasn't on it, so she confronted Dave in the meeting two days ago. He talked around it, telling her that I took her name off the slides. She then went to Jerry, who came to me this morning, but I had already gotten the story from my guy who wants off the team."

"What else?" asked John, finishing his coffee and putting down his cup.

"That pretty much sums it up; there are more incidents and other details, but the bottom line is Dave is not the guy we thought he was. He can't be trusted. I can't trust him."

"I agree, he doesn't belong here," said John, glancing at his watch. "I'm sure Melanie has left for the day; let's take a walk over to Jack's office and see if we can shut this operation down tonight. Dave's only been here about ten or eleven months, right?" Frank nodded. "Good, this shouldn't be much of a problem. Melanie can draw up the letter tomorrow."

Frank could see the lights were still on in the executive wing and felt relieved. As they headed down the hall, they ran into Victoria, Jack Garrideb's secretary, leaving for the day. "Hi," said John. "Is Jack still in?"

"You know he is, John," smiled Victoria. "Mr. Garrideb never gets out before the cleaning folks arrive."

"Yeah, you're right about that," said Frank, smiling. "Is he busy?"

"He has someone in his office. I didn't see who; they must have come in while I was at the copier. But you can hang out and wait if you like."

"I think we will," said Frank, smiling at Victoria as she left.

John and Frank took seats near Victoria's desk, positioning themselves so they could see when Jack finished his meeting and opened the door. They took the time available to review their material on Dave and strategize how they were going to inform Jack. Given what they now knew about Dave, there were few options. In fact, they saw only one. They agreed on what each would say, and Frank took notes.

Twenty minutes went by. Occasional sounds of laughter came from Jack's office. Frank and John smiled at each other, remembering the first time they heard Jack's laugh at a company function. Their attention then turned back to the door and the meeting they were waiting for.

Jack's voice got louder as he had risen from behind his desk and was approaching the door to let his visitor out. Frank and John collected their notes and rose. "So we'll have that drink another time, right?" asked Jack, heftily patting his visitor on the back.

"You bet," said Dave, shaking Jack's hand vigorously, and turning to walk out of the office.

It was one of the slow motion, car crash moments when their eyes met Dave's. Frank and John stood mute, barely keeping their mouths from dropping open. Dave paused, smiled broadly, and with a twinkle in his eyes said, "Hi, guys, always good to see you," before he walked past them out toward the corridor.

11

The Fifth Column
PSYCHOPATHS IN OUR MIDST

Ellyn carried her daughter up the three flights of stairs to her apartment. The little one was asleep after a long day in her mother's arms. Kicking the door closed behind her, Ellyn went directly to the bedroom, put her daughter in the crib, and kissed her on her forehead.

Returning to the kitchen, she filled the teapot with water, turned on the gas, and sighed. The door opened and her mother came in. "Shhhh, she's asleep," Ellyn warned. "I'm making some tea for us." Mom took off her old blue coat and hung it on the peg behind the front door.

They sat at the kitchen table, drinking tea and chatting excitedly about the day. "Good haul," said Ellyn, pulling a roll of bills from her shirt pocket and dropping it in the middle of the kitchen table.

"Impressive," said Mom, smiling. Together, they started to sort the money into piles. Most were singles, but there were a lot of fives and tens as well.

Hearing the sound of a key in the lock, Ellyn got up to open the door. "Hey, baby," said Mark, her husband, kissing her as he entered. Mark carried the folding card table into their apartment and leaned it against the counter. He took the playing cards from his shirt pocket and placed them on the counter with his keys. "How'd we do?" he asked, eyeing the pile of money on the table.

"I think we might have beat you today," she said as the women laughed. "Mom deserves an Academy Award! You should have seen her on Forty-third. One old lady had tears in her eyes as she handed me this!" Ellyn picked up the fifty-dollar bill and waved it in Mark's face.

"Great job, Mom," he said, kissing his mother-in-law on the forehead. "Usually it's only the 'suits' who give us a fifty!"

Mom rose slightly and took a mock bow as Mark and Ellyn applauded. "Oh, shhhh, she's asleep," warned Ellyn, remembering their young daughter in the next room.

"Well, I did pretty well myself," bragged Mark, taking a huge roll of singles from his backpack and adding it to the table. "Where would we be without people's greed?" he joked, grabbing a beer from the fridge and taking a seat.

"And guilt," added Mom, sipping her tea, a Cheshire cat smile on her lips.

"Lots of tourists today. And the heat wasn't bad either," he said, commenting on the absence of cops most of the day.

The team proceeded to count the money, and Ellyn made a note in her ledger book. "I say we hit Midtown early evening tomorrow," she suggested. "There's a three-day convention in town."

They laughed as Mom picked up the neat pile of money and placed it in a shoebox. Ellyn headed to the stove to begin cooking dinner, and Mark got another beer from the fridge.

Because of recent publicity about our work on psychopaths, we have received many questions from the public about how to handle them in the workplace. Most questions have to do with handling a "psychopathic" boss, but we have also heard about psychopathic peers, subordinates, and coworkers. Without a lot more information than we typically receive, it is impossible to determine whether the individual described is psychopathic. Recall that psychopathy refers to a potent mix of personality traits and behavioral patterns (see chapter 2), and that a proper assessment is made only by qualified professionals. We therefore strongly advise readers to be very careful about their use of the term, particularly in discussions with others. However, if you are working for or with an individual who appears to have psychopathic features, we offer some suggestions in this chapter.

It is important to understand that psychopaths derail your career by attacking the two most important aspects of your reputation: your competence and your loyalty. *Competence* is how well you do your job or the tasks assigned to you. It is the basic reason you have a job in the first place. While your ability to perform a task suits their purpose (that is, you are considered a *pawn* or *patron* in support of their *psychopathic fiction)*, psychopaths will continue to charm and groom you to support them. They may use unorthodox tactics (as they tend not to have good leadership skills), but you have value to them (albeit temporary), so your competence does not pose a direct threat.

Loyalty is an intangible trait that is often measured in terms of how supportive you are of the company and, conversely, how supportive the company is of its employees. Companies begin to build loyalty during recruitment and orientation by describing the successes the company has achieved and the opportunities afforded those who wish to build a career with the company. The company maintains loyalty by increasing feelings of company pride (such as when the company celebrates a major success in the marketplace); feelings of personal belongingness (through things like team achievement awards and company picnics); opportunities for personal and professional growth (such as through company-sponsored training programs and challenging assignments); or career advancement (as in salary increases, promotions, and achievement bonuses). For the employee's part, loyalty to the company is demonstrated through productivity, quality output, regular attendance, adherence to policies and procedures, and an above-and-beyond effort on behalf of the work unit and company, and so forth.

Once you are no longer of use to the psychopath or you pose a threat to him, he will discard you and attempt to overtly and covertly *neutralize* you in the eyes of upper management, coworkers, or anyone else who has influence. If a psychopath sees you as too competent (that is, a rival) or senses any hint of disloyalty on your part, you may be attacked. The attacks involve *disparaging the perceptions of your competence and loyalty in the eyes of others in the company*, particularly members of upper management.

Recall that perceptions of you by those in power—that is, your *reputation*—are based on the *impressions* you make. However, if you do not have ready access to those in power (for example, through participation in meetings or by making presentations to upper management), your reputation in *their* eyes can only be based on reports from others, primarily your boss. If your boss is a psychopath, then the odds are good that he or she has been spreading negative information about you.

Industrial psychopaths, be they manipulators, bullies, or puppetmasters, operate best in secret, so your reputation can be destroyed *without your even being aware that anyone has doubts about your competence and loyalty*. This puts you at a clear disadvantage. Should you try to complain about your psychopathic coworker or boss, you may very likely find that the waters have been poisoned against you, and every effort you make to remedy the situation may be seen as confirmation of the "problem employee" reputation that you now have. Once you have lost your credibility, you are essentially defenseless against the psychopath, short of taking legal action, which in many cases is a very costly, uphill battle. It is therefore incumbent on you to take *preventative measures* to assure that your competence and loyalty are never questioned.

Rule 1: Do Not Label Anyone a "Psychopath"

As noted earlier, it is not useful to label someone a psychopath; in fact, to label your boss a psychopath may make the situation worse for you than it already is. Even if you have reviewed all the traits of the psychopath and believe your boss or coworker demonstrates them, your company may not be in a position to take your side. Companies are very pragmatic and respond to information about *behaviors* relevant to the work at hand rather than subjective feelings about another person.

Rule 2: Build and Maintain Relationships

One psychopathic technique is to create conflict among staff members. Claiming that one person said something negative or derogatory about another is a common approach. The success of this approach relies on the tendency for individuals to avoid confronting others who they think have spoken ill of them. This "divide and control" technique increases tension and distrust among individuals, effectively shutting down communication and providing cover for the psychopath. A psychopathic boss can use this technique to control and isolate employees from each other and to hide his or her abusive behavior.

The best defense is to take every opportunity to interact with others on the job and develop a reputation as a friendly, talented, competent, and loyal person. Seek out opportunities to interact with members of upper management. While they may not routinely visit your workplace, their occasional appearances allow them brief chances to mingle with employees. Unfortunately, many such meetings end up like elementary school dances (no one asks anyone to dance) or "bitch" sessions (someone starts complaining and others join in).

You can take advantage of these occasional meetings by coming prepared with a serious question that is not embarrassing, confrontational, or self-serving. Ask a question about the business, the competition, or a new product line. The more maturity and practical understanding of business you demonstrate by your question, the more favorably the executives will remember you.

In addition, you should also always be prepared with what is referred to in business language as an "elevator speech" to use with any member of higher management you happen to meet. Assume you have 30 seconds in an elevator alone with an executive. Luckily, people often don't talk to each other in an elevator. Take this opportunity to introduce yourself to the executive (this shows initiative and a willingness to interact with people above you) and give your one-sentence talk (tell him or her what you do; comment on the business, the latest annual report, or the new office construction; and thank the executive for something, even just for visiting the site). Here is an example of a real elevator speech: "Hi, Mr. Johnson, I'm John Smith, I work in the lab on the ABC project. I really liked what you said in the latest annual report about the investment the company is making. Thanks. We appreciate your support for the project." You will be surprised at the positive reaction you receive. If you are asked questions, give brief, fact-based answers. Many executives rely on the impromptu input from employees for information they cannot get elsewhere. As this is your first meeting, always make it positive and supportive; avoid anything that may be embarrassing (to you, the company, or the executive), but be *sincere*. And, if your executive is like many we have known, he or she will remember your name and where you work. This can only help your career; it communicates competence and loyalty to someone who really matters.

Of course, this is also precisely what a psychopath would do! The difference is that the psychopath's intent is malevolent, while yours is to genuinely get along and fit in.

Rule 3: Understand Options Your Company May Offer

If you have not read your company policy manual, then do so. Many companies distribute copies to their staff and may even offer orientation programs to answer questions. Be familiar with your obligations to the company, as well as any policies or procedures in place to handle complaints and issues. For example, many American companies have policies against sexual harassment. Some have anti-bullying provisions that you should also note. Do not be afraid to ask questions about policies and procedures you do not understand.

Rule 4: Avoid Being Labeled a Complainer

Nobody likes someone who is always complaining. Reserve your complaints for something that is important to you. Learn how to pick your battles and, more important, learn how to rephrase your issues positively. A reputation as a complainer hurts your long-term credibility and plays nicely into the hands of the psychopath who merely has to reinforce what others already think about you.

How to Handle a "Psychopathic" Boss

One of the most debilitating things for your personal and professional life is to work for a psychopathic boss. He or she can make your life hell. Unfortunately, companies are filled with bosses who are unschooled in the management and supervisory techniques needed to effectively lead their departments or teams; these individuals can look and act like psychopaths, but in reality they are not. The real deal is much worse. Here are our thoughts on how to make the best of your situation should you have the misfortune of working for a real psychopath.

1. BUILD AND MAINTAIN A REPUTATION AS A GOOD PERFORMER

Bosses are expected to use power, influence, and leadership to motivate employees to perform their jobs up to specific standards of quality and productivity. While there may be differences in personal style and mismatch between your expectations and your boss's approach, the company is expected to take the side of your boss in most disagreements over *your* performance. This fact alone makes it very difficult to handle a boss with psychopathic tendencies, because he or she already has more power than you do and is expected to make management judgments about you, your performance, and your career. In the hands of a psychopathic boss, your own less-than-optimal performance is a tool that can (and will) be used against you. The best defense is to *always* perform up to your capabilities and do whatever tasks are assigned to you unless they are clearly illegal, unethical, or violate safety or security procedures. In addition, be open to regular feedback about your performance, and ask for feedback on a regular basis if it is not forthcoming.

2. PUT IT IN WRITING

In many, but not all, companies, assignments and objectives are given in writing. If this is not the case where you work, then you can always follow up each verbal directive with a written memo of your understanding. This memo should be short, well written, and focused. Simply state what you understand the assignment to be, the timetable, resource requirements, and assistance you expect from the boss or others working on the project. If possible, ask to meet with your boss to review it, take notes, and, of course, keep a copy of all documents for yourself. If you make this a regular part of your interactions with all your bosses—that is, part of your style of working—upper management will readily understand and accept it; in fact, it is a sign of a mature, well-motivated employee.

Sometimes objectives are open to negotiation, and you should take advantage of these opportunities. If an assignment is too big or your current assignments need to be reprioritized in order to complete the additional work in a timely manner, then ask to meet with your boss to discuss how this can be accomplished. Always come to these meetings with several solutions of your own; this demonstrates initiative and the fact that you seriously want to achieve the same results your boss does. You may not always get your way, but the key is to build a good working relationship with your boss, whether you think he or she is a psychopath or not.

You should document other things as well. For example, any positive or negative feedback you receive from your boss should be noted in your calendar or date book. A simple note that documents the meeting, what was said, and your response should be sufficient.

Any threats your boss makes should be noted either in your date book or a "memo to file," which you should keep (more on this later).

3. MAKE GOOD USE OF YOUR PERFORMANCE APPRAISAL

Many supervisors do not like writing or giving performance appraisals. Some find them time consuming (especially if the supervisor has many employees to review); others find them hard to write properly; and still others do not like to give negative feedback to their staff members, even if it is valid. Because the performance review becomes a part of your record, what is written down on this document is very critical to your career. Unscrupulous bosses can use the review as a way to derail your career by including inaccuracies and distortions; take the process seriously and try to participate as much as possible.

To facilitate the review process, some companies allow employees to submit information to the supervisor—a self-assessment—to be used as notes as they write the review. While no supervisor is required to accept this self-report of performance, it does help many supervisors to remember details they might have forgotten and may enlighten them to differences in understanding about objectives. Take advantage of this opportunity if it is made available to you. But remember to keep your self-evaluation focused, balanced, accurate, and succinct. This is also a good time to reflect on your developmental needs, and be open to hearing about them during your review.

When you receive your performance review (face to face is best) you will be better prepared to participate in the discussion if you have carefully reviewed your own performance. During the review meeting, you should ask questions about points you do not understand, correct misunderstandings, and, of course, take notes.

A well-written review should contain few generalities (such as "John is a poor performer," or "John is a team player"). Instead, it should contain specific behaviors that can be repeated (if positive) or changed (if negative), such as "John handed in the report three weeks late" or "John's status reports at team meetings were always accurate." If something on your review is not clear, ask your boss to give you actual examples of any incidents or behaviors that are mentioned. To the degree that your review is an accurate reflection of your true performance, the official record will better support your reputation for being competent and loyal.

Some performance reviews allow the employee to add written comments or submit an addendum for inclusion in the personnel file. Even if your review is outstanding, you should add a note. If your review contains inaccuracies, and your boss does not want to modify the final document, then this may be your only chance to correct the record. Do not write something in haste. Instead, carefully write down your view of the events in question. Make sure your note is professional and without emotion or inflammatory language. You may wish to have a friend read it and offer suggestions for improvement before you send it to human resources. Should your performance, reputation, or credibility ever be called into question, your performance reviews are the record the company will turn to first.

4. AVOID CONFRONTATIONS

Having a blowout with your boss in public is never a good idea; taking on a psychopath can only lead to disaster. Psychopaths will set you up to explode—by pushing your hot buttons—when it suits their purpose. Do not take the bait. As hard as it may be, you should always remain cool and calm when being attacked, however unfairly. We are not suggesting that you be submissive, but rather that you rely on your strengths—through assertiveness, not aggressiveness—when confronted. The safest, although not always practical, position is to minimize or avoid all contact with a boss you believe to be a psychopath. When you must interact, make sure there are others in the area that can witness your calm, professional stance and the psychopath's ranting. Then document the interaction in your date book in accurate, unemotional terms.

Psychopaths will sometimes berate their subordinates in front of their superiors to demonstrate their own "leadership." Because they are uninformed about true leadership, they think that this will help their careers; in most cases, it does not. Seasoned executives know that berating subordinates in public, especially during management meetings, is bad management. It shows them that the boss is not in control of him- or herself or the situation, and this sign of weakness is not lost on those higher up. However, you should never get angry and retaliate against your boss (that is, take the bait) in these situations. Rather, defend your decisions, judgments, or results by stating the facts. If you are in the wrong, admit it, apologize, and ask to be allowed to try again. If others are clearly at fault (for example, another department did not deliver material on time), mention it but do not come across as shifting blame to others. Make sure to note that you made every effort within your power (including asking for your boss's help) to achieve the goal or objective. To the best of your ability, you should come across as competent and loyal, even to the boss who just berated you in public.

Psychopaths, especially the bullying kind, seem to enjoy dressing down subordinates in the privacy of their own offices. This is an especially difficult situation to handle. These confrontations are meant to establish or reestablish the psychopath's dominance over you. During these "meetings," you should calmly state the facts as you know them (again, assertively, not aggressively). If you are clearly in the wrong, then you should not shift the blame.

You should also take good notes of what your boss says. Some nonpsychopathic bosses and many psychopathic ones will use profanity. Many corporations do not tolerate this form of verbal abuse; it is almost never appropriate, except perhaps when someone is about to do something dangerous on the job (for example, push the wrong button on a nuclear reactor). In the majority of cases, however, the use of profane language works against the speaker, and it should be noted verbatim in your date book, for future reference.

If you truly believe that you are in a meeting with a psychopath, then your only tactic is to take it. It is rarely, perhaps never, advisable to walk off the job. If the psychopath has targeted you as a rival or a threat, then this plays into his hands. It may be better to get out of the meeting and regroup.

5. MAKING A FORMAL COMPLAINT

Before you make a formal complaint, you should assess your situation very carefully. What is the perception of your boss in the company; what is his or her *reputation*? Is he or she seen as *competent* and *loyal*? Is he or she well connected in the power hierarchy? Recall that the industrial psychopath has established a *psychopathic fiction* in the minds of those in power: *I am the ideal leader.* Understand and anticipate that the psychopath has already disparaged *your* reputation in the eyes of those same people: John is *incompetent, disloyal,* and a *complainer.* Now, consider your options. You may have to accept the fact that you cannot prevail in this situation.

You may find that your organization has provisions for employees bringing issues to the attention of human resources or upper management. Read and understand these procedures carefully, and weigh them against the abuse you have received. Some companies have anonymous hotlines or tip lines that employees are encouraged to call should they witness any illegal (such as stealing company funds or lying on production records) or abusive behavior (such as sexual harassment or bullying). Learn more about these options and the proper way to take advantage of them should the need arise for you to make a report.

Confidentiality is an important part of organizational life. But it is important to understand that *you may not be afforded confidentiality* should you complain about your boss or coworker. If you feel threatened or fear retribution, you should make your report anonymously; you can always come forward later if you choose. However, keep in mind that some companies do not place much credence on anonymous complaints, considering them rumors or hearsay; your complaint may go unheard in these cases. Sometimes it takes multiple complaints about the same boss to get any attention.

It is also important to understand that just because you complain, the company need not take action, or the action they take may not be what you expected. You should be prepared for the fact that the company has put trust in the boss's supervisory judgment. It will take a lot to change this. If you are dealing with a psychopath, he or she may be better entrenched than you think. Your complaint may bring to the surface a history of your *own* poor performance or disloyalty, as carefully and consistently created by your psychopathic boss. You may end up losing your own job in the process.

6. LEAVE ON YOUR OWN TERMS

In the days of the psychological contract, employees expected to have jobs for life, or at least until retirement. Times have changed and so should your approach to employment. It is wise to always have an up-to-date résumé, with a list of your completed projects, achievements, and performance reviews on hand. It is your security

blanket. It might be fruitful to check the local newspapers or the
Internet occasionally for openings elsewhere. You do not have to be
actively looking or even thinking of leaving; this is just good career
management.

If you are truly working for a psychopathic boss, your only re-
course may be to distance yourself by applying for a transfer or, in
the worst case, leaving the company. Many companies have job-
posting bulletin boards on which positions in other departments and
locations are advertised. Learn about the posting process and take advantage of it *early*. Should you apply for an internal transfer, keep in
mind that the hiring manager will read your past performance reviews and seek a reference from your boss. It behooves you to try to
maintain a good relationship with your boss—psychopath or not—
for the length of your tenure. You may be surprised that your psychopathic boss may help you get the new job, especially if it is seen
as an easy way to take care of a rival or threat. If you worked on in-
terdepartmental teams, you should ask individuals from other areas
to be internal references. If you received commendations for doing a
good job, for instance, an employee of the month award or a gain-
share award, make sure these are in your personnel file. When you
weigh your options—and only you know how you feel about your
situation—you may opt for a lateral move rather than wait for a promotional position. If you have taken courses in a new field—for example, you currently work in the accounting department but are
working toward a master's degree in marketing—then a junior-level
position in the marketing department may be a good choice for you
as well as for the company. The key is to keep your options open at
all times and be attuned to changes in the perception others have of
you because of the machinations of your boss.

There may come a time when you decide that the best course of
action is to leave your employer. Because this decision concerns your
spouse and family as well, make sure all bases are covered before you
act. The ideal situation is to already have a new job lined up before
you announce your intent to leave.

If you are asked to leave, then it is important that you understand the benefits due you at your termination. Things like termination pay, health insurance coverage, unemployment insurance, accrued vacation, and sick time pay may be due you. Your human resources representative has the responsibility to apprise you of these things.

You may be given the opportunity to resign, or you may ask for this opportunity, because having been fired can be problematic down your career road. You will most likely be asked to sign a release form in that event. It is wise to seek legal counsel before you sign anything so you fully understand what you are agreeing to.

You may be asked to give your reasons for leaving, usually during an *exit interview*. Here you must use good judgment, and seeking the advice of legal counsel is not out of the question. It is always appropriate to state "personal reasons" and leave it at that. But you may feel the need to apprise the company of the difficulties you have had with your boss. You may find that they already know about his or her behavior; they may even offer you an incentive to stay if they realize that you have been competent and loyal and an asset to the company (do not count on this, however). Always leave on good terms; do not burn any bridges.

7. GET ON WITH YOUR LIFE AND YOUR CAREER

Once you are out of the grips of the psychopathic relationship, you will feel many things, some of which were described earlier. Most of all you will feel relief, as if some great burden has been taken off your back. Put your previous job and the psychopath behind you. Seek counseling if you need to, but move on with your life. Consider the experience as one of life's hard lessons and take on your new job with enthusiasm and eyes wide open.

Handling a "Psychopathic" Coworker

You may be working with a psychopath in the next cubicle and never know it. However, you may have suspicions based on how he behaves toward you or others. Whether or not you choose to do something is largely a function of the nature of the interactions you have with him.

Clearly, all the suggestions noted above on handling a psychopathic boss apply to this situation as well. To protect yourself, make sure you invest energy in managing your own reputation, build open and honest relationships with peers and your boss, work up to your abilities, and follow applicable policies and procedures. Be sensitive to and resist manipulation attempts, such as those described in earlier chapters of this book.

Try to keep your distance from psychopaths. However, if you are required to work closely with them, avoid doing their work for them, and resist their attempt to get you to hide their own poor performance. These forms of collusion are quite common and will be used against you should a psychopath decide you are no longer useful to his or her career. And, above all, do not confront the coworker you believe to be a psychopath.

1. DO NOT LABEL A COWORKER A "PSYCHOPATH"

Avoid labeling a coworker a "psychopath." It will get you nowhere and may lead to those in authority wondering about you. Psychopathy itself is not illegal, despite the problems it causes for those around individuals with these traits. Behavior, however, can be illegal, unethical, hurtful, and so forth. It is paramount that you focus on the *actual behavior* of the individual whom you believe to be a psychopath. Observe it, document it, and if you are intimidated or feel that you are in danger, bring it to the attention of those in authority or, at least, someone you trust.

2. CONSIDER REPORTING ABUSIVE BEHAVIOR

If you observe illegal behavior or flagrant abuse of others, bring it to the attention of your boss, but *only* if you have a strong, supportive relationship with him or her. Otherwise, send an anonymous letter to him or her. You may choose to make use of the company's reporting procedures, but do so anonymously, if you can. Reporting illegal, immoral, and abusive behaviors is typically viewed as a form of loyalty to the company, the industry, and in major cases, the country. However, do not assume that you will heralded as a hero, because the psychopath is constantly managing the perceptions of those around him or her, and you may have already been compromised. Recall that a successful corporate psychopath will already have established a strong influence network, and may already have planted seeds of doubt about your competence and loyalty.

If you are personally abused, seek advice from family, friends, or professionals outside the company, and then take steps to end the relationship, as noted above. This may involve telling your boss what is happening, reporting the abuse to human resources, or using other avenues available at your company. Make sure you fully understand the proper procedure to use and the ramifications for yourself. Proceed with caution, and remember never to confront the psychopath. Document everything.

3. CONSIDER LEAVING

In general, putting as much distance as possible between you and your psychopathic coworker is the best solution. If the situation is untenable, consider a transfer, or, as a last resort, leave the company.

How to Handle a "Psychopathic" Subordinate

Managing people is hard enough without one of them being a psychopath. Employees come in all shapes and sizes. Some are talented, others are not; some are motivated, others are sluggish; some work hard, others just put in their time. Unfortunately, supervisors cannot always choose the employees on their staff, but have to manage them nonetheless. Based on what we understand about psychopaths, they rarely, if ever, make good employees. Their parasitic nature, tendency to lie, and reliance on conning and manipulation to get what they want makes them the antithesis of the ideal employee. What is a supervisor who suspects he or she has a psychopath on staff to do?

1. CONTINUOUSLY IMPROVE YOUR LEADERSHIP AND MANAGEMENT SKILLS

The more you know about leading and managing people, the better off you will be when handling a psychopath. There are two reasons for this. First, your informed management style will serve you in good stead when applied to others on your staff. They will be productive and quality conscious, and deliver what you ask. This will not go unnoticed by your own boss and will go a long way to building and maintaining your *reputation* as a good leader or manager. Remember, that the psychopathic employee will attack your reputation, spread disinformation about your effectiveness and style, and sabotage your efforts to build and manage your team. To the degree that you can forestall this negative press by having a track record of good performance, you will receive better support from those above you in the organization.

Psychopath as Client

Psychopaths are not the favorite clients of defense attorneys. Hare recently took part in a symposium with Lenny Frieling, a criminal defense attorney and municipal court associate judge in Boulder County, Colorado. Frieling offered some valuable advice for lawyers with a psychopath as a client, and his comments are paraphrased, with his permission, as follows:

1. Get paid up front. If you lose the case, you will be blamed and unpaid. If you win the case, the client will take the credit and you will *still* be unpaid.

2. Be very careful about boundaries. The client is not your friend, and will collect and use against you whatever information is obtained. (This includes information related to the case *and* related to you personally.)

3. Remain in charge. A psychopathic client will attempt to run the show and to manipulate you and the system, making your job much harder.

4. Don't take at face value the client's description of events or interactions with others. Check everything out.

5. Be aware that the client will distort and minimize his or her criminal history. When confronted with the inaccuracies, the client will offer excuses that place the blame on defense attorneys, a corrupt system, or others.

6. The client will flatter you as long as things are going smoothly. If the case goes sideways, often because of the client's tendency to take charge and to ignore advice, you will become the enemy.

7. Keep copious notes on *everything*.

---

2. BUILD AND MAINTAIN RAPPORT WITH YOUR STAFF

While this is also part of being a good manager, it is so important to handling psychopathic manipulation that it deserves mention on its own. Psychopaths are good at setting people against each other, particularly when the lines of communication are inadequate. To the degree that you can keep open lines of communication between you and your staff members, the more likely they will come to you when they observe behaviors of the sort described in this book. This is the heads-up that you will need in order to stay one step ahead of the psychopathic subordinate.

You must keep an open mind, though. Sometimes we believe that the things we hear from subordinates are blown out of proportion because they are important to them but not necessarily to us. But it is just as likely that your subordinates' reports are accurate because they have more contact with their peers than you do. It is important to take all reports seriously and investigate to the best of your ability.

At the very least, you should keep detailed notes of all issues that come to your attention, and review them with your own boss during private meetings.

3. BUILD AND MAINTAIN A STRONG RELATIONSHIP WITH YOUR BOSS

The relationship you have with your boss is critical, not only to your own ability to get your job done, but to your chance to address issues before they become problems. Having a strong relationship with your own boss is necessary in order to deal with psychopathic manipulation. This relationship should be based on ready sharing of information about what is going on in the department and on projects. Make every effort to keep your boss in the loop.

There are many ways to keep the lines of communication open. Some bosses like to meet weekly with their staff members to review progress, project status, or issues. Others take a more relaxed approach, having lunch occasionally, or stopping by the office to get the latest information. Take advantage of these opportunities to give and receive information, particularly information about a potential problem employee on your staff.

4. KEEP GOOD NOTES AND DOCUMENTS

Despite the change from bureaucracy to the more modern transitioning organization models, the need to keep good records has remained a vital part of running a business. Learn to prepare concise, accurate, and timely reports. Even if they are not a part of your boss's requirements, write and keep them for yourself. Keep a record of what was discussed and agreed to in all meetings you attend. Keep records of both the "good" and "bad" performance of your staff members, and provide them positive and constructive feedback on a regular basis (these meetings should also be documented).

Keeping good records can be onerous, especially if you do not like to write or you do not have the time. You may want to take a time management course or get help with report writing, as there are skills and techniques available that can make the task far easier, less boring, and more a regular part of your management routine.

5. USE YOUR COMPANY'S PERFORMANCE MANAGEMENT PROCESS

Performance reviews serve the purpose of officially communicating feedback to employees about their performance. By documenting good performance, the supervisor communicates that he or she is paying attention to employees and has respect for their contributions. By documenting less-than-optimal performance, the supervisor communicates the fact that employees need to improve. Regular performance reviews, whether formal or informal, reinforce the relationship between the supervisor and employee and help to keep lines of communication open. Performance reviews are invaluable when managing or dealing with a psychopathic employee, especially if they are tied to a formal process of setting annual performance objectives, and measuring interim results.

In some cases, performance reviews may be the only way to deal with a psychopathic employee. If you are a supervisor who has ever wanted to discipline or terminate an employee, you no doubt have been asked by human resources to demonstrate the employee's poor performance in a performance review. If you have not completed a review or have neglected to document performance deficiencies, you may not be able to move forward as quickly as you would like. In the case of a psychopathic subordinate, the official performance record—written review and face-to-face discussion—is vital to managing them.

6. SEEK ADVICE FROM HUMAN RESOURCES

Many of the businesspeople who attend our talks and seminars are human resources professionals. Virtually all of them have recognized the traits and characteristics of the psychopath in one or more of their employees, either in their current companies or in past jobs. They tell us that their hands are sometimes tied because of supervisors who do not come to them with issues early on. Others note that performance reviews are poorly written and do not measure up to the level of detail they need in order to handle (in their words) "disruptive," "counterproductive," "dysfunctional," or "problem" employees.

Corporate Jerks

The individuals described in this book often are referred to by the police as *jerks*. The same appellation is used by Gloria Elliott, an organizational development consultant who organizes "jerk training" seminars. She estimates that 10 percent of those in the workplace are full-time jerks.

Research at the University of British Columbia suggests that jerks are sexually more successful than nice guys, who often do tend to finish last. Psychologist Paul Trapnell defines jerks as "manipulative, arrogant, boastful, calculating, quarrelsome, and sly." They are cold enough not to worry about their effect on others. But why are they so successful at attracting women? Part of the reason is that they have fewer social inhibitions, try harder, and sell themselves better than do the rest of us.

For example, most men whose advances to a woman are rebuffed will slink away, their ego and self-image validated or damaged. They are unlikely to try again, unless the signs of interest from a woman are unmistakable. A jerk/psychopath, on the other hand, knows he is perfect and is not worried about being rejected: "It's her problem, not mine." He simply moves on to the next woman.

The same principles apply to other aspects of human interaction, including attempts to scam or manipulate others.

After your direct supervisor, the human resources professional is perhaps the best person to talk to about questionable or suspicious behavior. You need not label someone a psychopath, but you can document and report behavior that is abusive, counterproductive, or does not live up to the standards of performance, job requirements, or code of conduct expected of all employees.

The world is made up of many types of people, some of them, unfortunately, psychopaths. In an ideal world, we would be able to get along with everyone, and accept them as equals; our gut feeling tells us that this is the right path to take. But, reality is often less than ideal, and our desires for an enlightened approach to business and professional relationships are often frustrated. It is our hope that this book will help readers avoid psychopathic manipulation on and off the job, and can assist those who have become embroiled in the psychopathic fiction to break free and get back on the path of a normal, happy, and productive life.

Nothing New

"The man without moral feeling is the kind who will take an oath with no sense of responsibility. . . . By nature he is a base kind of person, lacking the most elementary sense of decency and capable of absolutely nothing. He leaves his mother without support in her old age. . . . knows the inside of the town jail better than his own house. . . . In court, he is capable of playing any role: defendant, plaintiff, or witness. He knows a good many rascals."

—Theophrastus, c. 280 B.C.

ACT V, Scene III

THE RISE AND THE FALL

Dave sat on his deck admiring the trees in his backyard. He had called in sick that morning, deciding to lay low for a few days.

That branch needs to be cut, he thought, spotting a dead limb on an oak at the edge of the woods.

He watched his e-mail most of the day for anything interesting and wondered what was going on back at the site. Finally, he typed a note to his secretary. "Denise, Feeling a bit better, but still coughing," he wrote. "Anything going on I need to know about before the weekend?"

A few moments later he got the response he had been fishing for, "Frank has just been let go! Marge is in her office crying, and the rest of us are in shock," she wrote.

Dave smiled and picked up his phone and dialed. He practiced his cough as the tones went through. "Oh my God, Denise. They didn't!" he exclaimed, when Denise answered.

"Yes, Dave, it just happened. We don't know why," she said, holding back tears.

Dave asked what she had heard, and she told him all she knew. He had many questions and seemed to relish every detail Denise could provide. Dave assured her that things were going to be okay and then they hung up.

Dave breathed deeply, enjoying the fresh air, and then dialed Jack Garrideb. "Hi, Jack. How did it go?"

"As well as could be expected," answered Jack, wearily. "Word will travel fast, I'm sure."

"Yeah, Denise just called me, lots of folks in shock, apparently. Anything about me?" asked Dave in anticipation.

"Nothing yet. I'll have HR send you the draft announcement about your promotion for you to review. You may want to add in more about your background. Get it back to the communications department by Monday. We'll release it on Tuesday, after things quiet down a bit."

"Yes, certainly," assured Dave.

Dave hung up the phone and smiled. He poured himself another glass of wine and walked to the edge of the deck. He gazed out over his yard and silently toasted the oak with the dead limb.

"Sometimes you just have to cut out the deadwood," he said aloud, taking a sip. "Life *is* good."

NOTES

Numbers in boldface indicate page locations.

5 "Nice Suit." Special thanks to Dr. Michael Walton, a UK based Chartered Psychologist, for providing material for this case.

18 "Psychopathy, Sociopathy, and Antisocial Personality Disorder" *American Psychiatric Association. Diagnostic and Statistical Manual of Mental Disorders,* 4th ed. Washington, D.C.: Author, 1994.

20 "A pioneer in the early years . . ." Cleckley, H. *The Mask of Sanity,* 5th ed. St. Louis: Mosby, 1976.

22 "He describes these efforts . . ." Hare, R. D. *Without Conscience: The Disturbing World of the Psychopaths Among Us.* New York: Guilford Press, 1998.

24 "Nature? Nurture? Both!" Blonigen, D. M., Carlson, S. R., Krueger, R. F., & Patrick, C. J. A twin study of self-reported psychopathic personality traits. *Personality and Individual Differences,* 35(1), 179–197, 2003.

24 "Nature? Nurture? Both!" Larrson, H., Andershed, H., & Lichstenstien, P. (in press). A genetic factor explains most of the variation in the psychopathic personality. *Journal of Abnormal Psychology.*

24 "Nature? Nurture? Both!" Viding, E., Blair, R. J. R., Moffitt, T. E., & Plomin, R. Evidence for substantial genetic risk for psychopathy in 7-year-olds. *Journal of Child Psychology and Psychiatry,* 46(6), 592–597, 2005.

25 "The most reliable, valid . . ." Hare, R. D. *Manual for the Revised Psychopathy Checklist,* 2nd ed. Toronto, Ontario: Multi-Health Systems, 2003.

26 ". . . the shorter PCL: Screening Version . . ." Hart, S. D., Cox, D. N., & Hare, R. D. *Manual for the Psychopathy Checklist: Screening Version (PCL: SV).* Toronto, Ontario: Multi-Health Systems, 1995.

For additional information about biological and genetic research on psychopathy, see www.Hare.org.

42 "When Bad is Good" Bing, S. *What Would Machiavelli Do?* New York: HarperCollins, 2000.

54 "Consider these words by Jack Abbott . . ." Abbott, J. *In the Belly of the Beast: Letters from Prison.* New York: Random House, 1981.

55 "In several functional magnetic resonance. . . ." Kiehl, K. A., Smith, A. M., Hare, R. D., Mendrek, A., Forster, B. B., Brink, J., & Liddle, P. F. Limbic abnormalities in affective processing by criminal psychopaths as revealed by functional magnetic resonance imaging. *Biological Psychiatry,* 50(9), 677–684, 2001.

56 "Praise the Lord" Hare, R. D. The psychopathic offender. Presentation at the Judicial Symposium on Child Sexual Abuse, Bethel, Maine, May 11–12, 1995.

65 "On a recent Oprah Winfrey program . . ." Bird, A. *Blood Brother: 33 Reasons My Brother Scott Peterson is Guilty.* New York: ReganBooks, 2005.

66 "Where Was the Emotional Connection?" Curtis, K. "Scott Peterson: Portrait of a Psychopath." (The Associated Press). *The Desert Sun,* March 20, 2005.

76 "Giving Them What They Want" Steinbeck, J. *East of Eden.* New York: Viking Press, 1952.

89 "On Sunday he prayed . . ." On Sunday he prayed on his knees, on Monday he preyed on his fellow man. *Vancouver Sun,* May 20, 2000.

92 "I Felt Like I Was Lunch" Meloy, J. R., & Meloy, M. J. Autonomic arousal in the presence of psychopathy: A survey of mental health and criminal justice professionals. *Journal of Threat Assessment*, 2(2), 21–34, 2003.

94 "The Corporation as Psychopath" *The Corporation*. A film by Mark Achbar, Jennifer Abbott, & Joel Bakman.

94 "The Corporation as Psychopath" Babiak, P., & Hare, R. D. *The B-Scan 360: Research Version*. Toronto, Ontario: Multi-Health Systems, 2005.

118 "The Psychopath in the Next Cubicle" Adams, S. *Dilbert*. Andrews McMeel Publishing, 2002.

124 "The Dark Triad" Nathanson, C., Paulhus, D. L., & Williams, K. M. Predictors of a behavioral measure of scholastic cheating: Personality and competence but not demographics. *Contemporary Educational Psychology*, 31(1), 97–122, 2006.

124 "The Dark Triad" Paulhus, D., Hemphill, J., & Hare, R. D. (in press). *The SRP-III*. Toronto, Ontario: Multi-Health Systems.

135 "Corporate Fraud in the Boardroom" Skalak, S., Nestler, C., & Bussmann, K. Global Economic Crime Survey, 2005. Pricewaterhouse-Coopers

Special thanks to Michael MacDougall, MBA, MEd, former Director of PricewaterhouseCooper's Centre for Career Management (Vancouver) for his assistance.

163 "But I'm Not as Bad as the Others" *National Post*, September 15, 2005.

178 "Disordered Personalities at Work" Board, B. J., & Fritzon, K. Disordered personalities at work. *Psychology, Crime and Law*, 11(1), 17–32, 2005.

185 "Variations on a Theme" Hervé, Hugues, F.M. The Masks of Sanity and Psychopathy: A cluster analytical investigation of subtypes of criminal psychopathy. Unpublished doctoral dissertation, 2003.

187 "They Just Don't Get It" Erin McClam, The Associated Press, June 21, 2005.

190 "Researcher Paul Frick and his colleagues . . ." Frick, P. J., & Marsee, M. A. (2006). Psychopathy and developmental pathways to antisocial behavior in youth. In C. J. Patrick (Ed.), *Handbook of Psychopathy*. New York: Guilford Press. Frick et al.

190 "Donald Lynam and his colleagues . . ." Lynam, D. R., & Derefinko, K. J. (2006). Psychopathy and personality. In C. J. Patrick (Ed.), *Handbook of Psychopathy* (pp. 133–155). New York: Guilford Press. Lynam et al.

195 "The Dark Side of Charisma" Hogan, R., Raskin, R., & Fazzini, D. "The Dark Side of Charisma." In K. E. Clark & M. B. Clark (eds.), *Measures of Leadership* (pp. 343–354). West Orange: Leadership Library of America, Inc., 1990.

211 "Fictional Resumes" Peterson, M. "A resume distinguished by what it didn't mention." *New York Times,* September 6, 2001.

214 "Faking It" Eichenwald, K. and Kolata, G. "A Doctor's Drug Trials Turn Into Fraud." *New York Times,* May 17, 1999.

228 "The Emotional Disconnect" Abbott, J. (with Zack, N.). *My Return.* Buffalo NY: Prometheus Books, 1987. King County Sheriff's Office, DVD on Interrogation of Gary Ridgeway. Seattle, WA, 2003.

230 "B-Scan" For more information about research with the B-Scan, see www.B-Scan.com.

232 "Look Me in the Eye" Enron Annual Report, 1998.

237 " 'Please God, Help Me Plunder' " Barrow, B. "The Cartier Lifestyle of a Secretary who Stole from Bosses." *The Daily Telegraph,* January 21, 2004. Wordsworth, A. "Honest Greed." *National Post,* April 21, 2004.

287 "Love Fraud" For more information, see www.LoveFraud.com.

ACKNOWLEDGMENTS

When I met my first psychopath, I was a young industrial-organizational psychologist finding my way as a consultant who had stumbled upon something that was troubling. Robert D. Hare responded to my call for guidance, and our working relationship has grown since into a valued friendship. Working with Bob on this book has only strengthened my respect for his scientific rigor, subtle wit, and warm sense of humor.

The manuscript of this book would not have passed muster without the able critiques of Marian Babiak and Dr. John Babiak, who never held back their probing questions and insightful advice. The inspiration of Drs. H. Karl Springob, ABPP, and Paul W. Thayer, advisers from years past, continues to reassure me that personality is a critically important part of business performance, and education and personal awareness are the keys to improvement.

A special thanks to my mother, Mrs. Julia Babiak, for her continued and unending love and support. Joan Bedard, my life partner, made writing far easier than expected by providing the love, support, and encouragement I needed to get the job done. I am forever thankful to her for making each day an adventure.

Paul Babiak

New York, 2006

During my years of research on psychopathy, I have had the privilege of working with many outstanding students and colleagues. I thank them all. Since I began work in this area four decades ago, things have changed dramatically. Instead of a few academics and clinicians working in isolation, there now are many hundreds of researchers around the world, many in contact with one another and all dedicated to understanding the nature and implications of psychopathy. A significant event was the recent formation of the Society for the Scientific Study of Psychopathy (SSSP), an organization that will do much to facilitate international and interdisciplinary collaboration in the study of psychopathy and its impact on society.

Scientific research and debate and their applications to mental health and criminal justice certainly are important, but at the same time, the general public must learn as much as it can about psychopathy. It was for this reason that I wrote *Without Conscience: The Disturbing World of the Psychopaths Among Us.* My editor for the book was Judith Regan, publisher of the current volume. While writing *Without Conscience,* I had my first discussions with Paul Babiak. He had provided me with a case study which I included in a chapter on "White Collar Psychopaths." Since then, I have had the great pleasure of working with Paul on a number of projects, one of which is this book.

I would like to thank Kylie Neufeld for her able assistance with my research and writing endeavors over the past decade. My wife and best friend, Averil, continues to provide me with a nurturing environment, sound counsel, trenchant insights, and enlightened debates about things of importance. Our beloved daughter, Cheryl, taught us much about courage, dignity, and grace in the face of adversity.

Robert D. Hare

Vancouver, 2006

INDEX